A System for

Discrete Event Modelling on Simula

G. M. Birtwistle

Professor of Computer Science,
University of Calgary, Canada

DEMOS

A System for

Discrete Event

Modelling on Simula

Springer Science+Business Media, LLC

First published 1987 by
MACMILLAN EDUCATION LTD
London and Basingstoke

Library of Congress Cataloging in Publication Data
Birtwistle, G. M. (Graham M.)

   Discrete event modelling on simula.
   Bibliography: p.
   Includes index.
   1. SIMULA (Computer program language)   2. Digital
computer simulation.   I. Title
QA76.73.S55B57   1987   001.4'34   87-12892

ISBN 978-1-4899-6687-2   ISBN 978-1-4899-6685-8 (eBook)
DOI 10.1007/978-1-4899-6685-8

CONTENTS

This book is a primer on discrete event simulation modelling using the DEMOS package. It is written in informal style as a teaching text and is not meant as a reference manual. It should thus be read from start to finish and not dipped into at random. The book covers DEMOS fairly completely and uses it as a vehicle in which to describe several simulation models. As we have not aimed to produce a general text, no attempt has been made to cover the statistical side of discrete event simulation.

DEMOS is implemented in the general purpose language SIMULA (an extension to ALGOL 60). Thus DEMOS programs may be run on any computer that supports SIMULA (see references [3 - 10]). The SIMULA source code for DEMOS and a 270 page reference manual are available from the author. See page 146 for more detail.

SIMULA (Dahl et al. [1]) itself contains simulation primitives sufficient to build any simulation model, but leaves it to the user himself to flesh out the primitives in the style of his choice. While this puts the SIMULA expert in an enviable position, it is at first sight unfortunate for the beginner or occasional user of SIMULA. For it would seem that he has to acquire considerable expertise in SIMULA before he can start building out these primitives and actually get down to describing the simulation model itself. But this is not so. The situation was foreseen by the designers of SIMULA and they provided a way round the problem, namely the CONTEXT (= block prefix) mechanism. A context is a package written in SIMULA which extends that language towards a specific problem area. It will define the basic concepts and methods associated with the area, but leaves it to the modeller to apply them in his own way.

DEMOS is a context intended to help beginners in discrete event simulation get off the ground. It augments SIMULA with a few building blocks which provide a standardised approach to a wide range of problems. DEMOS invites model description in terms of ENTITIES and how they compete for RESOURCES. Written in terms of these concepts, DEMOS programs are bona fide SIMULA programs, but SIMULA programs which conform to a very simple format. They can thus be written and understood without a specialist knowledge of SIMULA. (This is very typical of contexts: their use requires much less SIMULA expertise than their writing.)

Format of this book

This book is based on material developed for undergraduate and postgraduate courses in Discrete Systems given at Bradford University, England, and for other courses given to industry. It has been written in tutorial style, each new feature being first motivated and then used in an illustrative example. Inevitably with a book written in this style, one or two DEMOS facilities could not be fitted in (a list of these is given in chapter 8, page 142). The DEMOS Reference Manual (Birtwistle [14]) covers the implementation of DEMOS in full; it gives proper documentation and SIMULA source listings for all the facilities of DEMOS.

For nearly all the DEMOS models in this book, we have first outlined our solution pictorially by means of activity diagrams and then given the corresponding DEMOS code. Input and output details are also recorded where appropriate. The main text is spread over eight chapters. Chapter 1 provides a brief introduction to discrete event modelling, and explains why DEMOS came to be written.

Chapter 2 provides a tutorial on that small sub-set of SIMULA we require (a check list of SIMULA declaration and statement types is given in appendix A). N.B. The reader is assumed to have a working knowledge of ALGOL 60. ALGOL 60, SIMULA and DEMOS programs all take the form

```
BEGIN
   declarations;
   statements;
END;
```

ASIDE: All programmers have idiosyncrasies and one of the author's is to include semicolons before each END after the final statement in a block or compound statement, and also after the final END. These are optional in SIMULA, and hence in DEMOS.

Chapter 3 illustrates the basic DEMOS approach to discrete event simulation model building (which has been inherited from SIMULA). With this approach, a system is described in terms of its constituent components (we call them

Preface

ENTITIES) and a full action history describing its behaviour pattern is given for each entity. The separate entity descriptions are pieced together to describe the behaviour of the system as a whole. This approach enables the system modeller to focus his attention on the description of one entity at a time and is very natural.

In discrete event simulations, entities may compete with each other for system resources, cooperate with each other to perform a sequence of tasks, or even interrupt one another. Chapters 4, 5, 6 and 7 consider these basic synchronisation problems in turn, and show how they can be described in terms of DEMOS mechanisms.

In chapter 8, we first tidy up a few loose ends and then remark on the implementation of DEMOS as a package in SIMULA.

Each chapter contains several exercises which are best attempted when met in the text. They form an important part of the book: several reinforce or extend points just made in the main text, and some form a lead into the next section. Answers to all but two exercises are given at the end of the book. Regretfully, space considerations prevented us from including activity diagrams and output for all our solutions. That would have been nice.

Many individuals have helped make this book possible by their advice and encouragement through the years. Very special thanks are due to my gurus over several years: Kristen Nygaard (for imparting the SIMULA ethos) and Robin Hills (the same for discrete event simulation). Alan Benson, Ole-Johan Dahl, Roy Francis, Lars Enderin, Paul Luker, Mats Ohlin, Rod Wild and Norman Willis read the manuscript and helped remove several errors and infelicities of style. Any remaining errors are solely mine. Sorry.

DEMOS itself, and all the programs contained in this book, were developed on the Leeds University DEC System 10 computer using the excellent SIMULA compiler written by the Swedish Defense Research Establishment, Stockholm. Thanks are due to the Leeds University Centre for Computer Studies for permission to use their machine, and to several individuals there for their able, cheerful, and willing assistance. Thanks are due too to Jim Cunningham, Henk Sol, and Jean Vaucher for spotting errors in the original release and sending fixes.

Typesetting

This manuscript was prepared by the author using the DEC
utilities SOS and RUNOFF. The page size of 50 lines by 62
characters has meant some compromises. Firstly not all our
diagrams could be fitted on to a single page: these we have
managed to split in a reasonable manner. Secondly program
listings, which can usually be spread over 72 columns, have
had to be narrowed down. However, because SIMULA is a
free-format language, only a few programs seem to have
suffered. Finally, the output from DEMOS programs also
reckons on a 72 character line. Accordingly all output
listings have been 'doctored' by squeezing out some
unnecessary blanks.

In the formal description of SIMULA there are several
symbols which are not reproducible on standard line printers.
The representation of SIMULA programs in this book follows the
recommendations of the SIMULA Standards Group. Key words are
reserved and written in upper case (e.g. BEGIN, PROCEDURE,
IF). Other changes are: array brackets('[' replaced by '('
and ']' by ')'), exponentiation ('**'), integer division
('//'), greater than or equal ('>='), less than or equal
('<='), not equal (NE), logical and (AND), logical or (OR),
logical not (NOT), and power of 10 (E).

1 INTRODUCTION

All around us in everyday life are complex systems of men and machines. Automobile plants, steel foundries, telephone exchanges, ticket reservation systems, banking systems, air flight control systems, local transport systems, etc. spring to mind. For these to function properly, we need to be able to understand them and how they react to emergencies (perhaps a bus breaks down in the rush hour), continual high pressures (rush hour traffic) as well as under normal circumstances (traffic in off-peak periods). Since the world is continually changing, systems have to adapt to new circumstances, e.g. how does the building of a new town nearby affect the local bus company? Which extra services should be provided and thus how many extra buses and crew will be needed? We may also need to implement totally fresh systems - how then do we justify and test our designs?

For all but the very simplest systems, we cannot just go ahead, implement a change and see what happens. It may prove too costly (who would build a new metro system in a town 'just to see if it is needed'?); it may even prove catastrophic (a new air traffic control system, or a new control program for a chemical plant). We have thus a distinct need to be able to experiment with adaptations of existing systems and test proposed designs without actually disturbing them or building them respectively. Here simulation can help.

Simulation is a technique for representing a dynamic system by a model in order to gain information about the underlying system. If the behaviour of the model correctly matches the relevant behaviour characteristics of the underlying system, we may draw inferences about the system from experiments with the model and thus spare ourselves any disasters.

Practical simulation work involves:

1. specification of the problem and satisfactory answers to such questions as: "Is it worth doing?", "Can it be done within our time scale and budget?", etc.

2. building a model which describes the system. We have used an adaptation of the well known activity diagram technique (explained in chapter 3) to represent pictorially the logic of the models developed in this book. In real life situations, it is important to have such a high level representation of the model so that the modeller can discuss his understanding of reality with the specialists who run the actual system. Whoever they are, be they managers, foremen, or workers, they are unlikely to understand computer programs and so cannot be expected to read a program text and point out logical flaws in a model. Yet feedback from them is essential. They must understand (at least) how their part of the system is represented in the model and so be able to confirm what has been done correctly, point out what has been omitted, and draw attention to those parts which do not function exactly as the official rule book states. Not many systems work exactly as planned and the modeller has to describe a given system as it actually is.

3. converting the model into an operating DEMOS program. This step is quite straightforward, almost mechanical, from the appropriate activity diagram - a second important reason for using them. Indeed, activity cycle diagrams can be used as high level flow charts for simulations written in activity, event, process or transaction mode.

4. validating the model by checking its consistency with the underlying system before any changes are made. The success of this validation establishes a basis of confidence in the results that the model generates under new conditions. Inadequate consistency will cause the modeller to try again from step 2 or step 3 above.

5. using the computer simulation program as an experimental tool to study proposed changes in the underlying system that the program represents.

This book makes no attempt to cover the steps 1, 4, or 5 above. For thorough accounts of the important topics of model validation, output analysis, and the design of experiments, etc., the reader is instead referred to the excellent texts of Fishman [32] and Shannon [37].

In this book we cover steps 2 and 3, first representing our models by activity diagrams and then presenting the corresponding DEMOS programs.

Unlike most languages used for discrete event simulation, SIMULA does not force the user into one style of modelling. (See Birtwistle [15, chapters 2 and 3], or Hills [13] for non-trivial models coded in activity, event, and process modes.) The designers of SIMULA included a standard context called SIMULATION which contains a sort of common denominator to all these three styles, but left it to the user to build this out. Thus if SIMULATION is to be used as it stands, a style of model building has to be developed and the user has to write his own synchronisation routines, data collection routines, etc. Some of these prove to be fairly subtle.

DEMOS extends SIMULATION by a few basic concepts which provide the operational research worker with a standardised approach to a wide range of discrete event problems. These are primarily the ENTITY for mirroring major dynamic model components whose complete life cycles warrant description in the model, and the RESOURCE for representing minor components. In addition, DEMOS automates as much as possible (scheduling, data collection, report generation), and provides event tracing to help in model validation and debugging. Happily these turn out to be the very areas in which the deepest knowledge of SIMULA itself is required. Along with the simplifications inherent in a prescribed model structure, this means that DEMOS programs can be written in a surprisingly small sub-set of SIMULA. Teaching experience has shown that this can be learnt quickly, and the beginner is very soon able to concentrate his attention squarely on the construction of the model.

The approach to model building that we have used remains viable as the range of problems widens and their degree of difficulty sharpens. Importantly, nothing learnt by the beginner need be unlearnt as his experience grows. But DEMOS is not the panacea for all discrete event problems: eventually the user will surely run into a problem which is not capable of being modelled cleanly in complete detail in DEMOS. Then the user can fall back on the host language SIMULA. Because DEMOS programs are SIMULA programs, all the power of SIMULA is directly available behind the building blocks provided by DEMOS. Any feature not provided by DEMOS can be written directly into a DEMOS program as SIMULA code. Again, any user can add or even replace DEMOS features by standard SIMULA mechanisms. Notice that at this stage of his career, the user will have already written several DEMOS (= SIMULA) programs and picking up the required expertise in SIMULA proper is no longer such a problem. Much has been absorbed by osmosis.

DEMOS has taken some time to evolve. Vaucher [19] long ago suggested writing a GPSS-like package in SIMULA and implemented such a package himself. The author did the same and learnt some valuable lessons. In particular, GPSS allows only one transaction type (which closely parallels a process in SIMULA or an entity in DEMOS). For many examples this is sufficient, but the rest have to be bent into this format. It certainly concentrates the mind wonderfully well. Experience with GPSS teaches one how to do a lot within a simple framework - how to separate out and de-emphasize minor components and resist the urge to overmodel. GPSS also teaches the value of resource types, and standard methods of synchronisation, automatic report generation and data collection.

About this time, the author collaborated for a while with Robin Hills. Hills already had a considerable background in both practical simulation work and simulation language design (see Hills [22, 23]). This background in activity based languages proved especially valuable when we sought for ways of tackling models involving complicated decisions - an area in which GPSS is weak. The product of our joint efforts, called SIMON 75 (see Hills and Birtwistle [16]), used WAITUNTIL statements to make the scheduling of events as easy as possible and in a uniform style. Waits until are expensive on machine time, but the package had some merit in that it was easy to learn and resulted in concise yet readable programs.

It came as a pleasant surprise when some 50 or so non-trivial SIMON 75 programs were analysed by the author for their usage of wait until. They proved necessary in only a few cases, and it was at once apparent that a much faster new version could be implemented which would retain the ease of learning and textual clarity of the old. Along with a few other improvements, this was developed into DEMOS.

Despite its modest design aims, DEMOS has been successfully used to tackle some realistic industrial simulations. The author has applied DEMOS to problems in the steel industry, for work on operating systems (segmentation and paging algorithms), and designing real time processes (long haul and local area networks, multiple cpu configurations). At the time of writing, DEMOS is used in the oil, gas, steel, aerospace, space, and hardware industries, and at a score of research institutes and at universities.

This chapter is a short introduction to the highlights of
SIMULA. It is not meant to be exhaustive: it merely aims to
give the reader with little or no prior knowledge of SIMULA
enough understanding to follow through the later chapters on
DEMOS. Full accounts of SIMULA are found in Birtwistle et
al. [11] and Rohlfing [12]. The central new ideas in SIMULA
are those of the OBJECT and of the CONTEXT. An OBJECT is used
in SIMULA to mirror the characteristics and behaviour of a
major component in the system under description. For example,
a boat in a harbour simulation or a furnace in a steel mill
simulation. Objects with similar characteristics and the same
behaviour pattern have the same single definition called a
CLASS DECLARATION. A CONTEXT is roughly a library of object
definitions common to one particular topic, e.g. a HARBOUR
context may contain class declarations for boats, cranes,
tugs, the tide, etc., and a TRAFFIC context may contain class
declarations for cars, trucks, etc. Once defined, a context
serves as a library of predefined building blocks. It is
available to any number of programs by its very occurrence
(almost, see later) as prefix to a program, e.g.

```
TRAFFIC
BEGIN
   program using cars, trucks, etc.;
END;
```

The remainder of this chapter is a tutorial on the purpose and
usage of objects and contexts.

2.1 OBJECTS

Objects are used in SIMULA programs to mirror major components
in the actual system under investigation. Each major
component in the actual system is mapped into a corresponding
object in the SIMULA program. As an example, consider a
harbour simulation involving boats, lorries, etc. Each actual
boat will be represented in the SIMULA program by a
corresponding boat object. It follows that the boat object
has to reflect all those features of the actual boat deemed

relevant in the model: not only its physical characteristics
such as its tonnage, current load, etc., but also the actions
it carries out as it wends its own way through the harbour
system.

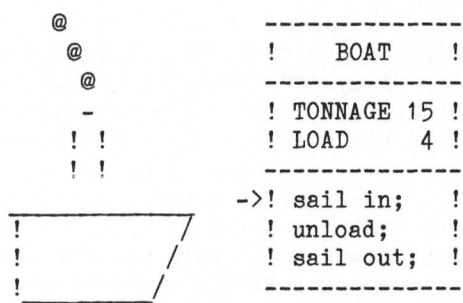

Figure 2.1 A boat and the corresponding boat object.

      Figure 2.1 introduces our standard way of depicting
objects - as rectangular boxes divided into three levels. The
top level gives the class of the object (here BOAT), the
middle level gives the ATTRIBUTES (data characteristics) of
the object (here TONNAGE and LOAD shown with current values of
15 and 4 respectively, perhaps in units of 1000 tons), and the
bottom level gives the life history of the boat object as a
sequence of actions. Here, these are informally shown as

              sail in; unload; sail out;

N.B. The middle and bottom layers may be empty, in which case
they will be omitted.

      Where it sheds light on the situation, the current action
of an object will be marked with an arrow, thus '->'. This
marker is called its LOCAL SEQUENCE CONTROL (or LSC for
short). The boat object in figure 2.1 represents an actual
boat sailing in. Figure 2.2 shows how a real world situation
involving three boats (one sailing out, one sailing in, and
one unloading) and one lorry (loading) would be mapped into a
SIMULA program. Notice how the LSCs of the boat objects move
on in tandem as the actual boats they represent progress
through the harbour system.

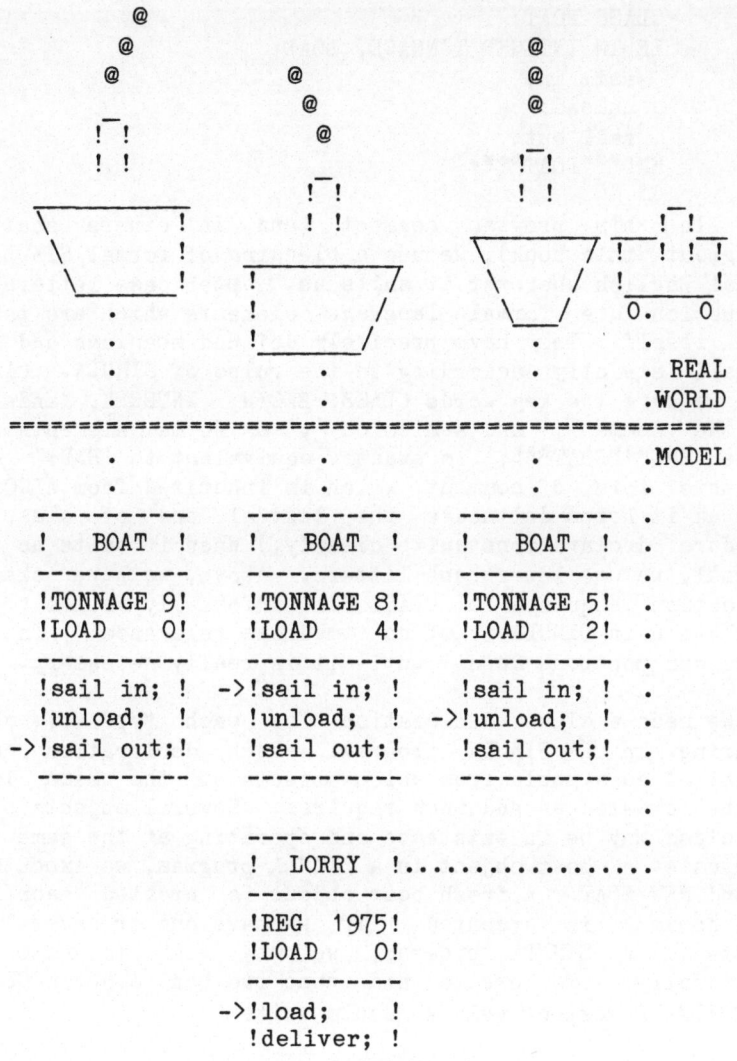

Figure 2.2 Objects representing 3 boats and 1 lorry.

Now although their individual data values are different, and they are currently performing different actions, the three boat objects have exactly the same layout of attributes and the same action sequence. The objects are said to be 'of the same class' and are defined by a single CLASS DECLARATION. Here it is in SIMULA (partly informally)

```
CLASS BOAT;
BEGIN INTEGER TONNAGE, LOAD;
  sail in;
  unload;
  sail out;
END***BOAT***;
```

N.B.   In this program segment (and in others scattered
throughout this book), we use a blending of formal SIMULA and
natural English wherever it suits us. Upper case letters and
punctuation are formal language elements which are part of
SIMULA itself. They have precisely defined meanings and must
be used strictly according to the rules of SIMULA. (In the
above we have the key words CLASS, BEGIN, INTEGER, and END,
and the comma ',' and semicolon ';' as formal elements. The
phrase 'END***BOAT***;' is exactly equivalent to 'END;' - we
use this form of comment, which is inherited from ALGOL 60,
often as it helps delineate the textual end of class and
procedure declarations quite clearly.) When it suits us to be
informal, we use lower case letters. Above, we have sketched
the action sequence of CLASS BOAT informally as its precise
formulation in SIMULA is of no immediate relevance.   In this
way we can postpone detail until it is really necessary.

     We need a class declaration for each type of object
appearing in a SIMULA program.   Each declaration can be
thought of as a mould from which objects of the same layout
can be created as and when required. Several objects of the
same class may be in existence and operating at the same time.
To   create a boat object in a SIMULA program, we execute the
command NEW BOAT. A fresh boat object is created each time
this command is executed.   If we have one or several boat
objects in a SIMULA program, we may wish to name them
individually.   To create and name two boat objects QE2 and
MARIECELESTE respectively we would write

        QE2   :- NEW BOAT;
        MARIECELESTE :- NEW BOAT;

(:- is read 'denotes').   QE2 and MARIECELESTE are SIMULA
variables of a type not found in ALGOL 60. They are REFERENCE
VARIABLES of type REF(BOAT) (which is read as 'ref to BOAT')
and are declared so

     REF(BOAT)QE2, MARIECELESTE;

QE2 and MARIECELESTE are variables capable of referencing boat objects. Similarly, should we wish to create and name a lorry L, we would declare REF(LORRY)L; and execute the reference assignment

        L :- NEW LORRY;

EXERCISES 2

    1. Give an informal declaration of CLASS LORRY based on the lorry object depicted in figure 2.2, page 7.

    2. Give an informal declaration of CLASS CUSTOMER describing the actions of customers who enter a barber's shop for a haircut. Draw a customer object which represents an actual customer whose hair is currently being cut.

CLASS VEHICLE

We now start to put things on a more formal footing. Consider the class of road vehicles. Although vehicles are of many shapes and sizes and are built for different purposes, they do have certain characteristics in common. We let them be typified (fairly arbitrarily) by their 'year of registration', their 'unladen weight', and by whether or not they are currently 'broken down'.

    The program below declares the prototype for such vehicles (lines 2-6), declares a pair of reference variables (FIAT and ROLLS) capable of referencing vehicle objects (line 8) and then creates a 1974 vehicle of weight 0.8 tons (FIAT) and a 1930 vehicle of weight 3.0 tons (ROLLS). Neither vehicle is broken down.

```
    BEGIN
      CLASS VEHICLE(REGISTERED, WEIGHT);
           INTEGER REGISTERED; REAL WEIGHT;
      BEGIN BOOLEAN BROKENDOWN;
         IF REGISTERED < 1885 OR WEIGHT <= 0.0 THEN error;
      END***VEHICLE***;

      REF(VEHICLE)FIAT, ROLLS;

      FIAT  :- NEW VEHICLE(1974, 0.8);
      ROLLS :- NEW VEHICLE(1930, 3.0);
    L: END;
```

In this program, the informal call on the undefined PROCEDURE
error indicates that corrective action is to be taken should
the actual parameter values to an object under creation prove
to be invalid.

```
------------------------------
!   MAIN PROGRAM BLOCK   !
------------------------------
!CLASS VEHICLE            !          --------------------
!FIAT              ---!----->!      VEHICLE      !
!ROLLS             ---!---    --------------------
------------------------------ !   !REGISTERED     1974!
!FIAT :-                  !  !   !WEIGHT          0.8!
! NEW VEHICLE(1974,0.8);! !   !BROKENDOWN    FALSE!
!ROLLS:-                  !  !   --------------------
! NEW VEHICLE(1930,3.0);! !   !IF REGISTERED<1885!
!L:                       !  !   !  OR WEIGHT <= 0.0!
------------------------------ !   !  THEN error;     !
                                !   --------------------
                                !
                                !
                                !   --------------------
                          --->!      VEHICLE      !
                                --------------------
                                !REGISTERED     1930!
                                !WEIGHT          3.0!
                                !BROKENDOWN    FALSE!
                                --------------------
                                !IF REGISTERED<1885!
                                !  OR WEIGHT <= 0.0!
                                !  THEN error;     !
                                --------------------
```

Figure 2.3 Two terminated vehicle objects.

     Figure 2.3 is a representation of the structures created
at the label L. Initially there are no objects in the system
and the reference variables FIAT and ROLLS each take the
standard value of NONE, which represents no object *1). Two
vehicle objects are created by our program (lines 10 and 11).
We detail the creation of the first object by following
through the reference assignment on line 10, namely
----
*1). In SIMULA all declared variables have standard initial
values according to their type. Booleans are initialised to
FALSE, arithmetics to zero, and reference variables to NONE.

```
        FIAT :- NEW VEHICLE(1974, 0.8);
```

First an object is created with layout as defined by CLASS
VEHICLE. The parameter values 1974 and 0.8 are transmitted
(by VALUE in the ALGOL 60 sense), and its local variable
BROKENDOWN is set to the standard initial value FALSE. Then
the actions of the object are entered. These perform a rough
check on the validity of the parameters. Once the actions of
the object have been exhausted, their LSCs are no longer
required, and the objects are said to be TERMINATED. Program
control returns to the generator NEW and the whereabouts of
the object is assigned to the reference variable FIAT.

       The second object is created in much the same way, and so
at the label L, FIAT and ROLLS will reference two distinct
vehicle objects. We can now access the current data values of
their attributes (parameters and local data values) from the
main program by the DOT NOTATION. Below we tabulate all the
possible accesses, their current values and their types.

Access	Value	Type
FIAT.REGISTERED	1974	INTEGER
FIAT.WEIGHT	0.8	REAL
FIAT.BROKENDOWN	FALSE	BOOLEAN
ROLLS.REGISTERED	1930	INTEGER
ROLLS.WEIGHT	3.0	REAL
ROLLS.BROKENDOWN	FALSE	BOOLEAN

Possible statements in a main program using these accesses are

```
        [INTEGER VINTAGE;  REAL TONNAGE;]

        IF ROLLS.REGISTERED < 1930 THEN VINTAGE := VINTAGE+1;
        IF FIAT.BROKENDOWN THEN take FIAT off the road;
        TONNAGE := FIAT.WEIGHT + ROLLS.WEIGHT;
```

The dot notation can be used to reassign attribute values as
well as read them. Should the unthinkable happen and the
ROLLS later break down, we would write

```
        ROLLS.BROKENDOWN := TRUE;
```

in our program.

Notice that when the program action is inside a particular object - such as when carrying out the parameter checking on object creation - the object refers to its own attributes directly, e.g. WEIGHT and REGISTERED. When the action is in the main program, we have to specify the particular object we require as well as the name of the attribute. These remote accesses have the format

<object reference>.<attribute name>

A run time (= execution time) error results if the value of the object reference in a remote access is NONE. The null object certainly has no attributes. Accordingly, the program will stop executing and print out a suitable error message.

The remote access problem has its analogues in everyday life. For example, when requiring the telephone number London 123 4567, we dial 123 4567 from inside London itself, but 01 123 4567 from the rest of Britain. 01 is the dialling code for London. When outside London, omitting the 01 prefix gives us quite a different value. Indeed it may not even exist (compare asking for BROKENDOWN within the main block).

EXERCISES 2 (continued)

3. Write the declaration of CLASS CAR. Each car object is registered, has a weight, and may or may not be broken down. In addition to these VEHICLE attributes, it has a maximum speed and some seats. Remember to check as many parameter values as you can.

Write SIMULA code to create a 1970, 1.2 ton car with a maximum speed of 240 kph and 2 seats referenced by REF(CAR)JAG. Cause JAG to breakdown. Draw the object referenced by JAG, filling in its attribute values to represent its status after the breakdown.

4. Write a declaration for CLASS BOAT. Each boat object has a tonnage, a current load (not a parameter), and a crew. The owners man the boats according to the formula: 5 permanent officers (including the captain), plus one seaman for every 200 tons of tonnage (rounded).

Write SIMULA code to create a boat object B of tonnage 2600 tons and then load it with 1600 tons. Use the actions of the class body to compute the size of the crew. Draw the object.

5. Give another everyday analogue of the remote access
problem in addition to the one given in the text (telephoning
a number in London).

SUB-CLASSES OF VEHICLE

We now turn our attention to defining more specific kinds of
road vehicles, for example, cars, trucks and pick-ups. All
are vehicles and will be registered, have an unladen weight
and   (hopefully) will be roadworthy.   But they have
distinguishing qualities too - trucks carry loads, cars carry
passengers and pick-ups have cranes for towing. We could
start from scratch and define

```
        CLASS TRUCK(REGISTERED, WEIGHT, MAXLOAD);
            INTEGER REGISTERED; REAL WEIGHT, MAXLOAD;
        BEGIN BOOLEAN BROKENDOWN, JUGGERNAUT;
          REAL LOAD;
          IF REGISTERED < 1885 OR WEIGHT <= 0.0 OR
            MAXLOAD <= 0.0 THEN error;
          JUGGERNAUT := MAXLOAD >= 25.0;
        END***TRUCK***;
```

and in the same way

```
        CLASS CAR(REGISTERED,WEIGHT,MAXSPEED,SEATS);...;

        CLASS PICKUP(REGISTERED,WEIGHT);..............;
```

But we have done so much of this work before. If trucks,
cars, and pick-ups really are 'vehicles plus' we should be
able to build on the definition of vehicle that we have
already worked out. This we can do in SIMULA by employing the
PREFIX NOTATION. We simply declare

```
        VEHICLE CLASS TRUCK(MAXLOAD); REAL MAXLOAD;
        BEGIN BOOLEAN JUGGERNAUT;
          REAL LOAD;
          IF MAXLOAD <= 0.0 THEN error;
          JUGGERNAUT := MAXLOAD >= 25.0;
        END***TRUCK***;

        VEHICLE CLASS CAR(MAXSPEED, SEATS);
                INTEGER MAXSPEED, SEATS;
        BEGIN
          IF MAXSPEED < 50 OR SEATS < 1 THEN error;
        END***CAR***;
```

```
VEHICLE CLASS PICKUP;
BEGIN
  REF(VEHICLE)VICTIM;

  PROCEDURE TOWIN(V); REF(VEHICLE)V;
  BEGIN
    IF V.BROKENDOWN THEN VICTIM :- V ELSE
        false alarm;
  END***TOW IN***;

END***PICK UP***;
```

TRUCK, CAR, and PICKUP are said to be SUB-CLASSES of VEHICLE. Figure 2.4 shows the attribute structures of the four types of object we have defined so far and typical accesses. Objects of the three sub-classes TRUCK, CAR, and PICKUP are compound objects which inherit all the attributes and all the actions of their prefix VEHICLE. When such objects are created, the actions of the prefix level(s) are executed first, and then the actions at the new level. Prefixing can be carried out to any depth, and so we may now use TRUCK, CAR, or PICKUP as prefix if we wish.

Trucks initially carry no payload. They are deemed juggernauts if their maximum payload is 25 tons or over. To create a 1970, 5 ton truck with a maximum payload of 37.5 tons we may write

```
        T :- NEW TRUCK(1970, 5.0, 37.5);        [REF(TRUCK)T;]
```

Note that each new truck object requires 3 parameters - two are inherited from the VEHICLE prefix. Later, to give T a load of 16 tons, we write

```
        T.LOAD := 16.0;
```

Cars have maximum speeds and seats as attributes in addition to VEHICLE attributes. We create a new 1969, 1.5 ton car with a top speed of 145 kph and with 5 seats by

```
        C :- NEW CAR(1969, 1.5, 145, 5);        [REF(CAR)C;]
```

```
-----------
! VEHICLE !<---REF(VEHICLE)V
-----------
!REGISTERED!      V.REGISTERED
!WEIGHT    !      V.WEIGHT
!BROKENDOWN!      V.BROKENDOWN
-----------


-----------
!   CAR   !<---REF(CAR)C
-----------
!REGISTERED!      C.REGISTERED
!WEIGHT    !      C.WEIGHT
!BROKENDOWN!      C.BROKENDOWN
-----------
!MAXSPEED  !      C.MAXSPEED
!SEATS     !      C.SEATS
-----------


-----------
!  TRUCK  !<---REF(TRUCK)T
-----------
!REGISTERED!      T.REGISTERED
!WEIGHT    !      T.WEIGHT
!BROKENDOWN!      T.BROKENDOWN
-----------
!MAXLOAD   !      T.MAXLOAD
!JUGGERNAUT!      T.JUGGERNAUT
!LOAD      !      T.LOAD
-----------


-----------
! PICKUP  !<---REF(PICKUP)P
-----------
!REGISTERED!      P.REGISTERED
!WEIGHT    !      P.WEIGHT
!BROKENDOWN!      P.BROKENDOWN
-----------
!VICTIM    !      P.VICTIM
!TOWIN     !      P.TOWIN(C)
-----------
```

Figure 2.4 Attribute structures and accesses.

Finally, pick-up objects are furnished with a reference
VICTIM to the current vehicle (if any) that they are towing.
VICTIM is initially NONE. The PROCEDURE TOWIN is the means of
supplying a suitable value to VICTIM. It may be any vehicle,
truck, car or pick-up object. Local procedures, such as
TOWIN, are treated as attributes in just the same way as are
parameters and local data values. They too are accessible via
the dot notation. We create a 1976, 4 ton pick-up by

     P :- NEW PICKUP(1976, 4.0);   [REF(PICKUP)P;]

If C breaks down (REF(CAR)C), P can be deputed to tow in C by
such a coding sequence as

     C.BROKENDOWN := TRUE;
     P.TOWIN(C);
   L:

```
    ---------------        ------------------
    !MAIN  PROGRAM!  --->!      PICKUP      !
    ---------------   !    ------------------
    !CLASS VEHICLE!   !    !REGISTERED  1976!
    !CLASS CAR    !   !    !WEIGHT       4.0!
    !CLASS TRUCK  !   !    !BROKENDOWN FALSE!
    !CLASS PICKUP !   !    ------------------
    !P        ---!---    !VICTIM       ---!---
    !C        ---!---    !PROCEDURE TOWIN !  !
    ---------------   !    ------------------   !
    !............!   !                         !
    !P.TOWIN(C);  !   !                         !
  ->!L:           !   !    ------------------   !
    ---------------  --->!      CAR        !<--
                          ------------------
                          !REGISTERED  1969!
                          !WEIGHT       1.5!
                          !BROKENDOWN  TRUE!
                          ------------------
                          !MAXSPEED     145!
                          !SEATS          5!
                          ------------------
```

Figure 2.5 Result of the call P.TOWIN(C).

Figure 2.5 pictures the situation at the label L.   When the
PROCEDURE TOWIN is called, the actual parameter value C is
passed by REFERENCE - a mechanism not found in ALGOL 60.

Informally this method of passing reference parameters is
equivalent to the reference assignment

    ⟨formal parameter⟩ :- ⟨actual parameter⟩;   (here V :- C;)

and is subject to the compatibility checks outlined in the
next sub-section. Rather interestingly, if P now breaks down,
another pick-up (Q say) can be instructed to tow in P (and C!)
by

        P.BROKENDOWN := TRUE;
        Q.TOWIN(P);

    In our examples, the actions belonging to an object have
been concerned with checking parameter values on object
creation and initialising local quantities. Furthermore, they
have been executed at once. Their scope is much broader than
this and they may be used to describe complete life histories
as indicated earlier. Such action sequences may be executed
all at once, or more usually, as a sequence of separate
sub-sequences or active phases. Between two active phases of
a given object, any number of active phases of other objects
may occur. Since this is the very basis of the process
approach, we leave its development to the next chapter.

SECURITY OF DATA ACCESS

N.B. For the examples of this section we assume the class
declarations of the previous section and the existence of the
reference variables

               REF(VEHICLE)V;

      REF(TRUCK)T; REF(CAR)C; REF(PICKUP)P;

So far we have concentrated on the objects themselves. We now
turn our attention to reference variables and reference
assignments. Reference variables are given a QUALIFICATION on
declaration, e.g. the qualification of REF(VEHICLE)V is
VEHICLE and of REF(TRUCK)T is TRUCK. This qualification
restricts the kind of object to which a reference variable is
allowed to refer. The typical reference assignment is

       ⟨reference variable⟩ :- ⟨object expression⟩;

Reference variables may be assigned to reference

a)   objects of their qualifying class
      e.g. V :- NEW VEHICLE(1976, 1.4);
            T :- NEW TRUCK(1974, 5.0, 37.2);

b)   objects of classes prefixed by their qualifying class
      e.g. V :- NEW PICKUP(1970, 10.0);
            V :- T;   (an existing object or NONE)

c)   no object at all
            V :- NONE;

By means of qualification, a SIMULA compiler can check the
compatibility of the left and right hand sides. (NONE can be
thought of as having a universal qualification here.) Such
attempted assignments as

            T :- NEW CAR(1939, 1.4, 100, 4);
            C :- NEW VEHICLE(1976, 1.9);

must always fail this compatibility check. This is sensible
because later, apparently good attempts to access (such as
T.LOAD or C.SEATS above) would be in error.   There is one
genuine case of doubt exemplified by the reference assignment

            T :- V;

which may be valid. It is valid if V currently references a
truck object or NONE: but is illegal if V currently
references a vehicle, a car, or a pick-up object. This check
can only be made during program execution. On meeting such
assignments in the source program, the SIMULA compiler prints
a warning message and plants a run time check which is carried
out when the assignment is actually attempted.   If this
compatibility check fails, execution of the program stops at
once. The compiler can thus guarantee that, at run time, a
reference variable refers either to NONE, or to an object of
its qualifying class, or to an object prefixed by its
qualifying class.   That is, if a REF(A) variable does
reference an object, then that object is at least 'A sized'.

     The qualification of a reference variable acts as a key
opening up the inside of the object it currently references.
In a remote access such as C.SEATS, we are guaranteed that C
references NONE (causing a run time error) or that the object
referenced by C, being at least CAR sized, must possess an
INTEGER attribute SEATS.   The qualification CAR of C gives
both the offset of SEATS within the object and its type

(INTEGER).   The compiler can also use qualification to reject such attempted accesses as C.DRIVER or T.SEATS as undefined, or such attempted illegal uses as

$$C.BROKENDOWN := C.BROKENDOWN + 1;$$

The prefix notation permits a useful flexibility in object referencing typified by the PROCEDURE TOWIN local to CLASS PICKUP. Any vehicle object, or object of a class prefixed by VEHICLE, is a suitable potential victim. This is very desirable. A weak qualification permits a wide range of objects to be referenced at the cost of run time checks on the validity of all remote accesses to attributes declared at stronger levels. We do not go into this aspect of SIMULA here as we never need to use it in the sequel. Indeed it is not frequently required in DEMOS programs. The reader is referred to Birtwistle et al. [11, chapter 4 on QUA, INSPECT, and VIRTUAL].

==, =/=, IS and IN

To complete this section on security of access, we introduce four more operators: ==, =/=, IS and IN. Because such a remote access as

V.BROKENDOWN   [REF(VEHICLE)V;]

causes a run time error if the value of V is NONE, it is important to have a means of checking against that eventuality. To this end, SIMULA includes the REFERENCE COMPARATORS == and =/=. Let V and W be references to objects or NONE.   Then

V == W is TRUE only if V and W reference the same
        object, or both are NONE.

V =/= W is equivalent to NOT(V == W).

Typical uses are furnished by

a) IF V == ROLLS THEN special treatment ELSE
      send V to end of queue;

where only ROLLS gets special treatment, and

b) inside the PROCEDURE TOWIN (page 14) local to CLASS PICKUP

where we ought to check the actual parameter against NONE each
time TOWIN is called. A better formulation would be

```
PROCEDURE TOWIN(V); REF(VEHICLE)V;
BEGIN
  IF V == NONE THEN parameter none ELSE
  IF VICTIM =/= NONE THEN pick-up engaged ELSE
  IF V.BROKENDOWN THEN VICTIM :- V ELSE
    false alarm;
END***TOWIN***;
```

in which IF V == NONE guards against the actual parameter
value being NONE (either explicitly or, more likely, as a
reference variable with value NONE), and IF VICTIM =/= NONE is
used to check that this pick-up is not already busy towing in
a victim. Only if these two checks are passed do we enter the
third IF condition.

IS and IN may be used to ascertain at run time the type
of object a variable is currently referencing. We use them in
conditions of the formats (a little restricted)

<reference variable> IS <qualification>, e.g. V IS CAR

<reference variable> IN <qualification>, e.g. V IN VEHICLE

Given CLASS A and REF(A)X. Then at run time the value of X
can only be a) NONE, b) an A object, or c) an object of a
class prefixed by A.

X IS A is TRUE only if X references an A object; it is
        FALSE if X has the value NONE or X references an
        object of a class prefixed by A.

X IN A is TRUE if X references an A object or an object of
        a class prefixed by A; it is FALSE if X == NONE.

We could thus extend the PROCEDURE TOWIN to

```
PROCEDURE TOWIN(V); REF(VEHICLE)V;
BEGIN
  IF ........ ELSE false alarm;
  IF V IS CAR THEN tow to nearest garage ELSE
  IF V IS TRUCK THEN tow to its owner ELSE
    tow to my garage;
END***TOWIN***;
```

where a call on this new TOWIN not only locates the victim as
before, but takes it to the nearest garage if it is a car, to
the victim's owning garage if it is a truck, and to the
rescuer's garage if the victim is either another pick-up or a
vehicle object.

EXERCISES 2 (continued)

   6. Define a CLASS ORDER which describes a class of
objects each of which possesses a serial number, an arrival
number, a set-up time, and a processing time.

   Define a CLASS BATCH which describes a class of objects
which have all the attributes of ORDER objects plus a batch
size.

   Define a CLASS SINGLE which describes a class of objects
which have all the attributes of ORDER objects plus a
finishing time and a weight.

   Define a CLASS PLATE which describes a class of objects
which have all the attributes of ORDER objects plus weight,
length, width, and finishing time.

N.B. In our suggested solution, all attributes are given as
local variables and none as parameters.

2.2 CONTEXTS

A SIMULA program must contain the class declarations which
give the patterns of the objects it uses. For example, a
traffic simulation involving the classes we developed in the
last section, would have the format

             BEGIN
                CLASS VEHICLE..............;
                VEHICLE CLASS CAR..........;
                VEHICLE CLASS TRUCK........;
                VEHICLE CLASS PICKUP.......;
                other relevant declarations;
                actions involving objects of
                   the above classes;
             END;

N.B. In a proper SIMULA program, the declarations must, of

course, appear in full. We have used the dots for brevity's
sake, a device we will often resort to in the sequel.

When working in a particular problem area, e.g.   traffic
simulation, it is clear that the same basic declarations may
be useful over a whole range of programs. It is tiresome and
error prone to prepare much the same program several times.
Instead, the inter-related definitions of vehicle types can be
collected together in SIMULA   to define a CONTEXT.   In this
case, we choose to call it TRAFFIC and define it by

```
            CLASS TRAFFIC;
            BEGIN CLASS VEHICLE..........;
               VEHICLE CLASS CAR..........;
               VEHICLE CLASS TRUCK........;
               VEHICLE CLASS PICKUP.......;
            END***TRAFFIC***;
```

Normally, TRAFFIC would now be separately compiled and the
object code be retained in a library. Users with an interest
in this particular field (and with access to the library) can
pick up the compiled context code by an EXTERNAL DECLARATION
as below

```
            BEGIN EXTERNAL CLASS TRAFFIC;
               TRAFFIC
                  BEGIN  other relevant declarations;
                     actions  involving   objects   of
                     classes defined in this block and
                     in TRAFFIC;
                  END;
            END;
```

As a particular example, the user wishing to write a   program
involving 2 cars and 1 pick-up merely codes

```
            BEGIN EXTERNAL CLASS TRAFFIC;
            TRAFFIC
               BEGIN REF(CAR)C1, C2;
               REF(PICKUP)AUTOREX;
               C1       :- NEW CAR......;
               C2       :- NEW CAR......;
               AUTOREX :- NEW PICKUP...;
               ....................
               END;
            END;
```

All the concepts defined inside TRAFFIC (namely VEHICLE, CAR,
TRUCK, PICKUP) are directly available within the user-defined
block. The ordinary user may restrict himself to using the
problem-oriented and familiar concepts as constituent building
blocks in his programs. He need not know the full SIMULA
language. But the experienced programmer has the general
language available and may extend the application language by
his own new concepts should he wish. For example,

```
        EXTERNAL CLASS TRAFFIC;

        TRAFFIC CLASS POLICE SURVEILLANCE;
        BEGIN
           CLASS TRAFFIC_LIGHTS...........;
           VEHICLE CLASS BLACK MARIA......;
           CAR CLASS POLICE CAR...........;
           ..............................
        END***POLICE SURVEILLANCE***;
```

Any block prefixed by this new context, e.g.

```
        POLICE SURVEILLANCE
           BEGIN
           ..............
           END;
```

has available all the definitions at the TRAFFIC level plus
the new ideas of traffic lights and police vehicles. Notice
that black marias and police cars may be towed in by pick-ups
when broken down since their respective class declarations
both contain the prefix VEHICLE (directly in the case of CLASS
BLACK_MARIA, and implicitly in the case of CLASS POLICE CAR
since its explicit prefix CAR is itself prefixed by VEHICLE).
Trafficants unconcerned by police activities will continue to
use TRAFFIC as prefix to their programs.

EXERCISES 2 (continued)

      7. Which items would you like already defined in a
context for a harbour simulation? Write down the skeleton of
its definition in SIMULA and how you would use it.

We begin with an analogy. Consider splitting the text of a play (= a system) into separate texts for each role (= each entity). For example, Act 1, Scene 1 of Shakespeare's Macbeth starts

> 1 Witch. When shall we three meet again.
> In thunder, lightning, or in rain?
> 2 Witch. When the hurlyburly's done,
> When the battle's lost and won.
> 3 Witch. That will be ere the set of sun.
> 1 Witch. Where the place?
> 2 Witch. Upon the heath.
> 3 Witch. There to meet with Macbeth.
> ....

This can be split into three separately described roles, as below. (Asterisks represent pauses in between speeches.)

> 1 Witch. When shall we three meet again.
> In thunder, lightning or in rain?
> *
>
> Where the place?
> *
>
> ....
>
> 2 Witch. When the hurlyburly's done,
> When the battle's lost and won.
> *
>
> Upon the heath.
> *
>
> ....
>
> 3 Witch. That will be ere the set of sun.
> *
>
> There to meet with Macbeth.
> *
>
> ....

The separate roles are sequences of active speaking phases and passive waits until it is one's turn again. In much the same way, when we come to describe a simulation

model, we first split the totality into suitable components
(cf. 1 Witch, 2 Witch, 3 Witch, ... in Macbeth), and provide
an object with a full life history to act out the role of
each. Once we have sorted out how each object synchronises
its actions with other objects (a major modelling problem),
the description of the rest of an object's life history can be
completed separately. We simply psyche ourselves into each
role in turn and then write out its actions from its own
viewpoint.

3.1 THE FIRST MODEL

EXAMPLE 1: PORT SYSTEM

A port has 2 jetties each of which can be used for unloading
by one boat at a time. Boats arrive at the port periodically
and must wait if no jetty is currently free. When a jetty is
available, a boat may dock and start to unload. When this
activity has been completed, the boat leaves the jetty and
sails away. The port authority has a pool of 3 tugs. Two are
required for docking: only one when a boat leaves its jetty.

It is instructive to hand simulate the system with some 'easy'
numbers. Assume that

- boats arrive at times 0, 1, 15
- tug manoeuvres take 2 time units
- unloading takes 14 time units.

Figure 3.1 gives a full TRACE of the Port System using
this data. We have named the boats B1, B2, and B3. As the
state of the system changes only at certain critical times,
only these times have been recorded (hence DISCRETE EVENT
simulation). The trace records the essential behaviour of the
system as a time ordered sequence of events. The first three
columns of figure 3.1 give the 'when', the 'who' and the
'what' of each event. The who of each event is ALWAYS a boat,
and so the behaviour of the complete system can be rephrased
in terms of the actions and interactions of B1, B2, and B3.
We follow this lead in figure 3.2 and split the trace
narrative into three separate columns, one for each boat.
Notice that each and every event appears once under the
appropriate boat name, and that no events have been omitted.
The whole is precisely the sum of its parts.

```
TIME ! BOAT ! CURRENT ACTION  ! NEXT EVENT
-------------------------------------------
 0.0 ! B1  ! arrive          !
     ! B1  ! request 1 jetty !
     ! B1  ! seize 1 jetty   !
     ! B1  ! request 2 tugs  !
     ! B1  ! seize 2 tugs    !
     ! B1  ! start docking   !  2.0
 1.0 ! B2  ! arrive          !
     ! B2  ! request 1 jetty !
     ! B2  ! seize 1 jetty   !
     ! B2  ! request 2 tugs  !
 2.0 ! B1  ! release 2 tugs  !
     ! B1  ! start unloading ! 16.0
     ! B2  ! seize 2 tugs    !
     ! B2  ! start docking   !  4.0
 4.0 ! B2  ! release 2 tugs  !
     ! B2  ! start unloading ! 18.0
15.0 ! B3  ! arrive          !
     ! B3  ! request 1 jetty !
16.0 ! B1  ! request 1 tug   !
     ! B1  ! seize 1 tug     !
     ! B1  ! start leaving   ! 18.0
18.0 ! B2  ! request 1 tug   !
     ! B2  ! seize 1 tug     !
     ! B2  ! start leaving   ! 20.0
     ! B1  ! release 1 tug   !
     ! B1  ! release 1 jetty !
     ! B1  ! quit            ! ****
     ! B3  ! seize 1 jetty   !
     ! B3  ! request 2 tugs  !
     ! B3  ! seize 2 tugs    !
     ! B3  ! start docking   ! 20.0
20.0 ! B2  ! release 1 tug   !
     ! B2  ! release 1 jetty !
     ! B2  ! quit            ! ****
     ! B3  ! release 2 tugs  !
     ! B3  ! start unloading ! 34.0
34.0 ! B3  ! request 1 tug   !
     ! B3  ! seize 1 tug     !
     ! B3  ! start leaving   ! 36.0
36.0 ! B3  ! release 1 tug   !
     ! B3  ! release 1 jetty !
     ! B3  ! quit            ! ****
-------------------------------------------
```

Figure 3.1 Trace of the Port System.

```
-------------------------------------------
!                     !         TIME        !
! EVENT   SEQUENCE ---------------------------
!                     ! B1  !  B2  !  B3   !
-------------------------------------------
! arrive              !  0.0 !  1.0 ! 15.0 !
! request 1 jetty     !  0.0 !  1.0 ! 15.0 !
! seize 1 jetty       !  0.0 !  1.0 ! 18.0 !
! request 2 tugs      !  0.0 !  1.0 ! 18.0 !
! seize 2 tugs        !  0.0 !  2.0 ! 18.0 !
! start docking       !  0.0 !  2.0 ! 18.0 !
! release 2 tugs      !  2.0 !  4.0 ! 20.0 !
! start unloading     !  2.0 !  4.0 ! 20.0 !
! request 1 tug       ! 16.0 ! 18.0 ! 34.0 !
! seize 1 tug         ! 16.0 ! 18.0 ! 34.0 !
! start leaving       ! 16.0 ! 18.0 ! 34.0 !
! release 1 tug       ! 18.0 ! 20.0 ! 36.0 !
! release 1 jetty     ! 18.0 ! 20.0 ! 36.0 !
! quit                ! 18.0 ! 20.0 ! 36.0 !
-------------------------------------------
```

Figure 3.2 Table of event times for each boat.

Figure 3.2 is just a rehash of the trace in which we have
followed through the actions of each boat as an individual.
Importantly, the action sequence of each boat may be framed in
exactly the same way - as the sequence of activities

        dock; unload; leave;

and clearly invites the declaration of a CLASS BOAT
(informally)

```
        CLASS BOAT;
        BEGIN request 1 jetty;
          seize 1 jetty;
          request 2 tugs;
          seize 2 tugs;
          dock;
          release 2 tugs;
          unload;
          request 1 tug;
          seize 1 tug;
          leave;
          release 1 tug;
          release 1 jetty;
        END***BOAT***;
```

from which three boat objects will be created. (Notice that
arrival will be taken care of by executing NEW BOAT at
appropriate times in the main program; quitting is
automatically taken care of by the SIMULA system when a boat
object exhausts its action sequence.)

EXERCISES 3

    1. Give another class declaration - role analogue
besides the one given in the text (Macbeth).

3.2 ACTIVITIES

Before developing DEMOS code for CLASS BOAT, we take a closer
look at the notion of an ACTIVITY. The life history of each
boat is a sequence of three such activities and their general
pattern would seem to be:

    ACQUIRE (= REQUEST and then SEIZE) the extra resources
needed for the forthcoming task.   The extra resources are
usually requested one at a time, and each request may be
followed by a wait until sufficient of the resource is
available and can be seized. N.B.   This being understood,
from now on we will usually use ACQUIRE for this joint phase
instead of separating it into a REQUEST followed by a SEIZE.

    HOLD all resources (both those just seized and those
previously acquired) while carrying out the task.

    RELEASE those resources no longer required and continue
with the next activity, if any.

NAME OF ACTIVITY	RESOURCES TO BE ACQUIRED	DURATION OF HOLD	RESOURCES TO BE RELEASED
DOCK	1 jetty and 2 tugs	2.0	2 tugs
UNLOAD	none	14.0	none
LEAVE	1 tug	2.0	1 tug and 1 jetty

Figure 3.3 The three activity patterns in detail.

Figure 3.3 tabulates these activity stages in the context of
our PORT system. If all the extra resources required for the
start of an activity are free, they can be seized in turn
immediately and the activity starts at once (e.g. B1 when
docking). When a resource is not available, then a request is
followed by a wait, and the boat object issuing the request
has to wait until any current user(s) have freed sufficient
for it to proceed (e.g. at time 1.0, B2 can seize a jetty,
but must wait for 2 tugs as only 1 is then free. Again, at
time 15.0, B3 must wait for a jetty to be released. When this
occurs at time 18.0 (released by B1), B3 does not have to wait
further to seize its tugs).

Notice that each boat object retains the same jetty
throughout its lifespan, but releases the tugs before
unloading. In general, resources may be retained through an
arbitrary number of activities. Also note that if no extra
resources are required, as for 'unload' (because the jetty has
already been seized), the pattern simplifies as the acquire
phase drops out and there can be no waiting. Such activities
are called BOUND as they are bound to follow straight on from
the previous activity.

This activity pattern of ACQUIRE (with the implicit wait
until resources are available), HOLD, and then RELEASE turns
out to be very common in discrete event model building -
indeed, CSL (Buxton and Laski [20]) and ECSL (Clementson [21])
were founded upon it. The activity pattern can be represented
neatly by ACTIVITY DIAGRAMS. These were introduced by Tocher
and Hills, but we can simplify them due to SIMULA's object
feature. Activity diagrams are essentially high level flow
charts which encapsulate the main features of a model. They
are important because they provide good bases for model
presentation and discussion (especially with people unfamiliar
with programming languages): and also for the eventual coding
of the model. In activity diagrams, we depict model resources
by circles labelled with the initial value of the item they
represent, e.g.

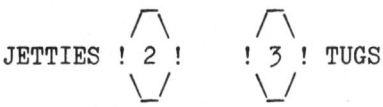

JETTIES ! 2 !   ! 3 ! TUGS

(Sorry - this is the best we can do.) Each activity is
represented by a rectangular box labelled with the appropriate
task, e.g.

```
    ---------------
    !   DOCK    !
    ---------------
```

The activities are considered one by one. If extra resources
are required for an activity, then we draw directed lines from
the appropriate resource circle into the top edge of the
activity box (if time is taken to flow down the page).

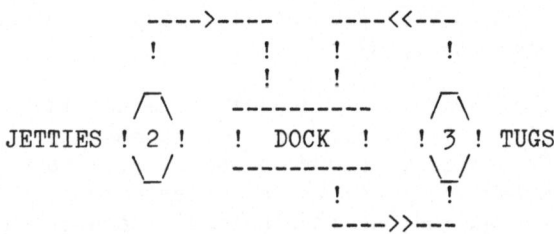

Figure 3.4   The activity DOCK.

Directed lines leading from the bottom edge of the activity
box back into resource circles represent resources no longer
needed when the activity has been completed. Figure 3.4 shows
the diagram for the activity DOCK. Notice that we have used
double arrows from and into the resource TUGS to indicate that
two tugs are required.

     The full activity diagram for each boat's behaviour is
obtained by stringing together the separate activity drawings
in the correct time ordered sequence (see figure 3.5). In the
same figure we have included the outline of CLASS BOAT (with a
request followed by a seize shortened into acquire). Notice
that the class declaration can be written down from the
activity diagram in a quite mechanical way. Indeed,
Clementson [21] and Matthewson [26] have automated similar
processes.

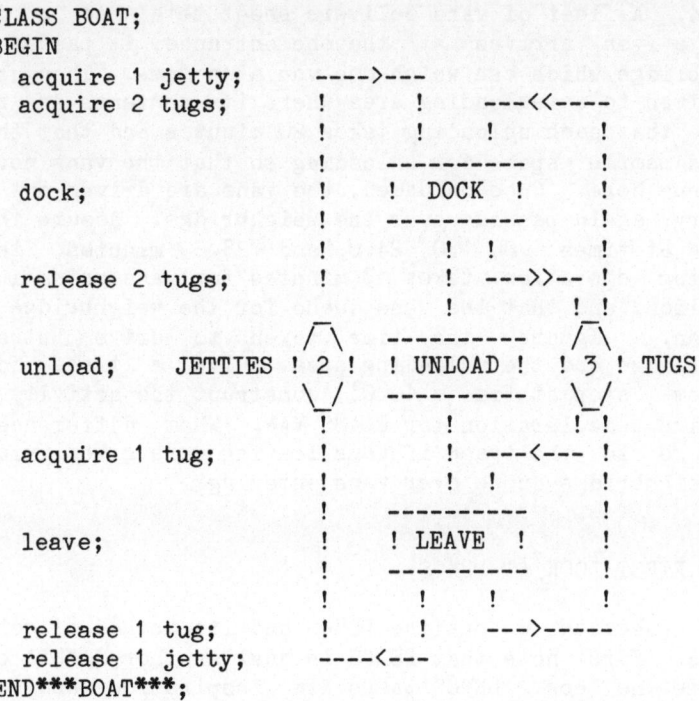

```
CLASS BOAT;
BEGIN
    acquire 1 jetty;        ---->---
    acquire 2 tugs;        !      !    ---<<----
                           !      !    !        !
                           !      ----------    !
    dock;                  !      ! DOCK  !    !
                           !      ----------    !
                           !      ! !        !
    release 2 tugs;        !      !   --->>--  !
                           !      !         ! !
                  /\      ----------       /\
    unload;  JETTIES ! 2 ! ! UNLOAD ! ! 3 ! TUGS
                  \/      ----------       \/
                           !      !         ! !
    acquire 1 tug;         !      !   ---<---  !
                           !      ! !        !
                           !      ----------    !
    leave;                 !      ! LEAVE  !    !
                           !      ----------    !
                           !      !  !        !
    release 1 tug;         !      !    --->-----
    release 1 jetty;       ----<---
END***BOAT***;
```

Figure 3.5 Port System activity diagram.

EXERCISES 3 (continued)

2. Customers arrive at a one man barber's shop for haircuts. If the barber is free, a haircut starts at once. If not, the customers wait on the first-come, first-served (henceforth FCFS) basis. Give a trace for the simulation in terms of the actions of the customers, assuming that four customers arrive at times 0, 20, 35, and 40 respectively and that each haircut takes 15 minutes. (Ignore the time taken to get seated, leave the chair and pay the barber.) Prepare an activity diagram for the model, and give an informal declaration for CLASS CUSTOMER.

HINT: let the barber be modelled as a resource, initially of size 1.

3. Repeat exercise 3.2 above for a two man barber's shop using the same customer arrival sequence and the same length of time per haircut.

4. A fleet of vans delivers sheet metal to a factory. When a van arrives at the one entrance, it passes overs a weighbridge which can weigh one van at a time. Then the van is driven to an unloading area where its contents are removed. Assume that each unloading takes 20 minutes and that there is always ample space for unloading so that the vans never need to queue here. Once unloaded, the vans are driven out of the factory, again passing over the weighbridge. Assume that vans arrive at times 0.0, 1.0, 24.0, and 25.0 minutes, that the weighing operation takes 3 minutes for vans going in either direction, and that the vans queue for the weighbridge in FCFS fashion. Ignore the time taken to drive between the weighbridge and the unloading area. Give a trace for this problem (stop at time = 40.0), construct the activity diagram and give a declaration for CLASS VAN. What difference would it make to the trace if vans leaving were given priority in the weighbridge queue over vans entering?

3.3 A FIRST LOOK AT DEMOS

In this section, we outline DEMOS and its method of scheduling events. First note that DEMOS is just another SIMULA context, no more, no less. DEMOS takes its inspiration and approach from SIMULA's standard CLASS SIMULATION (but does not use it). As with CLASS SIMULATION, DEMOS provides various behind-the-scenes structures such as an event list and primitive routines for entering entities into it and deleting entities from it. These are not meant to be used directly. Instead DEMOS provides some much higher-level classes and procedures for direct use. From the user's point of view, we can picture the declaration of the DEMOS context by

```
        CLASS DEMOS;
        BEGIN
          CLASS ENTITY(TITLE); VALUE TITLE; TEXT TITLE;
          BEGIN
            PROCEDURE SCHEDULE(T); REAL T;............;
            PROCEDURE CANCEL;.......................;
          END***ENTITY***;
          CLASS RES(TITLE, AVAIL);...................;
          PROCEDURE HOLD(T); REAL T;.................;
          REAL PROCEDURE TIME;......................;
          REF(ENTITY)PROCEDURE CURRENT;.............;
          ...................................
          set up the event list at clock time 0.0;
        END***DEMOS***;
```

(This skeleton suffices for the time being - other DEMOS facilities will be introduced as we go along. A more complete outline is given in appendix B.) DEMOS is used as a context in the usual manner

DEMOS BEGIN ..... END;

CLASS RES is used to model minor simulation elements, such as TUGS and JETTIES, where we don't need to give full role descriptions, but essentially record how much of the modelled resource is currently available. In the Port example, we declare REF(RES)TUGS, JETTIES; and create appropriate objects by

TUGS   :- NEW RES("TUGS"   , 3);
JETTIES :- NEW RES("JETTIES", 2);

RES objects require two parameters: the first is TEXT TITLE (enclosed in double quotes ") which is used in reports and traces; the second is INTEGER AVAIL which is used to fix the initial size of the resource pool. Thereafter, AVAIL is maintained by calls on ACQUIRE and RELEASE to record the current level of the resource pool (0 <= AVAIL <= initial size). After object creation, portions of a resource may be acquired in integer chunks, e.g.

JETTIES.ACQUIRE(1); TUGS.ACQUIRE(2);

Requests are considered on the first-come, first-served basis (this can be altered by use of PRIORITY, see chapter 4). A request is granted immediately if sufficient of the resource is free and no other entity is blocked. Otherwise the requester is himself blocked and is held in a hidden resource queue q (REF(QUEUE)q; see chapter 5) local to the RES object. There he remains until he is first in the queue and there is sufficient of the resource available for him to proceed.

When a current user releases his share, he sends a signal to the resource, e.g.

TUGS.RELEASE(2); JETTIES.RELEASE(1);

A call on RELEASE not only increments the resource pool, but also unblocks any waiting entities whose request can be granted. Each unblocked entity leaves the resource queue q and enters the event list behind its unblocker and at the same clock time (see figure 3.1, page 26, at times 2.0 and 18.0).

N.B.   Full   details   on ACQUIRE and RELEASE are delayed until
priority queueing has been introduced (page 62).

```
----------------------        -----------------------
!         RES        !        !         RES         !
----------------------        -----------------------
! TITLE       "TUGS" !        ! TITLE    "JETTIES" !
! AVAIL           3  !        ! AVAIL           2  !
! q                  !        ! q                  !
! PROCEDURE ACQUIRE(N)!        ! PROCEDURE ACQUIRE(N)!
! PROCEDURE RELEASE(N)!        ! PROCEDURE RELEASE(N)!
----------------------        -----------------------
```

Figure 3.6 The two RES objects.

     CLASS ENTITY is used as prefix to declarations of major
simulation components in DEMOS. Entity objects are given full
life histories and are the only objects that can be scheduled.
PROCEDURE SCHEDULE is used to enter an unscheduled (or
passive) entity into the event list. For example, NEW
BOAT("BOAT").SCHEDULE(15.0) enters a new boat object into the
event list at 'the current clock time + 15.0'. PROCEDURE HOLD
operates on the entity at the head of the event list and is
used to represent the duration of an activity.   Seen from
inside the calling object itself, it represents a period of
time in the same state and holding the same resources until it
takes   up its actions again.   Remember that the actual
parameter to both HOLD and SCHEDULE represents a delay.   We
can now complete our model description in DEMOS.

```
   BEGIN EXTERNAL CLASS DEMOS;
     DEMOS
       BEGIN REF(RES)TUGS, JETTIES;

          ENTITY CLASS BOAT;
          BEGIN
          DOCK:
            JETTIES.ACQUIRE(1); TUGS.ACQUIRE(2);
            HOLD(2.0);
            TUGS.RELEASE(2);
          UNLOAD:
            HOLD(14.0);
          LEAVE:
            TUGS.ACQUIRE(1);
            HOLD(2.0);
            TUGS.RELEASE(1); JETTIES.RELEASE(1);
          END***BOAT***;
```

```
        TUGS    :- NEW RES("TUGS"  , 3);
        JETTIES :- NEW RES("JETTIES", 2);
        NEW BOAT("BOAT").SCHEDULE(0.0);
        NEW BOAT("BOAT").SCHEDULE(1.0);
        NEW BOAT("BOAT").SCHEDULE(15.0);
        HOLD(36.0);
      END;
  END;
```

N.B. The labels DOCK, UNLOAD, LEAVE are not necessary - they
are inserted as documentation aids.

REMARKS ON EXAMPLE 1

We create the first boat object by executing NEW BOAT("BOAT").
This gives us a carbon copy of the class declaration as
depicted in figure 3.7 (the DEMOS system automatically gives
the boat objects a serial number, as shown). The ENTITY
prefix contains the user-accessible procedure SCHEDULE and
also the hidden mechanism for entry into and exit from the
event list. This behind-the-scenes mechanism is intended to
be used not directly, but indirectly through the standard
scheduling procedures HOLD and SCHEDULE. (We meet CANCEL
later.)

```
     ---------------------------
     !          BOAT           !
     ---------------------------
     ! PROCEDURE SCHEDULE(T) !   ENTITY PREFIX
     ! TITLE         "BOAT 1" !
     ---------------------------
   ->! DOCK:                   !
     !   JETTIES.ACQUIRE(1);   !
     !   TUGS.ACQUIRE(2);      !
     !   HOLD(2.0);            !
     !   TUGS.RELEASE(2);      !
     ! UNLOAD:                 !
     !   HOLD(14.0);           !
     ! LEAVE:                  !
     !   TUGS.ACQUIRE(1);      !
     !   HOLD(2.0);            !
     !   TUGS.RELEASE(1);     .!
     !   JETTIES.RELEASE(1);   !
     ---------------------------
```

Figure 3.7 The first boat object.

Because of a command within its ENTITY prefix, a freshly
created boat object is frozen with its LSC referring to the
first user-written action. It will not start executing this
action until scheduled to do so. In our program, all three
boat objects are scheduled as soon as they are created by the
calls on SCHEDULE. Thus they enter their user-written action
sequences at simulation clock times 0.0, 1.0, and 15.0
respectively. Thereafter, their lives are sequences of
resource requests with implied waits of locally unpredictable
(but possibly zero) length, and holds of known duration.

Objects which have been scheduled by a SCHEDULE or HOLD
are chained together behind the scenes in an EVENT LIST.
Associated with each such object is the known time of its next
event - the time at which it is due to be first released into
the simulation, or the time at which its current activity is
due to finish. (Objects awaiting the availability of
resources cannot be members of the event list.) Scheduled
objects are ranked according to the REAL value of their next
event time. Scheduling is framed so that the object at the
head of the event list (the one with the least event time) is
active. It has the standard reference REF(ENTITY)PROCEDURE
CURRENT and its event time is always available through a call
on the standard REAL PROCEDURE TIME.

We now illustrate how DEMOS's scheduling operates by
tracing out the changes in the event list as the program is
executed. Space does not allow us to draw out the objects in
full. Instead we use the format

object(event time),   e.g. B1(2.0)

to represent objects in the event list. We have named the
boats B1, B2, and B3; and the DEMOS block D (for further
explanatory notes, see page 158). We also record when objects
are blocked on a resource. We draw snapshots according to the
frame

TIME ! EVENT LIST   !TUGS!JETTIES

The snapshot at time 2.0 is thus

2.0 ! B1(2.0), B3(15.0), D(36.0)   !B2 !

B1 is CURRENT and B2 is awaiting the availability of 2 tugs.
B3 is scheduled to start its actions at time 15.0, and the
DEMOS block to resume its actions at time 36.0.

Consider the PORT system at time 0.0. The actions of the DEMOS context establish the event list, and enter the DEMOS block into it. D behaves just as though it were an entity.

    0.0 ! D(0.0)   !   !

The DEMOS block is CURRENT (the first object in the event list) and its actions are executed. These actions establish the resources TUGS and JETTIES and then schedule B1. B1 enters the event list at 'TIME + 0.0' behind D.

    0.0 ! D(0.0), B1(0.0)   !   !

The DEMOS block is still CURRENT and continues by scheduling B2 and B3 in turn.

    0.0 ! D(0.0), B1(0.0), B2(1.0), B3(15.0) !   !

The next action by D is its HOLD(36.0). This removes D from the head of the event list and replaces it at the bottom. B1 becomes the new CURRENT, but the clock time remains at 0.0 (the simulation clock time is always the event time of CURRENT).

    0.0 ! B1(0.0), B2(1.0), B3(15.0), D(36.0) !   !

B1 seizes 1 jetty and 2 tugs and then executes HOLD(2.0). This causes B1 to be re-inserted in the event list at time 2.0. B2 becomes the new CURRENT and the simulation time moves up to 1.0.

    1.0 ! B2(1.0), B1(2.0), B3(15.0), D(36.0) !   !

B2 seizes a jetty, but is then blocked as 2 tugs are not currently available. B2 is thus removed from the event list and waits passively for that resource.

    2.0 ! B1(2.0), B3(15.0), D(36.0)   !B2 !

B1 becomes the new CURRENT and the simulation clock moves up to 2.0. B1 continues by executing TUGS.RELEASE(2). This awakens B2 who can now proceed. B2 returns to the event list at once, but behind B1.

    2.0 ! B1(2.0), B2(2.0), B3(15.0), D(36.0) !   !

B1 continues (entering its unloading phase) by executing

HOLD(14.0).

2.0 ! B2(2.0), B3(15.0), B1(16.0), D(36.0)!   !

B2 becomes the new CURRENT at the same clock time 2.0. It now
seizes 2 tugs and starts docking.

4.0 ! B2(4.0), B3(15.0), B1(16.0), D(36.0)!   !

B2 remains CURRENT but the clock time moves up to 4.0.   B2
continues by releasing 2 tugs and then executes its
HOLD(14.0). The new frame is

15.0 ! B3(15.0), B1(16.0), B2(18.0),D(36.0)!   !

The simulation clock moves up to 15.0 with B3 as the new
CURRENT. Poor old B3 is immediately blocked as no jetties are
free. B1 becomes the new CURRENT and the clock time advances
to 16.0.

16.0 ! B1(16.0), B2(18.0), D(36.0)   !   !B3

B1 as CURRENT seizes 1 tug and starts leaving. It is
rescheduled in the event list at time 18.0, but behind B2.
N.B. In general, tie breaks in the event list are resolved on
the 'first scheduled for that event time, first taken'
principle. A HOLD thus re-inserts the caller in the event
list behind all other entities with events due to take place
at the same time.

18.0 ! B2(18.0), B1(18.0), D(36.0)   !   !B3

B2 becomes the new CURRENT and the simulation clock time moves
up to 18.0.   B2 seizes 1 tug and starts leaving. It is
re-entered into the event list at time 20.0. B1 becomes the
new CURRENT.

18.0 ! B1(18.0), B2(20.0), D(36.0)   !   !B3

B1 now releases 1 tug and then 1 jetty. This last action
awakens B3 who joins the event list immediately, but behind
B1.

18.0 ! B1(18.0), B3(18.0), B2(20.0),D(36.0)!   !

B1 now completes its user-written actions and is automatically
deleted from the event list by the DEMOS system. B3 becomes

the new CURRENT.

        18.0 ! B3(18.0), B2(20.0), D(36.0)   !   !

B3 now seizes 1 jetty and 2 tugs and executes a HOLD(2.0)
simulating the docking activity. B2 becomes the new CURRENT.

        20.0 ! B2(20.0), B3(20.0), D(36.0)   !   !

B2 releases 1 tug and 1 jetty, and is deleted from the event
list as its actions are now exhausted. The event list is now
down to two objects.

        20.0 ! B3(20.0), D(36.0)   !   !

B3 now releases 2 tugs and enters its unloading phase
executing its HOLD(14.0). It remains CURRENT, but the clock
time advances to 34.0.

        34.0 ! B3(34.0), D(36.0)   !   !

B3 now seizes 1 tug and starts leaving, rescheduling itself
for clock time 36.0. It is entered into the event list behind
the DEMOS block D.

        36.0 ! D(36.0), B3(36.0)   !   !

If the simulation were to end now, it would not be quite
complete as B3 has not yet released its resources. To allow
for this circumstance, the DEMOS block has been coded to
execute an extra hidden HOLD(0.0) before it closes down the
simulation. Thus the next frame is

        36.0 ! B3(36.0), D(36.0)   !   !

This trick causes the simulation run to end at the expected
simulation clock time, but in effect gives all other events
scheduled for that time precedence. B3 here continues its
actions by releasing 1 tug and 1 jetty. It is then deleted
from the event list. The final frame is

        36.0 ! D(36.0)   !   !

Finally then, the DEMOS block is re-entered. It automatically
issues a final report before closing down the simulation.

Once an entity has been created and scheduled, it decides
for itself what to do next until its action pattern has been
exhausted. It is then said to be TERMINATED and can never be
scheduled again. If not referenced (the attributes of
referenced terminated objects may be accessed, e.g. TUGS and
JETTIES), the object is automatically deleted from the model.
Thus boat objects are logically deleted at clock times 18.0,
20.0, and 36.0.

Notice that the scheduling style, which is inherited from
SIMULA, focusses our attention on CURRENT. We have not needed
to reference any of the boat objects in the model explicitly.
They are found implicitly either in the event list as CURRENT,
or at the head of a resource queue.

EXERCISES 3 (continued)

5. Give DEMOS code for the Barber's Shop model given as
exercise 3.2.

6. Give DEMOS code for the Factory model given as
exercise 3.4.

7. Give a frame by frame snapshot of the changes in the
event list as your program for exercise 3.6 above is executed.

8. Notice that all the boat objects in the Port System
(also customer objects in exercise 3.5 and van objects in
exercise 3.6) are created at clock time zero. This may be
tolerable in a small simulation involving only a few entities,
but in larger models this method of dealing with transient
entities is not acceptable. As an example, consider running
our model of the Port System over 10,000-20,000 time units.
Perhaps 1000 boats will pass through, but no more than 5 or 6
may be in contention at any one time. To create all the boat
objects at time zero wastes much space in the computer and
clutters up the event list. What can be done to improve
matters if we know the distribution of inter-arrival times of
the boats?

EXAMPLE 2: PORT SYSTEM REVISITED

We have followed through the construction of one model in
DEMOS and its execution by hand. The task was simplified by
our choice of 'easy' numbers. We now repeat the exercise with

more realistic data, and use standard DEMOS mechanisms to
introduce random behaviour into the simulation. We also take
the opportunity to show a standard method of dynamically
generating a stream of transient entities whose inter-arrival
pattern is known (exercise 3.8), and introduce event tracing.

Model data

Timings in hours:
```
  docking              CONSTANT:2.0
  unloading            NORMAL:mean=14.0,st.dev.=3.0
  leaving              CONSTANT:2.0
  boat inter-arrival   NEGEXP:mean=0.1/hour
```

Resources:
```
  TUGS                 RES:limit=3
  JETTIES              RES:limit=2
```

As before, docking and leaving are fixed length activities of
duration 2 hours. Unloading is a sample from a NORMAL
distribution with mean 14.0 and standard deviation 3.0. The
inter-arrival times are drawings from a negative exponential
(NEGEXP) distribution with a mean rate of one boat every 10
hours. The simulation model is run for 28 days.

```
BEGIN EXTERNAL CLASS DEMOS;
  DEMOS
    BEGIN
      REF(RES)TUGS, JETTIES;
      REF(RDIST)NEXT, DISCHARGE;

      ENTITY CLASS BOAT;
      BEGIN
        NEW BOAT("BOAT").SCHEDULE(NEXT.SAMPLE);
      DOCK:
        JETTIES.ACQUIRE(1);  TUGS.ACQUIRE(2);
        HOLD(2.0);
        TUGS.RELEASE(2);
      UNLOAD:
        HOLD(DISCHARGE.SAMPLE);
      LEAVE:
        TUGS.ACQUIRE(1);
        HOLD(2.0);
        TUGS.RELEASE(1);  JETTIES.RELEASE(1);
      END****BOAT****;
```

```
        TUGS     :- NEW RES("TUGS",    3);
        JETTIES  :- NEW RES("JETTIES", 2);
        READDIST(NEXT,       "NEXT BOAT");
        READDIST(DISCHARGE, "DISCHARGE");
        TRACE;
        NEW BOAT("BOAT").SCHEDULE(0.0);
        HOLD(28.0*24.0);
    END;
END;
```

***Input:
=========

NEXT BOAT NEGEXP 0.1
DISCHARGE NORMAL 14.0 3.0

***Output:
==========

```
                    CLOCK TIME =  0.000
****************************************************************
*                                                              *
*          T R A C I N G   C O M M E N C E S                   *
*                                                              *
****************************************************************

  TIME/CURRENT AND ITS ACTION(S)

 0.000 DEMOS   SCHEDULES BOAT 1 NOW
               HOLDS FOR 672.000, UNTIL 672.000
       BOAT 1  SCHEDULES BOAT 2 AT 26.574
               SEIZES 1 OF JETTIES
               SEIZES 2 OF TUGS
               HOLDS FOR 2.000, UNTIL 2.000
 2.000         RELEASES 2 TO TUGS
               HOLDS FOR 16.385, UNTIL 18.385
18.385         SEIZES 1 OF TUGS
               HOLDS FOR 2.000, UNTIL 20.385
20.385         RELEASES 1 TO TUGS
               RELEASES 1 TO JETTIES
               ***TERMINATES
26.574 BOAT 2  SCHEDULES BOAT 3 AT 33.116
               SEIZES 1 OF JETTIES
               SEIZES 2 OF TUGS
               HOLDS FOR 2.000, UNTIL 28.574
28.574         RELEASES 2 TO TUGS
```

```
                  HOLDS FOR 14.724, UNTIL 43.298
33.116 BOAT 3     SCHEDULES BOAT 4 AT 41.836
                  SEIZES 1 OF JETTIES
                  SEIZES 2 OF TUGS
                  HOLDS FOR 2.000, UNTIL 35.116
35.116            RELEASES 2 TO TUGS
                  HOLDS FOR 16.287, UNTIL 51.403
41.836 BOAT 4     SCHEDULES BOAT 5 AT 56.849
                  AWAITS 1 OF JETTIES
43.298 BOAT 2     SEIZES 1 OF TUGS
                  HOLDS FOR 2.000, UNTIL 45.298
45.298            RELEASES 1 TO TUGS
                  RELEASES 1 TO JETTIES
                  ***TERMINATES
       BOAT 4     SEIZES 1 OF JETTIES
                  SEIZES 2 OF TUGS
                  HOLDS FOR 2.000, UNTIL 47.298
.................................................
```

```
                   CLOCK TIME =  672.000
*****************************************************************
*                                                               *
*                      R E P O R T                              *
*                                                               *
*****************************************************************

                   D I S T R I B U T I O N S
                   **************************
```

TITLE	/	(RE)SET/	OBS/TYPE	/	A/	B/	SEED
NEXT BOAT		0.000	64 NEGEXP		0.100		33427485
DISCHARGE		0.000	58 NORMAL		14.000	3.000	22276755

```
                      R E S O U R C E S
                      *****************
```

TITLE	/	(RE)SET/	OBS/	LIM/	MIN/	NOW/	% USAGE/	AV.WAIT/	QMAX
TUGS		0.000	114	3	0	3	17.063	2.854E-02	1
JETTIES		0.000	56	2	0	0	78.566	5.498	6

REMARKS ON EXAMPLE 2

WARNING: It becomes tedious to repeat the necessary first card 'BEGIN EXTERNAL CLASS DEMOS;' and last card 'END;' for every DEMOS program in this book. Accordingly, in future

DEMOS examples and exercises, they will not be given explicitly, but are understood.

The input to the program is the specification of the two random streams. The output from the program is an event trace followed by a standard report on the use of user-created DEMOS facilities. In the report, two distributions (NEXT and DISCHARGE) and two resources (TUGS and JETTIES) are detailed. The output echoes the distribution definitions ('TITLE', 'TYPE', and its parameters under 'A' and 'B' (possibly empty)) and gives the number of calls (under 'OBS') on each. '(RE)SET' gives the simulation time at which the object was created. The column 'SEED' quotes the automatically determined value for each distribution. These come out in a mechanically predetermined sequence which can be overridden (see remarks in chapter 8).

Then the resource usages are detailed. The columns are headed 'TITLE' and '(RE)SET' (obvious), 'OBS' (which gives the number of calls on RELEASE), 'LIM' (which echoes the initial value of the resource represented), 'MIN' (minimum reached level of the resource, $0 <= MIN <= LIM$), 'NOW' (the currently available level of the resource), '% USAGE' (the time weighted average of the portions of the resource seized expressed as a percentage of the maximum possible usage; see also page 60), 'AV. WAIT' (the average wait time of entities which have completed calls on ACQUIRE. It includes zero waits.), and 'QMAX' (the maximum attained length of the queue of blocked requesters. Instant seizes - zero waits - ARE included).

N.B. Real values in reports are usually printed to 3 decimal places, but any real values which are too large to fit their allotted field or give only two significant places or less are printed floating point (see the 'AV. WAIT' column for TUGS).

Event tracing

Event tracing is initially off. It is switched on by a call TRACE, and continues to be on until switched off by a call NOTRACE. TRACE and NOTRACE are global routines which can be called from within entities as well as from the DEMOS block. Notice that the DEMOS system itself numbers the entities in the order of their creation. The user supplies a text (here "BOAT") and the DEMOS system appends to that text its serial number (taken modulo 100). In programs with several different entity classes, DEMOS will give each class its own sequence of serial numbers.

Because the DEMOS block itself behaves very much like an entity, it is simple to trace over a selected period. For example, should we wish to trace only the first 24 hours of the simulation, we replace the coding sequence

```
TRACE;
HOLD(28.0*24.0);
```

by the sequence

```
TRACE;
HOLD(24.0);
NOTRACE;
HOLD(27.0*24.0);
```

Pseudo-random number generation

The program contains two of DEMOS's random sampling mechanisms; several more will be met later *2).

Any simulation based on random behaviour naturally requires mechanisms for generating sequences of random numbers from various probability distributions. It is sufficient to have a sequence of random numbers from a uniform distribution available; for from it, by suitable mathematical transformations, it is possible to generate sequences of random numbers for other distributions. In turn, to obtain a sequence of uniform random numbers, it is sufficient to be able to generate a sequence Xk of integers in the range $[1,M-1]$ as the sequence Xk/M is approximately uniformly distributed over $(0,1)$. The simple examples below indicate how this can be done in SIMULA. Consider the sequences

$$S1 = 7, 3, 6, 1, 2,....$$

and

$$S2 = 4, 8, 5, 10, 9,....$$

Can you work out which number comes next in either sequence?
----
*2). A proper account of random number generation techniques is beyond the scope of this little book - see instead Fishman [32], Knuth [35], or Shannon [37].

In fact, both sequences have been produced mechanically by repeated application of the formula

$$X_0 = \text{any number in the range 1 through 10}$$
$$X_{k+1} = 2*X_k \text{ modulo 11} \quad (k = 0, 1, 2, \ldots)$$

($X_0 = 9$ for S1; $X_0 = 2$ for S2.) The full sequence is ($X_0 = 2$)

4, 8, 5, 10, 9, 7, 3, 6, 1, 2, 4 (repeats)

The sequence is said to have a CYCLE of length 10. It contains all the integers in the range 1 through 10, although in 'random' order.

The program segment below implements a uniform distribution based on this generator.

```
CLASS RANDOM(U); INTEGER U;
BEGIN
  REAL PROCEDURE NEXT;
  BEGIN
    U := 2*U;
    IF U > 11 THEN U := U-11;
    NEXT := U/11;
  END***NEXT***;
CHECK PARAMETER:
  IF U̅ < 1 OR U > 10 THEN error;
END***RANDOM***;

REF(RANDOM)S1, S2;

S1 :- NEW RANDOM(9);
S2 :- NEW RANDOM(2);
```

Successive calls on S1.NEXT produce the numbers .636, .273, .545,...; and successive calls on S2.NEXT the numbers .364, .727, .455,... Notice that if by ill luck we had chosen 7 as the starting value for S2, calls on S2.NEXT would have produced the sequence .273, .545, .091 .. which are too closely related to the output from S1.NEXT for comfort. The problem is less acute in proper generators as their cycle lengths are enormous; but it should not be ignored. Variates for a wide variety of theoretical and empirical distributions can be generated by building on the output from NEXT. We give three examples to illustrate the method: RANDINT which generates INTEGER values, NEGEXP which generates REAL values, and DRAW which generates BOOLEAN values.

To generate random integers in the range [A,B], we declare

```
RANDOM CLASS RANDINT(A, B); INTEGER A, B;
BEGIN
  INTEGER PROCEDURE SAMPLE;
  BEGIN
    SAMPLE := A + ENTIER((B-A+1)*NEXT);
  END***SAMPLE***;
  IF A > B THEN error;
END***RANDINT***;

REF(RANDINT)R;
R :- NEW RANDINT(9, 2, 5);
```

Successive calls R.SAMPLE produce the sequence - 4, 3, 4, 2, ... - integers in the range [2,5].

Similarly a negative exponential distribution may be implemented by

```
RANDOM CLASS NEGEXP(M); REAL M;
BEGIN
  REAL PROCEDURE SAMPLE;
  BEGIN
    SAMPLE := -LN(NEXT)/M;
  END***SAMPLE***;
  IF M <= 0.0 THEN error;
END***NEGEXP***;

REF(NEGEXP)N;
N :- NEW NEGEXP(2, 0.1);
```

Successive calls on N.SAMPLE produce the sequence of values 10.116, 3.185, 7.885, ... - a negative exponential distribution with a mean of 10 (supply 1/mean as the second actual parameter).

Finally, we define a simple truth distribution

```
RANDOM CLASS DRAW(P); REAL P;
BEGIN
  BOOLEAN PROCEDURE SAMPLE;
  BEGIN
    SAMPLE := P > NEXT;
  END***SAMPLE***;
END***DRAW***;
```

```
REF(DRAW)HEADS, SIXTHROWN;

HEADS     :- NEW DRAW(9, 0.5);
SIXTHROWN :- NEW DRAW(9, 0.1667);

IF SIXTHROWN.SAMPLE THEN ...
```

Successive calls on HEADS.SAMPLE produce the sequence of
values FALSE, TRUE, FALSE, TRUE, TRUE, ... - BOOLEAN values
with a 50% chance of being TRUE; successive calls on
SIXTHROWN.SAMPLE produce the sequence of values FALSE, FALSE,
FALSE, TRUE, FALSE, ... - BOOLEAN values with a 16.67% chance
of being TRUE.

The DEMOS random number generators

The basic random number generator used in DEMOS is a Lehmer
generator published by Downham and Roberts [31]. It is

$$X_o = \text{some seed generated by DEMOS}$$
$$X_{k+1} = 8192*X_k \text{ modulo } 67099547$$

and has a cycle length of 67099546. By noting that 8192 =
32*32*8, the generator can be coded in SIMULA in such a way as
not to overflow on a 32 bit (or longer) word computer since
67099547 < 2**26. Such random number generation algorithms
produce predictable sequences of numbers since each number is
fixed by its predecessor. Thus all numbers in a sequence are
completely determined by the initial value. To emphasise this
inherently non-random character, they are called PSEUDO-RANDOM
NUMBERS. But if the basic algorithm is carefully chosen, the
numbers possess sufficient of the properties of random
sequences to be capable of use as random sequences for many
practical purposes.

Three groupings of distribution are defined in DEMOS.
Six return REAL values and are sub-classes of RDIST (NORMAL,
UNIFORM, NEGEXP, ERLANG, CONSTANT, and EMPIRICAL); two return
INTEGER values and are sub-classes of IDIST (RANDINT,
POISSON); and one returns BOOLEAN values and is a sub-class of
BDIST (DRAW). More details are found in appendix C. In
example 2, we declared

```
REF(RDIST)NEXT, DISCHARGE;
```

and used PROCEDURE READDIST to create objects according to a

specification which was read in. READDIST takes two
parameters: the first is a variable qualified by RDIST,
IDIST, or BDIST, and the second a suitable TEXT title for the
object to be created. This user-given name is checked against
the input stream and a match must be found. Then the input
stream specifies the type of distribution (NORMAL, NEGEXP,
UNIFORM, ERLANG, CONSTANT, EMPIRICAL, POISSON, RANDINT, or
DRAW) followed by the appropriate parameters. In our case, we
have

```
NEXT BOAT     NEGEXP    0.1
DISCHARGE     NORMAL    14.0    3.0
```

To assist the inexperienced, the selection of appropriate
well-separated random seeds is done automatically by a special
routine in the DEMOS system. The routine is based on work by
Mats Ohlin [36]; for the theory behind the method, see Fuller
[34]. As noted before, these default values may be
overridden.

It can be shown that $8192**120633 = 36855$ modulo 67099547
(and $36855 = 3**4*5*7*13$), and so we can derive a stream of
seeds from the generator

```
Uo   = 907
Uk+1 = 36855*Uk modulo 67099547
```

which has cycle of length $33549773 = 67099546/2$. We can thus
take over 120000 drawings before one stream starts to overlap
with its successor, and this separation holds for more than
500 distributions.

Dynamic entity generation

Notice how the boats are generated and scheduled (see in the
trace at clock times 0.000 (twice), 26.574, 33.116, ...) and
that they are automatically numbered sequentially. The first
boat object is generated in the DEMOS block; thereafter, the
first action of each boat object is to generate the next in
sequence delay T (T = 26.574, 6.542, 8.720, ... in turn)
before continuing with its own actions. The values in the
sequence T (the boat inter-arrival times) are drawings from a
negative exponential distribution with a mean rate of 1 boat
every 10 hours. Using this device, we need keep only one as
yet unentered boat object in the event list at a time.

Deadlock

One has to be careful about the order in which entities are
allowed to request resources. For example, if we have two
resources A and B each of limit 1, and entities P and Q which
execute

a) P: A.ACQUIRE(1);   Q: B.ACQUIRE(1);
        HOLD(t1);   HOLD(t2);
        B.ACQUIRE(1);   A.ACQUIRE(1);

then the following sequence of actions could occur: P seizes
A and holds; then Q seizes B and also holds. Now both P and Q
are blocked forever as each has the very resource the other
one needs in order to continue. This situation is known as
DEADLOCK. It can be induced into example 2 (page 40) if
instead of the correct

b)   JETTIES.ACQUIRE(1); TUGS.ACQUIRE(2);

we miscode

c)   TUGS.ACQUIRE(2); JETTIES.ACQUIRE(1);

The distribution report at time 672.0 then reads

TITLE	/	(RE)SET/	OBS/TYPE	/	A/	B/	SEED
NEXT BOAT		0.000	64 NEGEXP		0.100		33427485
DISCHARGE		0.000	10 NORMAL		14.000	3.000	22276755

and the resource report reads

TITLE	/	(RE)SET/	OBS/	LIM/	MIN/	NOW/%	USAGE/AV.	WAIT/QMAX
TUGS		0.000	18	3	0	1	60.654	0.111 55
JETTIES		0.000	8	2	0	0	96.787	0.862 1

Deadlock has been caused by boats which own jetties and wish
to leave blocking boats which own tugs (or have a prior claim)
and want jetties.

    A good account of deadlock, containing several examples,
is found in Shaw [38]. The DEMOS system does not prevent
deadlock occurring nor attempt to recover from it if it sets
in. Deadlocked entities just grind to a halt while other
entities continue. When the simulation run has ended, future
DEMOS systems will check on the resource ownership and
requests from non-terminated entities, and a warning will

given if any are found to be deadlocked. In certain
elementary situations, the possibility of deadlock can be
checked in advance using a simple graphical technique (see
Shaw [38, chapter 8] for a more general method based on Petri
nets). We represent the state of the system by a graph in
which the nodes are resources and an arc from node A to node B
implies that an entity which holds resource A can request node
B. The node EMPTY represents the initial empty state of an
entity. Figure 3.8 gives resource graphs for the situations
labelled a), b), and c) above. The deadlock condition is
revealed by a closed loop in the resource graphs. Thus
possible deadlocks can be detected quickly and corrected prior
to coding a program. There is no way a context can do this
for you, but either a compiler or a pre-processor for DEMOS
could.

```
                    ---------
                    !       !
          -----<-----! EMPTY !----->-----
          !         !       !           !
-------           --------           ---------
!       !-------------------->!           !
!   A   !                     !     B     !
!       !<--------------------!           !
---------                     ---------
```

a) Deadlock: cycles A->B->A, B->A->B


```
---------        ---------        ---------
!       !        !       !        !       !
! EMPTY !----->!JETTIES!----->! TUGS  !
!       !        !       !        !       !
---------        ---------        ---------
```

b) No deadlock as no cycles


```
---------        ---------        ---------
!       !        !     !----->!       !
! EMPTY !----->! TUGS  !      !JETTIES!
!       !        !     !<-----!       !
---------        ---------        ---------
```

c) Deadlock: cycle TUGS->JETTIES->TUGS

Figure 3.8 Deadlock: resource graphs.

EXERCISES 3 (continued)

9. Write a sub-class to CLASS RANDOM which implements the normal distribution. For suggestions on the algorithm, see Fishman [32], Knuth [35], Pritsker and Kiviat [28], or Shannon [37].

10. Two types of customer arrive at a one chair barber's shop. Customers wanting a haircut only arrive at a mean rate of one every 40 minutes (NEGEXP distributed), and customers wanting both a haircut and a shave arrive at a mean rate of one every 60 minutes (again NEGEXP distributed). The barber serves on the first-come, first-served principle (FCFS). It takes him from 12-24 minutes (UNIFORMly distributed) to give a haircut only, and from 20-36 minutes (UNIFORMly distributed) to give both a haircut and a shave. The first haircut-only customer arrives at opening time, the first customer who wants both arrives 10 minutes later. Model the barber's shop and run it for 8 hours of simulated time.

HINT: model the barber as a RESource, and declare entity classes for both types of customer.

11. A tool crib is manned by two clerks who check out tools to mechanics. Mechanics use the tools to repair failed machines. The time to process a tool request depends on the type of tool. Requests fall into two categories

Type	Mechanic inter-arrival time	Service times in seconds
1	NEGEXP:mean=0.005/sec	UNIFORM:100.0->200.0
2	NEGEXP:mean=0.008/sec	UNIFORM: 75.0->150.0

At time 0.0, there is one request of each type pending. The clerks serve the mechanics in FCFS fashion independent of the type of request. Run the simulation model for 8 hours.

12. A small grocery store has three aisles and two checkout counters. Shoppers arrive at the store with a mean inter-arrival time of 100 seconds, NEGEXP distributed. on arrival, each takes a basket and may go down one or more of the three aisles selecting items for purchase as she/he proceeds. The probability of going down an aisle, the time required to shop an aisle and the number of items selected for purchase in the process are

Aisle	Prob	Time in seconds	No. of items
1	0.75	UNIFORM: 60.0->180.0	RANDINT:2->4
2	0.55	UNIFORM:120.0->180.0	RANDINT:3->5
3	0.82	UNIFORM: 75.0->165.0	RANDINT:6->8

When shopping has been completed, the customers queue up FCFS
fashion at one of two checkout counters. Here each chooses
another 1->3 impulse items (RANDINT distributed). A
customer's checkout time depends on the number of items she/he
has bought and is 10 seconds per item, plus 15->35 seconds
(UNIFORMly distributed) to pay and get the change. Run the
model for 8 hours.

HINTS: the ALGOL 60 construction

          IF condition THEN BEGIN statements; END

is also a part of SIMULA and hence DEMOS.

Also, you may care to use the global TEXT PROCEDURE EDIT which
accepts a TEXT T and an INTEGER N as actual parameters, and
combines them into a single text (e.g. EDIT("AISLE", 1)
returns "AISLE 1". If the text T is more than 10 characters
long then it is stripped down to 10; if the integer value of N
is not in the range 0 - 99 then ABS(N)//100 is accepted. It
is commonly used with RES etc. arrays which share the same
text as title.

    13. Consider the program below which models a doctor's
surgery.

```
    DEMOS
      BEGIN REF(RES)DOCTOR;

        ENTITY CLASS PATIENT;
        BEGIN NEW PATIENT("P").SCHEDULE(next);
          DOCTOR.ACQUIRE(1);
          HOLD(consultation);
          DOCTOR.RELEASE(1);
        END***PATIENT***;

        HOLD(540.0);  COMMENT***START AT 9 O'CLOCK;
        DOCTOR :- NEW RES("DOCTOR", 1);
        NEW PATIENT("P").SCHEDULE(0.0);
        HOLD(90.0);
      END;
```

The program has the first patient arriving at 9.00, and the doctor starting work at the same time. It closes abruptly at 10.30 whether the doctor is engaged in a consultation or not. Modify the program so that the surgery doors are locked at 10.30 (no more patients can then be admitted - arrange to cut off the arrival stream at this time), and let the doctor finish off his current consultation (if any) and also consult with any patients who are waiting but arrived before 10.30.

14. Suppose in exercise 3.13 above we have as initial conditions that 'n' patients are already waiting at time 9.00 when the doctor begins his work. It is not correct to replace the single statement

        NEW PATIENT("P").SCHEDULE(0.0)

in the DEMOS block by

        FOR K := 1 STEP 1 UNTIL n DO   [INTEGER K;]
          NEW PATIENT("P").SCHEDULE(0.0);

because then EACH of the n PATIENTs has as its first action the generation of another. Thus this code would model n separate streams of patients instead of the one stream required. Give a correct solution.

15. Go through the suggested solutions to exercises 3.10-3.12 and replace all the calls on READDIST by the equivalent explicit assignments. E.g. in example 2 on page 42

        READDIST(NEXT,   "NEXT BOAT");
        READDIST(DISCHARGE, "DISCHARGE");

could be replaced by

        NEXT   :- NEW NEGEXP("NEXT BOAT", 0.1);
        DISCHARGE :- NEW NORMAL("DISCHARGE", 14.0, 3.0);

The main task of this chapter is to show how minor resources are handled in DEMOS. Resource synchronisations are classified into one or other of two types: mutual exclusion and producer/consumer. In mutual exclusion synchronisations, items from a pool of resources are requested and released by the same entity. In producer/consumer synchronisations, producer entities make resources available to consumer entities (in the manner of relay runners handing on a baton).

Separate classes RES and BIN are defined in DEMOS to handle these cases. Although not absolutely necessary, this is desirable as it allows better error control and more explicit reporting. These two classes have much in common and we will often call items modelled by RES or BIN objects 'resources'.

4.1 CLASS RES

EXAMPLE 3:   READERS AND WRITERS

A file is used to record the current status of elements in a dynamic system. It could, for example, be flight records for an airport. The file is periodically updated by writer processes, each of which must have sole access to the file when carrying out an update. The file is also read from time to time by reader processes, any number of which may access the file at the same time.

This model reinforces our newly acquired knowledge of DEMOS, contains two ENTITY classes and introduces priority queuing for resources.

Let there be r readers and w writers. We can solve the file accessing problem very simply by means of a RES object of limit r, say

       FILE :- NEW RES("FILE", r);

A reader object gains access to the file by

```
        FILE.ACQUIRE(1);
        read;
        FILE.RELEASE(1);
```

and a writer object gains access to the file by

```
        FILE.ACQUIRE(r);
        write;
        FILE.RELEASE(r);
```

Thus reader objects do not block each other, but block any
writer object; a writer object will not only block other
writer objects, but reader objects too.

     The structure of the reader objects is basically a loop
comprising a period of access to the file to read the latest
information, followed by a sequence of actions based on that
information.   The writer objects are similarly structured.
The activity diagram for the model is given in figure 4.1
(notice how we have represented the cyclic nature of these
objects).

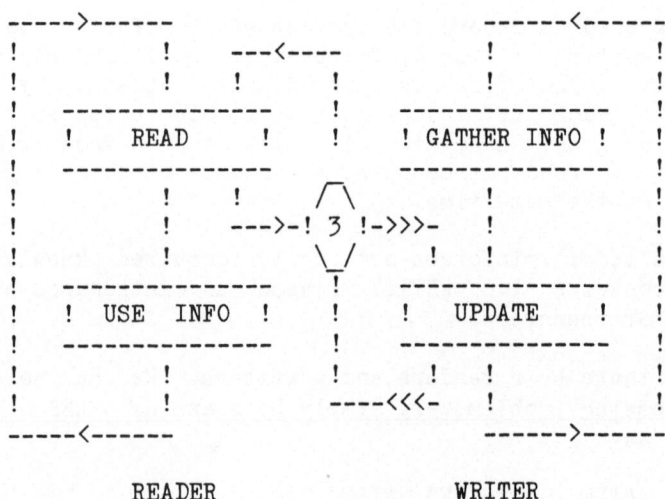

                    READER   WRITER

      Figure 4.1 Readers and writers activity diagram.

     A complete program for 3 readers and 2 writers is listed
below.   The 'read', 'use info.', 'gather info.', and 'update'
timings are explicitly listed in the program.   The program
introduces a new data collection device - the COUNT. COUNT
objects are used to record incidences.

        C.UPDATE(n);   [REF(COUNT)C;]

increments a counter local to C by n. As can be seen from the
program text, COUNT objects have but one parameter, a TEXT
title. This title, the reset time, and the sum of the n's are
recorded in the final report.

```
.DEMOS
   BEGIN
      REF(RES)FILE;
      REF(COUNT)READS, WRITES;

      ENTITY CLASS READER;
      BEGIN
      READ:
         FILE.ACQUIRE(1);
         HOLD(2.0);
         FILE.RELEASE(1);
         READS.UPDATE(1);
      USE_INFO:
         HOLD(5.0);
         REPEAT;
      END***READER***;

      ENTITY CLASS WRITER;
      BEGIN
      GATHER_INFO:
         HOLD(5.0);
      WRITE:
         FILE.ACQUIRE(3);
         HOLD(3.0);
         FILE.RELEASE(3);
         WRITES.UPDATE(1);
         REPEAT;
      END***WRITER***;

      READS  :- NEW COUNT("READS");
      WRITES :- NEW COUNT("WRITES");
      FILE   :- NEW RES("FILE", 3);
      TRACE;
      NEW READER("R").SCHEDULE(0.0);
      NEW WRITER("W").SCHEDULE(0.0);
      NEW READER("R").SCHEDULE(0.0);
      NEW READER("R").SCHEDULE(2.0);
      NEW WRITER("W").SCHEDULE(1.0);
      HOLD(25.0);
   END;
```

***Output:
==========

                    CLOCK TIME = 0.000
****
*   *
*   T R A C I N G   C O M M E N C E S   *
*   *
****

    TIME/CURRENT AND ITS ACTION(S)
    0.000 DEMOS   SCHEDULES R 1 AT 0.000
                   SCHEDULES W 1 AT 0.000
                   SCHEDULES R 2 AT 0.000
                   SCHEDULES R 3 AT 2.000
                   SCHEDULES W 2 AT 1.000
                   HOLDS FOR 25.000, UNTIL 25.000
          R 1   SEIZES 1 OF FILE
                   HOLDS FOR 2.000, UNTIL 2.000
          W 1   HOLDS FOR 5.000, UNTIL 5.000
          R 2   SEIZES 1 OF FILE
                   HOLDS FOR 2.000, UNTIL 2.000
    1.000 W 2   HOLDS FOR 5.000, UNTIL 6.000
    2.000 R 3   SEIZES 1 OF FILE
                   HOLDS FOR 2.000, UNTIL 4.000
          R 1   RELEASES 1 TO FILE
                   HOLDS FOR 5.000, UNTIL 7.000
          R 2   RELEASES 1 TO FILE
                   HOLDS FOR 5.000, UNTIL 7.000
    4.000 R 3   RELEASES 1 TO FILE
                   HOLDS FOR 5.000, UNTIL 9.000
    5.000 W 1   SEIZES 3 OF FILE
                   HOLDS FOR 3.000, UNTIL 8.000
    6.000 W 2   AWAITS 3 OF FILE
    7.000 R 1   AWAITS 1 OF FILE
          R 2   AWAITS 1 OF FILE
    8.000 W 1   RELEASES 3 TO FILE
                   HOLDS FOR 5.000, UNTIL 13.000
          W 2   SEIZES 3 OF FILE
                   HOLDS FOR 3.000, UNTIL 11.000
    9.000 R 3   AWAITS 1 OF FILE
   11.000 W 2   RELEASES 3 TO FILE
                   HOLDS FOR 5.000, UNTIL 16.000
          R 1   SEIZES 1 OF FILE
                   HOLDS FOR 2.000, UNTIL 13.000
          R 2   SEIZES 1 OF FILE

```
                    HOLDS FOR 2.000, UNTIL 13.000
         R 3        SEIZES 1 OF FILE
                    HOLDS FOR 2.000, UNTIL 13.000
13.000 W 1          AWAITS 3 OF FILE
       R 1          RELEASES 1 TO FILE
                    HOLDS FOR 5.000, UNTIL 18.000
       R 2          RELEASES 1 TO FILE
                    HOLDS FOR 5.000, UNTIL 18.000
       R 3          RELEASES 1 TO FILE
                    HOLDS FOR 5.000, UNTIL 18.000
       W 1          SEIZES 3 OF FILE
                    HOLDS FOR 3.000, UNTIL 16.000
16.000 W 2          AWAITS 3 OF FILE
       W 1          RELEASES 3 TO FILE
                    HOLDS FOR 5.000, UNTIL 21.000
       W 2          SEIZES 3 OF FILE
                    HOLDS FOR 3.000, UNTIL 19.000
                    .................
24.000 W 2          AWAITS 3 OF FILE
       W 1          RELEASES 3 TO FILE
                    HOLDS FOR 5.000, UNTIL 29.000
       W 2          SEIZES 3 OF FILE
                    HOLDS FOR 3.000, UNTIL 27.000
.................................


                    CLOCK TIME = 25.000
**************************************************************
*                                                            *
*                      R E P O R T                           *
*                                                            *
**************************************************************


                       C O U N T S
                       **********

            TITLE    /    (RE)SET/OBS
            READS         0.000    9
            WRITES        0.000    5


                    R E S O U R C E S
                    *****************
```

TITLE	/	(RE)SET	/OBS/	LIM/	MIN/	NOW/	% USAGE/	AV. WAIT	/QMAX
FILE		0.000	14	3	0	0	88.000	1.000	3

REMARKS ON EXAMPLE 3

A call on REPEAT (a procedure local to CLASS ENTITY), causes
the actions of the calling object to be repeated. The
procedure has to be more subtle than revealed in this example,
for very often the actions of an entity body take the form

```
        BEGIN
          initialising actions;
          repeated actions;
        END;
```

A call on REPEAT in an entity body must not cause ALL the
actions of such a body to be repeated, including the
initialising actions. To avoid this, place a label 'LOOP' on
the first statement of the actions to be repeated.

```
        BEGIN
          initialising actions;
        LOOP:
          repeated actions;
          REPEAT;
        END;
```

Note that the label identifier MUST be LOOP, and LOOP can have
no other meaning within an entity body. Should the entity
body contain no initialising actions, no explicit occurrence
of LOOP is needed.

In the report on FILE, the statistic % USAGE = 88.000 is
made up of nine completed reads of chunk size 1 and duration 2
plus five completed writes of chunk size 3 and duration 3 (the
fourteen completed usages recorded under OBS) plus one part
write (W2 at time 24.0) of duration 1. The total number of
space*time units comes to be 9*1*2 + 5*3*3 + 1*3*1 = 66 which
is 88% of the maximum possible usage 3*25.

EXAMPLE 4: READERS AND WRITERS WITH PRIORITY

Example 3 gave neither readers nor writers priority. Should
this be required, we can make use of a hitherto unmentioned
attribute of CLASS ENTITY, namely INTEGER PRIORITY. A local
variable, it is initially zero. When an entity enters any
queue, it is always ranked according to its current value of
PRIORITY (larger values in front of smaller values, but after
all other entities in the same queue with the same value). In

the first version of the readers and writers problem, readers and writers were queued on the FCFS principle as each and every PRIORITY was zero.

We can give reader objects priority by altering their declaration to (recording essential actions only)

```
ENTITY CLASS READER;
BEGIN PRIORITY := 1;
LOOP:
   FILE.ACQUIRE(1);
   HOLD(2.0);
   FILE.RELEASE(1);
   HOLD(5.0);
   REPEAT;
END***READER***;
```

and leaving the declaration of CLASS WRITER unaltered. The following segment from the trace shows its effect (no change until TIME = 7.000)

```
  TIME/CURRENT AND ITS ACTION(S)
                 .....
 7.000 R 1       AWAITS 1 OF FILE
       R 2       AWAITS 1 OF FILE
 8.000 W 1       RELEASES 3 TO FILE
                 HOLDS FOR 5.000, UNTIL 13.000
       R 1       SEIZES 1 OF FILE
                 HOLDS FOR 2.000, UNTIL 10.000
       R 2       SEIZES 1 OF FILE
                 HOLDS FOR 2.000, UNTIL 10.000
 9.000 R 3       SEIZES 1 OF FILE
                 HOLDS FOR 2.000, UNTIL 11.000
10.000 R 1       RELEASES 1 TO FILE
                 HOLDS FOR 5.000, UNTIL 15.000
       R 2       RELEASES 1 TO FILE
                 HOLDS FOR 5.000, UNTIL 15.000
11.000 R 3       RELEASES 1 TO FILE
                 HOLDS FOR 5.000, UNTIL 16.000
       W 2       SEIZES 3 OF FILE
                 HOLDS FOR 3.000, UNTIL 14.000
                 .....
```

The report on FILE is

TITLE /	(RE)SET/	OBS/	LIM/	MIN/	NOW/	% USAGE/	AV. WAIT/	QMAX
FILE	0.000	14	3	0	0	84.000	0.941	3

REMARKS ON EXAMPLE 4

As expected, with the shortest jobs getting priority (reading is faster than writing), the average wait time has decreased. Priority can be dynamically reassigned as often as desired. For example, we could give boat objects in example 2 (page 40) priority when entering the port by writing (informally)

```
ENTITY CLASS BOAT;
BEGIN PRIORITY := 1;
  dock;
  unload;
  PRIORITY := 0;
  leave;
END***BOAT***;
```

Now that we have met PRIORITY, we can present a more complete picture of RELEASE and ACQUIRE. (See page 155 for their semi-formal algorithms.) A call R.ACQUIRE(n) does not delay CURRENT should sufficient of R be available (R.AVAIL >= n) AND CURRENT have greater priority than any entity awaiting a share in R. In this case, R.AVAIL is decremented by n and CURRENT continues on. Otherwise, CURRENT is deleted from the event list and enters the queue for R (R.q for short) in priority order.

A call on R.RELEASE(n) increments R.AVAIL by n and enters E1 the entity (if any) at the head of R.q (E1==R.q.FIRST) into the event list at the current clock time, but as last entity scheduled for that time. When E1 becomes CURRENT, it tests to see if it can proceed (CURRENT == R.q.FIRST AND R.AVAIL >= n). If not, it is deleted from the event list and remains blocked in R.q. Otherwise, E1 leaves R.q, decrements R.AVAIL, and promotes E2 (the new first entity in R.q, if any) into the event list, but IMMEDIATELY after itself. E1 then continues on as CURRENT. When E2 becomes CURRENT, it goes through the same exercise. Thus, waiting entities which can now proceed are peeled off the front end of R.q in priority order after E1. Note that a call on RELEASE does not delay CURRENT nor cause it to lose its position at the head of the event list.

EXERCISES 4

1. Manufacturing widgets involves a relatively lengthy assembly process followed by a short fixing time in an oven. Several assemblers share a single oven which can hold only one

widget at a time. An assembler cannot begin assembling a new widget until he has removed the old one from the oven. Assume that there are 3 assemblers and that there is an infinite supply of raw widgets.

Model data
==========

Timings in minutes:
    Assemble widget   UNIFORM:25.0->35.0
    Fire in oven   NORMAL:mean=8.0,st.dev.=2.0

Run your model for a 40 hour week assuming no discontinuities within a day or in moving between consecutive 8 hour days.

    2. A machine is used to polish castings. The steps required to polish a casting are shown below (the timings are in minutes and all distributions are UNIFORM).

a) fetch a raw casting from the storage area (9.0->15.0). Assume an infinite supply of unpolished castings.
b) load raw casting on to the polishing machine (6.0->14.0).
c) polish the raw casting (60.0->100.0).
d) reposition the casting on the machine for a final polishing (8.0->22.0).
e) carry out the final polishing (80.0->140.0).
f) unload and store the finished casting (15.0->30.0).
Repeat from a).

    The castings are too heavy to be handled by an operator. He requires the use of an overhead crane for each of the steps a), b), d), and f) above. There is but one overhead crane which is also used to perform other tasks. Such tasks occur in the mean every 50 minutes (NEGEXP distributed), and the time taken to service each call is NORMALly distributed with a mean of 25.0 and a standard deviation of 5.0. Run your model for 400 hours of simulated time assuming no discontinuities, that the one polisher starts work at phase a) at time 0.0, and that the first 'other task' for the overhead crane occurs at time 20.0.

    3. Assembled TV sets move through a number of testing stations in the final stages of their production. At the last of these, the vertical control is tested. If it is wrong, the offending set is rerouted for adjustment (the setting is modified). After adjustment, the set is returned to the inspection station where it queues for retesting (with

increased priority each time it fails, if more than once).
After passing the test, the sets move on to a packing area.

Model data
==========

```
    Timings in minutes:
      set arrival rate    NEGEXP:mean=0.2/minute.
      inspection time     UNIFORM:6.0->10.0
      readjustment time   NORMAL:mean=30.0,st.dev.=5.0
    Resources:
      INSPECTORS          RES:limit=2
      ADJUSTERS           RES:limit=1
```

The chance of a set passing the inspection is 90% whether it
be for the first, second, ... attempt. Run your model for 40
hours and estimate the staging space (space for waiting sets)
required ahead of both the stations.

   4.   Faulty units are sent for repair to a special section
in a factory. Repairs are carried out in two stages - first
the unit is stripped down, and then it is rebuilt.   Each
operation has its own work station. Work station 1
(stripping) can work on two units at a time, work station 2
(rebuilding) on one unit at a time. But storage is limited,
and at most four units can be queued in front of work station
1, and at most two in front of work station 2. If four units
are already queued in front of work station 1, a newly arrived
faulty unit is subcontracted. When a strip job is completed,
the unit is automatically moved to the area in front of work
station 2 when there is room (it takes 0.2 hours should the
area be empty, and 0.1 hours should there be one unit already
there) and a new strip job is started. Should the storage
area in front of work station 2 be full, work station 1 is
blocked until a space is freed.

Model data
==========

```
   Timings in hours:
    unit arrival rate NEGEXP:mean=4/hour
    strip down        NORMAL:mean=0.50,st.dev.=0.05
    rebuild           NORMAL:mean=0.25,st.dev.=0.1
    between stations  CONSTANT:0.2 if area empty, 0.1 if not
```

At the start of the day, both work stations are idle, and two
repair jobs are waiting. The next unit arrives at 0.5 hours.

Run the model for a working week of 136 hours assuming no discontinuities and report on how many units were subcontracted.

5. Repeat exercise 4.4 above with the following twist. Arrange for units arriving at the end of the week (after 134 hours) to be blocked. They are not subcontracted, but left as 'starters' for the following week. At this time, any other work in hand or pending is completed.

6. A production line involves 5 servers stationed along a conveyor belt. Items to be serviced arrive at a mean rate of 4 per minute (NEGEXP distributed). If unserviced they are carried along the conveyor passing a server every minute. If an item reaches an idle server, the item is picked off the conveyor, serviced (which takes UNIFORM 0.8->1.2 minutes) and stored away. If an item passes all the servers, then it is recirculated and reappears in front of server 1 after a delay of 5 minutes. Run the simulation for 480 minutes, and note the work rates of the servers and the number of recirculated items.

7. Repeat exercise 4.6 with the following change. Items are not recirculated. There is sufficient storage space allocated in front of server 5. Server 5 thus services all items that get past the other servers. Give an estimate of the storage space necessary in front of server 5.

4.2 CLASS BIN

We now introduce the second basic synchronisation, commonly called the 'producer/consumer' synchronisation. A simple manifestation occurs when we have two cooperating entities, the first of which produces items for the second one to consume. The main point being that the consumer is blocked if no item is currently available when one is needed, i.e. it is consuming items faster than they are being produced.

In DEMOS, we represent such a pool of available items by a BIN object. For this example, we could create an initial pool of two items by

ITEMS :- NEW BIN("ITEMS",2);   [REF(BIN)ITEMS;]

The first parameter TEXT TITLE (passed as "ITEMS") is used in reports and in traces; the second parameter INTEGER AVAIL

gives the initial size of the pool (here 2, as shown in figure
4.2).   Thereafter, as with CLASS RES, AVAIL is maintained to
record the current level of the available pool.   Note that
this AVAIL has no upper limit (0 <= AVAIL).

```
                     -------------------
REF(BIN)ITEMS--->!          BIN         !
                     -------------------
                     !TITLE     "ITEMS"!
                     !AVAIL          2!
                     !q                ! for blocked entities
                     !PROCEDURE TAKE(N)!
                     !PROCEDURE GIVE(N)!
                     -------------------
```

Figure 4.2 A BIN object.

The activity diagram for this simple model together with
corresponding DEMOS code is given in figure 4.3. Notice how
the BIN object has been represented in that figure: by
convention, its initial value is drawn inside a bucket.

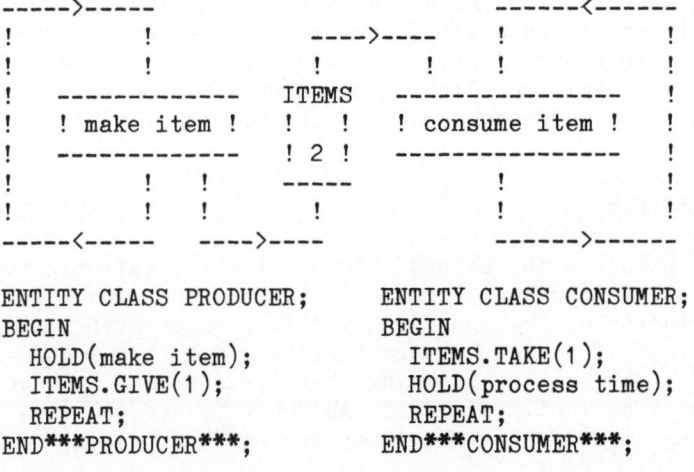

```
ENTITY CLASS PRODUCER;    ENTITY CLASS CONSUMER;
BEGIN                     BEGIN
   HOLD(make item);         ITEMS.TAKE(1);
   ITEMS.GIVE(1);           HOLD(process time);
   REPEAT;                  REPEAT;
END***PRODUCER***;        END***CONSUMER***;
```

Figure 4.3 Producer/consumer activity diagram.

The consumer obtains an item from the pool by ITEMS.TAKE(1);
If the pool is empty (AVAIL = 0), the consumer waits in a
hidden queue q local to ITEMS. When permission is granted,
the consumer reduces the pool size by the amount requested,
leaves the queue and is entered into the event list at the
current clock time, but behind CURRENT (the producer).

When the producer has completed an item, he updates the size of the pool by ITEMS.GIVE(1); This command also awakens the consumer should he be blocked and allows him to continue now (at the current clock time, but behind CURRENT). Then the producer makes a start on the next item.

N.B. Of course BIN portions larger than unity may be taken and given. The rules for TAKE and GIVE follow the pattern of those for ACQUIRE and RELEASE (see page 62). Their semi-formal algorithms are given on page 159.

EXAMPLE 5:   CAR FERRY

Motorists wishing to cross the strait between the mainland and a small island have to use a ferry. The ferry ties up on the mainland overnight and starts work promptly each day at 7.00. It shuttles to and fro between the mainland and the island until approximately 22.00 hours when the service closes down for the night. The ferry has a capacity limit of six cars. When the ferry arrives at a quay, the cars on the ferry are driven off, and then any waiting cars (up to the maximum of six) are driven on. When the ferry is fully loaded, or the quay queue is empty, the ferry leaves that side of the strait and starts another crossing. When the ferry has completed a round trip and deposited any passengers on the mainland, the captain checks the time. If it is 21.45 hours or later, he closes down the service for the night.

Model data

Timings in minutes:
car inter-arrival

on mainland	NEGEXP:mean=0.15/min
on island	NEGEXP:mean=0.15/min
crossing time	NORMAL:mean=8.0,st.dev.=0.5
drive on	CONSTANT:0.5 (per car)
drive off	CONSTANT:0.5 (per car)

Run the model for 1 working day under the following initial conditions: at time 7.00, there are 3 cars waiting on the mainland and 1 on the island.

Compute the average number of cars per trip, the number of fruitless (empty) crossings, and the average waiting time per car on each side.

There is clearly a great deal of symmetry in the model which we exploit by using arrays. We let the quantities on the mainland side have index 1, and corresponding quantities on the island side have index 2.

We are interested in how many cars are waiting, and not in how individual cars arrive, cross, and continue. Accordingly, we need not model cars as entities, but use a pair of BIN objects - Q(1) and Q(2) - to record the current queue length on each side of the strait.

Taking NEXT(1) and NEXT(2) as the car inter-arrival distributions, car arrivals can be taken care of by a pair of objects of CLASS ARRIVAL.

```
ENTITY CLASS ARRIVAL(SIDE); INTEGER SIDE;
BEGIN HOLD(NEXT(SIDE).SAMPLE);
  Q(SIDE).GIVE(1);
  REPEAT;
END***ARRIVAL***;
```

The ferry starts from the mainland and repeats the sequence of actions 'load; cross; unload;' until it is time to close down. A skeleton of CLASS FERRY is

```
ENTITY CLASS FERRY;
BEGIN INTEGER SIDE, C;
  FOR SIDE := 1, 2 DO
  BEGIN load;
    HOLD(crossing time);
    unload;
  END;
  IF TIME < 21.45 o'clock THEN REPEAT;
END***FERRY***;
```

We now examine 'load' and 'unload' in turn. Let INTEGER C, local to CLASS FERRY, maintain the number of cars currently on board. The loading activity takes place while there is at least one car in the queue and the ferry capacity limit of 6 has not been reached. In SIMULA, this is

```
C := 0;
WHILE C < 6 AND Q(SIDE).AVAIL > 0 DO
BEGIN Q(SIDE).TAKE(1);
  HOLD(0.5);
  C := C + 1;
END;
```

Unloading is easier. It merely consists of letting all the cars (and there are C of them) drive off.

```
HOLD(C*0.5);
```

This is the second case (see also exercise 3.13, page 53) in which the closing down time of the simulation cannot be predicted in advance. We synchronise via another BIN object, initially zero, named SHUTDOWN. After initialising the system, the DEMOS block calls SHUTDOWN.TAKE(1) and is blocked. It is left to the FERRY object to decide when to shut down the system. This it does by executing SHUTDOWN.GIVE(1) as its last action. This awakens the DEMOS block at precisely the right moment.

```
DEMOS
  BEGIN
    REF(BIN)ARRAY Q(1:2);
    REF(RDIST)ARRAY NEXT(1:2);
    REF(BIN)SHUTDOWN;
    REF(RDIST)CROSSING;
    REF(TALLY)LOAD;
    REF(COUNT)TRIPS, EMPTIES;

    ENTITY CLASS FERRY;
    BEGIN INTEGER SIDE, C;
      FOR SIDE := 1, 2 DO
      BEGIN
    LOADING:
        C := 0;
        WHILE C < 6 AND Q(SIDE).AVAIL > 0 DO
        BEGIN
          Q(SIDE).TAKE(1);
          HOLD(0.5);
          C := C + 1;
        END;
        LOAD.UPDATE(C);
        IF C = 0 THEN EMPTIES.UPDATE(1);
    CROSS:
        HOLD(CROSSING.SAMPLE);
    UNLOAD:
        HOLD(C*0.5);
      END;
      TRIPS.UPDATE(1);
      IF TIME < 1305.0 THEN REPEAT;
      SHUTDOWN.GIVE(1);
    END***FERRY***;
```

```
      ENTITY CLASS ARRIVAL(SIDE); INTEGER SIDE;
      BEGIN
        HOLD(NEXT(SIDE).SAMPLE);
        Q(SIDE).GIVE(1);
        REPEAT;
      END***ARRIVAL***;

      HOLD(420.0);   COMMENT***START AT 7.00;
      Q(1)     :- NEW BIN("MAINLAND", 3);
      Q(2)     :- NEW BIN("ISLAND",   1);
      SHUTDOWN :- NEW BIN("SHUTDOWN", 0);
      NEXT(1)  :- NEW NEGEXP("MAINLAND", 0.15);
      NEXT(2)  :- NEW NEGEXP("ISLAND",   0.15);
      CROSSING :- NEW NORMAL("CROSSING", 8.0, 0.5);
      TRIPS    :- NEW COUNT("TRIPS");
      EMPTIES  :- NEW COUNT("EMPTY TRIPS");
      LOAD     :- NEW TALLY("AV. LOAD");
      NEW ARRIVAL("ARR", 1).SCHEDULE(0.0);
      NEW ARRIVAL("ARR", 2).SCHEDULE(0.0);
      NEW FERRY("FERRY").SCHEDULE(0.0);
      SHUTDOWN.TAKE(1);
    END;
```

***Output:
==========

                    CLOCK TIME = 1315.296
****
*   *
*   R E P O R T   *
*   *
****

                   D I S T R I B U T I O N S
                   ****

TITLE /	(RE)SET/	OBS/TYPE /	A/	B/	SEED
MAINLAND	420.000	133 NEGEXP	0.150		33427485
ISLAND	420.000	146 NEGEXP	0.150		22276755
CROSSING	420.000	78 NORMAL	8.0000	0.050	46847980

                      C O U N T S
                      ****

TITLE /	(RE)SET/	OBS
TRIPS	420.000	39
EMPTY TRIPS	420.000	2

T A L L I E S
****

TITLE	/	(RE)SET/	OBS/	AVERAGE/	EST.ST.DEV./	MINIMUM/	MAXIMUM
AV. LOAD		420.000	78	3.487	1.634	0.000	6.000

B I N S
****

TITLE	/	(RE)SET/	OBS/	INIT/	MAX/	NOW/	AV. FREE/	AV. WAIT/	QMAX
MAINLAND		420.000	132	3	6	2	1.678	0.000	1
ISLAND		420.000	145	1	7	7	1.705	0.000	1
SHUTDOWN		420.000	1	0	1	0	0.000	895.296	1

REMARKS ON EXAMPLE 5

The output echoes the distribution definitions, then the
counts and tallies, and finally the BIN usages are listed.
The BIN report columns are headed 'TITLE', '(RE)SET' (both
obvious), 'OBS' (the number of completed calls on TAKE),
'INIT' (the initial level of this BIN), 'MAX' (the maximum
level of this BIN), 'NOW' (the current level of items
available for the taking), 'AV. FREE' (the time-weighted
average number of items available since the creation of this
BIN), 'AV. WAIT' (the average time spent queueing by entities
blocked on this BIN including zero waits), and finally 'QMAX'
(maximum number of blocked entities including zero waits).

The program introduces another data collection device -
the TALLY. TALLY objects are used to record time independent
variables. Observations are recorded by

        T.UPDATE(x);   [REF(TALLY) T;]

Various statistics are maintained over the readings $x1$, $x2$,
..., xn, as the report "T A L L I E S" shows. They include
the number of observations ('OBS'), their mean, their
estimated standard deviation, their minimum, and their
maximum.

When an entity becomes terminated, the DEMOS system
checks to see that it has released all the portions of RES
objects that it has seized. Otherwise, an error is reported.
This is not required for BIN objects (why?) and is a major
reason for implementing RES and BIN separately instead of
trying to make do with a single class.

EXERCISES 4 (continued)

8.   This simulation follows the (much simplified)
progress of a billet through a steel mill. Billets are long,
thickly sectioned steel bars which arrive at the mill from
another factory (we assume an inexhaustible stockpile). The
job of the mill is to convert each billet into steel plate.
To accomplish this, the billets are heated one at a time in a
furnace until they have reached a 'suitable' temperature.
Each billet is then transported on a railway bogie to a
soaking pit area (if no bogies are available, the current
billet is kept inside the furnace). The billet is unloaded
with the help of a crane. This frees the bogie which is then
shunted back to the furnace. Note that a billet will be
loaded straight from its bogie into a soaking pit should one
be free; otherwise the crane dumps it in the soaking pit area
and loads it later when a pit is free.

The billet is left in the soaking pit until it has
reached a uniform temperature throughout. It then becomes
eligible to be rolled, but is kept in the soaking pit until a
rolling mill is free. A crane is also needed for the
unloading operation. The billet passes through the rolling
mill several times and is shaped a little more on each pass.
Eventually it is squeezed into the desired shape of a flat
plate.

Use lower case letters to denote informally the activity
durations. Assume that bogie movements do not interfere with
each other and take a negligible time. Simulate with 12
soaking pits, 2 cranes, 9 bogies and 1 rolling mill.

9.   A small production line has three stages: the first
assembles the inner and outer rings of bearings, the second
greases the assemblage, the third packs them two to a box (the
packers take two greased assemblages at a time). There are 3
assemblers, 1 greaser, and 2 packers.

Model data
==========

Timings in minutes:
    inner arrival rate   NEGEXP:mean=6/min
    outer arrival rate   NEGEXP:mean=6/min
    assembling   NORMAL:mean=0.5,st.dev.=0.1
    greasing   CONSTANT:0.15
    packing   NORMAL:mean=0.6,st.dev.=0.1

Initially there are 10 inners and 10 outers.   Run   the   model
for 8 hours.

10.   A machine uses a type of part   which   fails
periodically.   Whenever this happens, the machine must be
switched off. The faulty part is then removed by its operator
and wheeled by him to the repair shop. The operator then
takes a replacement part (queueing if none are there) and
wheels it back to his machine. The operator then installs the
replacement part, and starts a fresh run.

Faulty parts are repaired by a repairman. He also has a
never failing supply of other jobs which occupy him when there
are no faulty parts to repair. Although these other jobs have
a lower priority, once started they cannot be interrupted.

Model data
==========

        Timings in hours:
          part life time   NORMAL:mean=36.0,st.dev.=7.0
          removal time   CONSTANT:0.4
          repair time   NORMAL:mean=2.0,st.dev.=0.5
          replacement time   CONSTANT:0.4
          other job time   UNIFORM:0.5->1.5

The removal and replacement times include the time spent
wheeling the parts to and from the repairman. There are
sufficient wheelbarrows in the factory for them not to cause
delays.

Run the model for a four week month assuming that there
are no discontinuities between shifts. Let there be three
machines (initially all in working order). At time 0.0, there
is one faulty part awaiting repair. Arrange for the machines
to break down at approximately 6 hours, 18 hours and 30 hours
respectively.

11. Two processes communicate with each other via a
buffer of capacity L. The sender process, S, deposits
messages of uniform size into one of the L buffer slots.   The
receiver process, R, extracts the messages one by one and
decodes them. R and S may not access the buffer at the same
time.

Model data
==========

Timings in minutes:
  message arrival rate   NEGEXP:mean=1/min
  deposit a message   CONSTANT:0.05
  extract a message   CONSTANT:0.05
  decode a message   UNIFORM:0.6->1.4

Write DEMOS programs to model this system under the assumptions

a) the buffer has an infinite capacity. S puts the messages into buffer slots 1, 2, 3, ... etc.

b) the buffer has a finite capacity and is organised cyclically. S puts messages into buffer slots 1, 2, ..., L, 1, 2, ..., L, 1, etc. Be careful to ensure that S does not overwrite a previous message before R has extracted it.

   12. A garage is open from 9.00 until (about) 17.00 weekdays and from 9.00 until (about) 13.00 on Saturdays for the maintenance and repair of motor cars. The garage has 5 service bays each of which can deal with one car at a time. Two classes of car are serviced by the garage

   a) private cars which are booked-in in advance and left by their owners outside the garage on the appointed day at or before 9.00.

   b) police cars which are repaired by the garage under a special contract. Police cars are in use 24 hours a day. When one is in trouble it is brought to the garage at once for an unscheduled but high priority repair.

Model data
==========

Timings in hours:
  Scheduled maintenance   UNIFORM:1.5->2.5
  Police car inter-arrival NEGEXP:mean=1/12 per hour
  Police car repair   NORMAL:mean=2.5,st.dev.=1
Resources:
  Bays   RES:limit=5
Scheduled bookings:
  Private car group size   RANDINT:12->20 weekdays
                                   :halved Saturday

The simulation runs over a four week period. Each
weekday the garage tries to shut at 17.00 hours. Any work
then in progress is completed, but work not yet started is
suspended until 9.00 the following day (and this includes work
on police cars). On Saturdays, the garage completes
outstanding services on all vehicles booked in before 13.00
before closing for the weekend. Any police cars arriving
while the garage is still open servicing this backlog will
also be serviced. Notice that if a private car is kept
overnight it takes precedence over the next day's intake of
private cars, but it may be overtaken the following workday
morning by a police car which has arrived overnight.

5 ENTITY-ENTITY COOPERATIONS

In the simulations we have described so far, an activity has always involved one entity and none or several minor components modelled by resources (RES or BIN objects). Sometimes this is not possible and an activity must be described as a coming together of two or more entities. We illustrate the problem by two simple modifications to the last example (CAR FERRY).

5.1 COOPT

Consider a ferry service similar to that of example 5 (page 67) except that this time the ferry transports lorries and can accommodate only one at a time. But, and here is the crux, we are interested in modelling the behaviour of the lorries as they cross to the island, deliver goods, and finally return to the mainland. So that we can concentrate on the one major point, we simplify the problem a little by insisting that the ferry always waits for a lorry should none be waiting, and that the ferry operates a 24 hour service round the clock.

We cannot now model the lorries as resources; they must be modelled as entities. Informal declarations of CLASS LORRY and CLASS FERRY are

```
ENTITY CLASS LORRY;            ENTITY CLASS FERRY;
BEGIN                          BEGIN INTEGER SIDE;
CROSS:                            FOR SIDE := 1, 2 DO
   await ferry;                   BEGIN
   load;  !                       ! load;
   cross; !--->SYNCHRONISE<---! cross;
   unload;!           !           ! unload;
DELIVER:               !           END;
   deliver goods;  !              REPEAT;
RETURN:                !        END***FERRY***;
   await ferry;       !
   load;  !           !
   cross; !--->-----!
   unload;!
END***LORRY***;
```

```
            !               !
        *** COOPT A         !
LQ(1)   ***====>======      !       L :- LQ(1).COOPT;
        ***    LORRY     "  !
    LQ(1).WAIT          ----------
                        ! load !    HOLD(load);
                        ----------
                            !
                        ----------
                        ! cross !   HOLD(crossing);
                        ----------
                            !
                        ----------
                        ! unload !  HOLD(unload);
                        ----------
            RESCHEDULE"  !
        ======<======    !          L.SCHEDULE(0.0);
        ! THE   LORRY    !
    ----------           !
    ! deliver !          !
    ----------           !
        !                !
       etc              etc

       LORRY            FERRY
```

```
ENTITY CLASS LORRY;        ENTITY CLASS FERRY;
BEGIN                      BEGIN INTEGER SIDE;
ARRIVE:                      FOR SIDE := 1, 2 DO
  LQ(1).WAIT;                BEGIN
DELIVER:                      L :- LQ(SIDE).COOPT;
  HOLD(deliver);              HOLD(load);
RETURN:                       HOLD(crossing);
  LQ(2).WAIT;                 HOLD(unload);
END***LORRY***;               L.SCHEDULE(0.0);
                            END;
                            REPEAT;
                          END***FERRY***;
```

Figure 5.1 LORRY/FERRY synchronisation.

Clearly the sequence of activities 'load; cross; unload;'
cannot take place without both a lorry and a ferry.
Representing two entities doing the same thing at the same
time by writing code which has both of them moving down the
event list can be quite difficult to achieve. It also
clutters up the event list. Instead, we arrange for one of

the entities to dominate and let it treat the other as a
resource to be coopted, retained as a passive slave throughout
the period of cooperation, and then be released for
independent progress at the end of this period of cooperation.
Only the master entity appears in the event list, and there
must be a corresponding hole in the life history of the slave
entity for each such period of cooperation (e.g. for both
CROSS and RETURN in the case of a lorry).

Figure 5.1 shows that part of the activity diagram
concerned with the ferry loading a lorry on the mainland side,
crossing the strait, and then unloading the lorry on the
island side. It also gives more complete outlines for LORRY
and FERRY. In our activity diagrams (see for example, figure
5.1), we depict WAITQ's by 3*3 blocks of asterisks.

We synchronise by means of two WAITQ objects - LQ(1) and
LQ(2)- the first representing the mainland queue, the other
the island queue.

```
---------------------------------
!          WAITQ          !<---REF(WAITQ)LQ(1)
---------------------------------
!TITLE           "MAINLAND"!
!slaveq                    ! for waiting victims
!masterq                   ! for waiting masters
!REF(ENTITY)PROCEDURE FIRST !
!REF(ENTITY)PROCEDURE LAST  !
!INTEGER PROCEDURE LENGTH   !
!PROCEDURE COOPT            !
!PROCEDURE WAIT             !
!PROCEDURE FIND(E, COND)    !
!BOOLEAN PROCEDURE AVAIL    !
---------------------------------
```

Figure 5.2 Result of LQ(1) :- NEW WAITQ("MAINLAND").

A WAITQ (see figure 5.2) has two subsidiary queues - one
(slaveq) holds potential victims (here, lorries), the other
(masterq) holds potential masters when the slaveq is empty.
Both queues contain entities which are ordered according to
PRIORITY. Accessible attributes include COOPT and WAIT (both
outlined below: see page 159 for their semi-formal
algorithms); LENGTH which returns the current length of the
queue of slaves; and FIRST and LAST which return references to
the first and last slave entities respectively. If the value
of LENGTH is zero, FIRST and LAST return NONE; if the value of

LENGTH is 1, then they return the same value. FIND is dealt
with later in this chapter on page 94; AVAIL is used in
chapter 6, page 107.

A lorry signals its readiness for its first crossing by a
call LQ(1).WAIT which puts it to sleep (out of the event list)
in the slaveq of LQ(1), and also awakens the ferry should it
be in the masterq of LQ(1) awaiting the arrival of a lorry.
From now on, the lorry rests passively until the ferry has
deposited it on the far bank. Its actions are re-entered at
the label DELIVER when scheduled again after the crossing.

The ferry awaits custom on the mainland side by calling
LQ(1).COOPT which causes it to wait in the masterq of LQ(1)
should the slaveq of LQ(1) be empty (i.e. if LQ(1).LENGTH =
0). A call on COOPT delays the caller until there is a slave
entity (i.e. it never returns NONE) and returns a reference
to the first entity in the slaveq when one is there; it also
removes the slave from that queue. Thus repeated calls on
COOPT do not return the same victim. The lorry L remains
passive during the ferry's subsequent

        HOLD(load); HOLD(crossing); HOLD(unload);

The ferry's next action, L.SCHEDULE(0.0), causes L to be
placed in the event list, at the current clock time, but as
the last entity scheduled for that time. Notice that the
simulation clock time is where it should be for both L and the
ferry. The ferry's next action is to start a fresh 'load' and
L is about to start delivering goods. The synchronisation on
the island side is, of course, very similar.

Notice that should LQ(n) be empty - n = 1 or 2 - the
ferry awaits the arrival of a lorry as the request was made as
LQ(n).COOPT and a call on COOPT implies a delay if no victim
is waiting in the slaveq. Should the ferry be required to
leave at once if no lorries are waiting, we have to put in a
test before calling COOPT, e.g.

```
            IF LQ(n).LENGTH = 0 THEN HOLD(crossing) ELSE
            BEGIN L :- LQ(n).COOPT;
              HOLD(load);
              HOLD(crossing);
              HOLD(unload);
              L.SCHEDULE(0.0);
            END;
```

Now we have to show how we can deal with the general case
of one master and several slaves. Consider a revamping of the
ferry problem with cars arriving, but no lorries. As in
example 5, the ferry can cope with up to 6 cars at a time, but
now we are interested in modelling the cars as entities as
they tour round the island and eventually return. The
solution is in the same style as above, but instead of
coopting just one object per crossing, this time we may coopt
up to six. The new problem is "Where do we keep them during
the crossing?" It is most convenient to place them in a queue
local to CLASS FERRY. A suitable declaration - CLASS QUEUE -
is defined in DEMOS (see figure 5.3). Most of the attributes
to CLASS QUEUE are similar to those of CLASS WAITQ.

```
-----------------------------
!          QUEUE           !<---REF(QUEUE)CARGO
-----------------------------
!TITLE            "CARGO" !
!slaveq                   ! for saved entities
!REF(ENTITY)PROCEDURE FIRST!
!REF(ENTITY)PROCEDURE LAST !
!INTEGER PROCEDURE LENGTH  !
-----------------------------
```

Figure 5.3 Result of CARGO :- NEW QUEUE("CARGO").

We declare REF(QUEUE)CARGO local to CLASS FERRY, and create
the queue by

         CARGO :- NEW QUEUE("CARGO");

Any coopted CAR object E can be placed in the queue (in
priority order, of course) by E.INTO(CARGO) and removed from
it and scheduled by E.OUT; E.SCHEDULE(delay). INTO and OUT
are additional ENTITY attributes. We let the cars queue for
the ferry in WAITQs CQ(1) and CQ(2). Thus the CAR and FERRY
class outlines are

```
         ENTITY CLASS CAR;
         BEGIN
         ARRIVE:
           CQ(1).WAIT;
         DELIVER:
           HOLD(tour island);
         RETURN:
           CQ(2).WAIT;
         END***CAR***;
```

```
ENTITY CLASS FERRY;
BEGIN INTEGER C, SIDE;
  REF(QUEUE)CARGO;  REF(ENTITY)E;
  CARGO :- NEW QUEUE("CARGO");
LOOP:
  FOR SIDE := 1, 2 DO
  BEGIN
LOAD:  C := 0;
     WHILE C < 6 AND CQ(SIDE).LENGTH > 0 DO
     BEGIN
       E :- CQ(SIDE).COOPT;
       E.INTO(CARGO);
       HOLD(load);
       C := C + 1;
     END;
CROSS:
     HOLD(crossing);
UNLOAD:
     WHILE CARGO.LENGTH > 0 DO
     BEGIN
       HOLD(unload);
       E :- CARGO.FIRST;
       E.OUT;
       E.SCHEDULE(0.0);
     END;
   END;
   .....REPEAT;
END***FERRY***;
```

Should the cars be unloaded according to the last-on-board, first-off rule we would replace the seventh last line above by E :- CARGO.LAST.

EXAMPLE 6: INFORMATION SYSTEM

This problem has been used in several papers and books and so provides an interesting comparison (see for example, Pritsker and Kiviat [28]). The model represents an information retrieval system with a number of remote terminals each capable of interrogating a single processor (CPU). A customer with a query arrives at one or other of the terminals and queues, if necessary, to use it. The terminals are physically far apart and so no queue jumping is possible. When the terminal is free, the user keys in his request, and then signals his presence to the system. He then awaits his reply.

The queries are picked up by a scanner which looks at each terminal in turn. If there is no query outstanding, the scanner rotates on to the next terminal in turn. If there is a query, the scanner locks on to that terminal and does not rotate further until it has succeeded in copying the query to a buffer unit capable of holding three such queries at a time. The copying process is blocked if no buffer slot is available. When the copying has been completed, the scanner starts to rotate again and leaves the cpu to deal with the request.

The CPU processes the query and places the answer in the buffer slot overwriting the query. The answer is returned to the terminal by the buffer unit (without using the scanner) and then that buffer slot is freed. The customer reads the reply and then quits his terminal.

Model data
==========

Timings in minutes:
inter-customer arrivals	NEGEXP:mean=5/min
enter a query	UNIFORM:0.3->0.5
transfer query to buffer	CONSTANT:0.0117
process a query on CPU	UNIFORM:0.05->0.10
transfer reply back	CONSTANT:0.0397
scanner rotation	CONSTANT:0.0027
scanner to test a terminal	CONSTANT:0.0027
customer to read reply	UNIFORM:0.6->0.8

Resources:
BUFFER	BIN:initially 3
TERMINAL(1:6)	RES:limit=1
REQUESTQ(1:6)	WAITQ:for pending queries

We can describe the model in terms of two entity classes - QUERY and SCANNER. CLASS SCANNER describes the actions of the real scanner as it rotates from terminal to terminal. If the current terminal has no request pending, the scanner moves on, otherwise it awaits a buffer and transfers the query into it before rotating on.

CLASS QUERY describes the roles of the customer, his request and the reply. On arrival, the customer keys in his request and awaits his reply. The query (same object) is eventually passed from the terminal to a CPU buffer by the scanner. Since these actions are already described inside CLASS SCANNER, they are not repeated here - instead each QUERY object is coopted by the scanner for this part of its life. When it resumes its own life history, the query is already in a buffer. Then the query is processed by the CPU and the reply sent back to the appropriate terminal for reading.

Now that we have outlined the roles to be played by scanner and query objects and decided upon their interactions, we can tackle their declarations separately. We begin by detailing CLASS SCANNER.

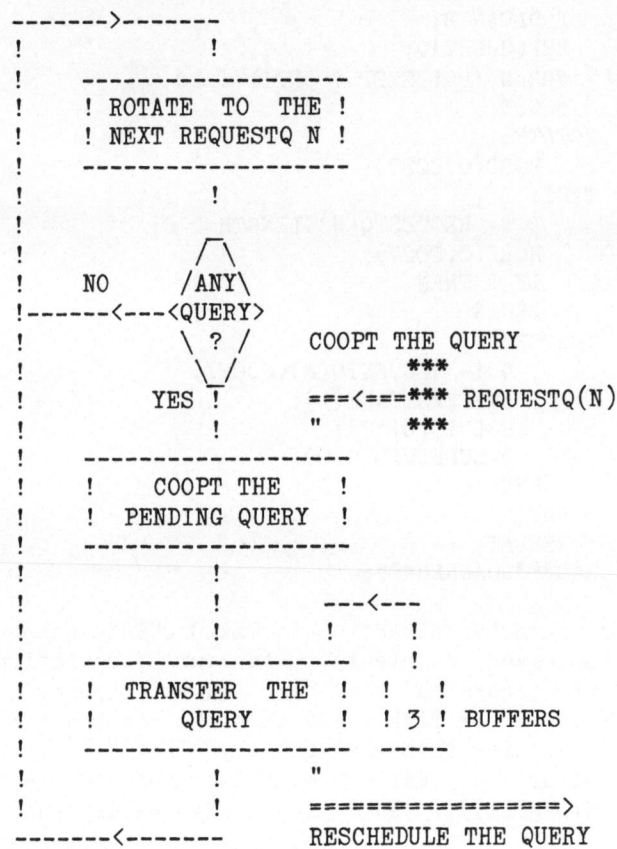

Figure 5.4 CLASS SCANNER activity diagram.

The scanner rotates from terminal 1 to terminal 6, and then repeats. At each terminal N (1 <= N <= 6), it rotates (HOLD(0.0027)) and then tests to see if any query is pending (B := REQUESTQ(N).LENGTH > 0). This test also takes 0.0027 minutes to complete. If there is a request, then the scanner locks on to that terminal, acquires a buffer (by BUFFERS.TAKE(1). This may imply a delay.), and then transfers the request to the buffer (HOLD(0.0117)). Once this has been accomplished, the query is then released (Q.SCHEDULE(0.0)) and the scanner is free to rotate to the next terminal.

The full declaration is

```
ENTITY CLASS SCANNER;
BEGIN INTEGER N;
   BOOLEAN B;
   REF(QUERY)Q;
   FOR N := 1 STEP 1 UNTIL 6 DO
   BEGIN
ROTATE:
      HOLD(0.0027);
TEST:
      B := REQUESTQ(N).LENGTH > 0;
      HOLD(0.0027);
      IF B THEN
      BEGIN
TRANSFER:
         Q :- REQUESTQ(N).COOPT;
         BUFFERS.TAKE(1);
         HOLD(0.0117);
         Q.SCHEDULE(0.0);
      END;
   END;
   REPEAT;
END***SCANNER***;
```

We now turn our attention to CLASS QUERY (whose activity diagram is given overleaf). In our formulation, a query object first generates the next query object, notes its arrival time (T := TIME), and then chooses its terminal (N). That terminal is then seized (by TERMINAL(N).ACQUIRE(1), perhaps after a wait), and the request is keyed in (HOLD(KEYIN.SAMPLE)). Now the query waits passively in REQUESTQ(N).

When it becomes active again, the scanner has acquired a buffer slot on its behalf and copied the request into that buffer. The request is now processed (HOLD(PROCESS.SAMPLE)) and the reply returned to the appropriate terminal (HOLD(0.0397)). After the transfer has been completed, the buffer slot is freed (BUFFERS.GIVE(1)), possibly unblocking the scanner. Then the reply is read and the terminal vacated

(TERMINAL(N).RELEASE(1)), which allows in the next query, if
any. Finally, a histogram of through times (THRU) is updated
by the elapsed time of this query through the system.

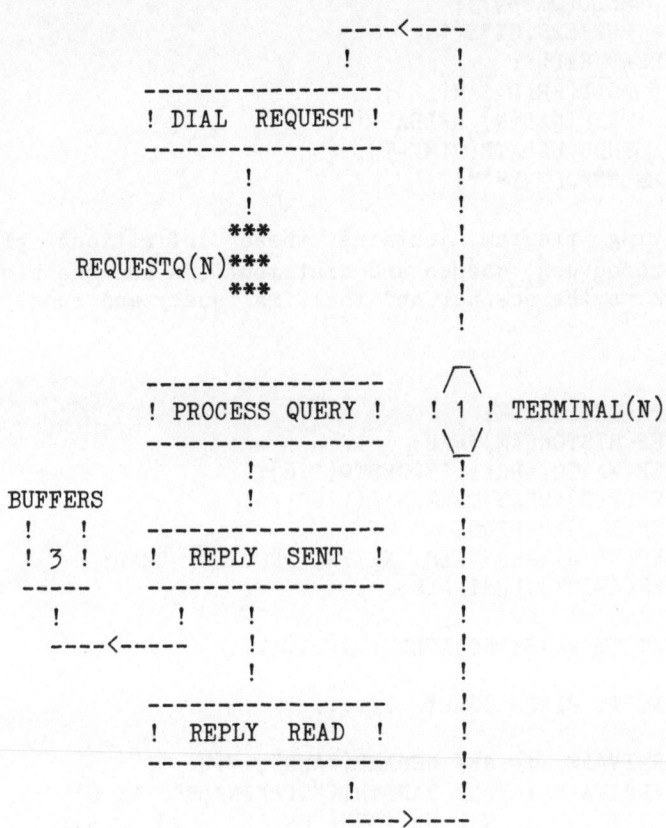

Figure 5.5 CLASS QUERY activity diagram.

```
      ENTITY CLASS QUERY;
      BEGIN
        INTEGER N; REAL T;
        NEW QUERY("QUERY").SCHEDULE(ARRIVALS.SAMPLE);
        T := TIME;
        N := TERMINALS.SAMPLE;
      JOIN QUEUE AND DIAL REQUEST:
        TERMINAL(N).ACQUIRE(1);
        HOLD(KEYIN.SAMPLE);
      AWAIT PROCESSING:
        REQUESTQ(N).WAIT;
```

```
        PROCESSING:
          HOLD(PROCESS.SAMPLE);
        SEND_REPLY:
          HOLD(0.0397);
          BUFFERS.GIVE(1);
        READ_REPLY:
          HOLD(READ.SAMPLE);
          TERMINAL(N).RELEASE(1);
          THRU.UPDATE(TIME-T);
        END***QUERY***;
```

The driving program contains these definitions plus the
various resources, queues and distributions and one histogram.
It generates the scanner and the first query and runs for 60
minutes.

```
    DEMOS
      BEGIN INTEGER K;
        REF(HISTOGRAM)THRU;
        REF(WAITQ)ARRAY REQUESTQ(1:6);
        REF(RES)ARRAY TERMINAL(1:6);
        REF(BIN)BUFFERS;
        REF(RDIST)ARRIVALS, KEYIN, PROCESS, READ;
        REF(IDIST)TERMINALS;

        ENTITY CLASS SCANNER...........;

        ENTITY CLASS QUERY.............;

        ARRIVALS   :- NEW NEGEXP("ARR", 5.0);
        TERMINALS :- NEW RANDINT("TERMINALS", 1, 6);
        KEYIN      :- NEW UNIFORM("KEYIN", 0.3, 0.5);
        PROCESS    :- NEW UNIFORM("PROCESS", 0.05, 0.10);
        READ       :- NEW UNIFORM("READ", 0.6, 0.8);
        THRU       :- NEW HISTOGRAM("THRU", 1.0, 11.0, 10);

        FOR K := 1 STEP 1 UNTIL 6 DO
        BEGIN
         REQUESTQ(K):-NEW WAITQ(EDIT("REQUEST",K));
          TERMINAL(K):-NEW RES(EDIT("TERMINAL", K),1);
        END;

        BUFFERS :- NEW BIN("BUFFERS", 3);
        NEW SCANNER("SCANNER").SCHEDULE(0.0);
        NEW QUERY("Q").SCHEDULE(0.0);
        HOLD(60.0);
      END;
```

```
***Output:
==========


                    CLOCK TIME =  60.000
*******************************************************************
*                                                                 *
*                        R E P O R T                              *
*                                                                 *
*******************************************************************



                 D I S T R I B U T I O N S
                 ************************


TITLE      /  (RE)SET/ OBS/TYPE    /      A/    B/      SEED
ARRIVALS       0.000   300 NEGEXP       5.000            33427485
TERMINALS      0.000   300 RANDINT          1     6     22276755
KEYIN          0.000   260 UNIFORM      0.300 0.500      46847980
PROCESS        0.000   257 UNIFORM  5.000E-02 0.100      43859043
READ           0.000   257 UNIFORM      0.600 0.800      64042082



                 H I S T O G R A M S
                 ********************


                    S U M M A R Y


TITLE      /  (RE)SET/ OBS/ AVERAGE/  EST.ST.DV/MINIMUM/MAXIMUM
THRU           0.000   254    4.392       3.347   1.080  17.292


CELL/LOWER LIM/  N/ FREQ/ CUM %
                              I-------------------------------
   0 -INFINITY    0  0.00    0.00 I
   1     1.000   73  0.29   28.74 I*****************************
   2     2.000   44  0.17   46.06 I******************
   3     3.000   29  0.11   57.48 I***********
   4     4.000   25  0.10   67.32 I*********
   5     5.000   21  0.08   75.59 I********
   6     6.000   15  0.06   81.50 I******
   7     7.000   11  0.04   85.83 I****
   8     8.000    7  0.03   88.58 I***
   9     9.000   11  0.04   92.91 I****
  10    10.000    3  0.01   94.09 I*
  11    11.000   15  0.06  100.00 I******
                              I-------------------------------
```

R E S O U R C E S
****

TITLE /	(RE)SET/	OBS	/LIM	/MIN	/NOW/	% USAGE/	AV. WAIT/	QMAX
TERMINAL 1	0.000	40	1	0	0	83.549	4.323	15
TERMINAL 2	0.000	45	1	0	0	96.128	6.677	18
TERMINAL 3	0.000	45	1	0	0	94.530	1.851	4
TERMINAL 4	0.000	42	1	0	0	89.087	2.133	6
TERMINAL 5	0.000	38	1	0	0	78.368	0.652	3
TERMINAL 6	0.000	44	1	0	0	89.604	3.323	7

B I N S
****

TITLE /	(RE)SET/	OBS	/INIT	/MAX	/NOW/	AV. FREE/	AV. WAIT/	QMAX
BUFFERS	0.000	257	3	3	3	2.457	0.000	1

W A I T   Q U E U E S
****

TITLE /	(RE)SET/	OBS	/QMAX	/QNOW/	Q AVERAGE/	ZEROS/	AV. WAIT
REQUEST 1	0.000	41	1	0	0.000	41	0.000
REQUEST 1 *	0.000	41	1	0	1.017E-02	0	1.488E-02
REQUEST 2	0.000	46	1	0	0.000	46	0.000
REQUEST 2 *	0.000	46	1	0	1.672E-02	0	2.181E-02
REQUEST 3	0.000	45	1	0	0.000	45	0.000
REQUEST 3 *	0.000	45	1	0	1.711E-02	0	2.281E-02
REQUEST 4	0.000	43	1	0	0.000	43	0.000
REQUEST 4 *	0.000	43	1	0	1.276E-02	0	1.780E-02
REQUEST 5	0.000	38	1	0	0.000	38	0.000
REQUEST 5 *	0.000	38	1	0	1.226E-02	0	1.936E-02
REQUEST 6	0.000	44	1	0	0.000	44	0.000
REQUEST 6 *	0.000	44	1	0	1.368E-02	0	1.866E-02

REMARKS ON EXAMPLE 6

The report on each wait queue details the delays caused to the
masters wishing to coopt victims (line 1) and to the victims
themselves (in the starred line 2). In lines 1, 'TITLE' and
'(RE)SET' are obvious, 'OBS' gives the number of completed
calls on COOPT for the WAITQ, 'QMAX' the maximum length of the

masterq (which includes zero waits), 'QNOW' the current length
of the masterq, 'Q AVERAGE' the time weighted average length
of the masterq, 'ZEROS' the number of zero waits (instant
coopts) in the masterq and 'AV. WAIT' the average wait time
of each master including zero waits. In the same manner, the
second line reports on the way slaves are delayed in the
slaveq. OBS must be the same for both lines.

As expected, the scanner is never delayed in a REQUESTQ
(see line 1 reports) as it makes sure a query is waiting
before calling COOPT.

We have used a histogram - THRU - to collect and display
the elapsed through times for each query. Having entered the
system, each query makes a local note of the current clock
time by T := TIME. The last action of each query object is to
update THRU by a call

THRU.UPDATE(TIME-T);

As can be seen from the report on THRU, a summary of the
update readings is printed followed by the histogram itself.
Each histogram object requires 4 parameters: a TEXT TITLE, a
REAL lower bound for the update values, a REAL upper bound for
the update values, and an INTEGER giving the number of
recording cells. Each cell has the same width = (upper bound
- lower bound)/number of cells. Thus

THRU :- NEW HISTOGRAM("THRU", 1.0, 11.0, 10);

establishes a histogram entitled THRU with 10 cells for
recording values in the ranges [1.0->2.0), [2.0->3.0), ...,
[10.0->11.0). There are also two extra cells for recording
underflow (here updates less than 1.0) and overflow (here 11.0
or greater). In this case, the underflow cell has no entries
recorded and the overflow cell 15 entries. The summary
records the minimum (=1.080) and the maximum (=17.292) through
times and these could be used in later runs to reset the
histogram bounds should this be desired.

N.B. A little paper and pencil work shows that assuming
no blocking the expected average terminal usage will be 0.400
+ (0.0027+0.0027)*3 + 0.0117 + 0.0750 + 0.0397 + 0.7000 =
1.2426. As we expect roughly 50 users per terminal per hour
this figure shows that the system design is inadequate and we
must expect queues to build up. Such rough and ready analyses
should always be performed on simulation models to give an

idea of through times etc. (or at least rough bounds for them)
for they pin point expected bottlenecks and may even obviate
the need to run the model. Notice also that the buffers are
reported as being under utilised. Was this to be expected?

EXERCISES 5

1. A library has an archive section containing specialist
books. Anyone requesting such a book must first fill out a
request slip and then present it to a librarian. The
librarian then goes into the archive stacks to locate the book
and return with it. The book is then checked out and handed
over to the reader. Assume that all requests are found in the
stack, and that each reader makes one request at a time. If
several readers are waiting, a librarian can pick up several
request slips at a time, up to a maximum of five. The
librarians are quite democratic and if more than one is free,
they divide the work amongst themselves as equally as
possible. (Devise a suitable strategy yourself and compare it
with the suggested solution. Yours may well be smarter.)

Model data
==========

Timings in minutes:
request rate	NEGEXP:mean=0.5/min
time to check request	CONSTANT:0.1
walk to stack	UNIFORM:0.5->1.5
locate n books	NORMAL:mean=n,st.dev.=n/5
return from stack	UNIFORM:0.5->2.0
check out each book	CONSTANT:0.5

Assume that there are three librarians and that each can
handle up to five requests at a time. Assume that the first
request arrives at time 0.0. Run your model for 8 hours.

HINT: If X is a sample from a normal distribution with mean 0
and standard deviation 1, then Y = m + sX is a sample from a
normal distribution with mean 'm' and standard deviation 's'.

2. Rewrite exercise 5.1 above with the following new
strategy for the librarians when collecting slips. The
librarians are queued for work on the longest-idle,
first-back-to-work principle. When they begin to accept
requests, they take as many as they can up to the maximum of
five before allowing the next free librarian (if any) to

accept any remaining requests.

    3. A steel mill furnace melts a load of steel, and then
pours it into batches of moulds. Then the furnace is reloaded
and its work cycle repeated. The molten steel in the moulds
is allowed to set (form a solid crust on the outside so that
it is self-supporting). Then the moulds are stripped away and
the ingots removed. The batch is then loaded into a soaking
pit where it is heated until it has achieved a certain uniform
temperature.   Meanwhile, the moulds are cleaned, reassembled
for further use, and returned to the furnace area.   When a
batch has reached the requisite temperature, it is noted as
ready for rolling. Rolling turns the ingots into slabs, the
end product of the mill.

    The furnace has a capacity of 300 tons which is enough to
fill 2 batches of moulds, one after the other. Each batch of
moulds is transported on its own railway bogie (there are
always 15 moulds to a batch). After a pouring, each batch of
moulds is shunted into a siding to set.   After setting, the
batch can be moved from the sidings. A team of strippers take
the bogie to the soaking pit area where, with the help of a
crane (there is one reserved for each team), they remove the
moulds and dump the ingots. The ingots await placement in a
soaking pit.   Meanwhile the strippers clean the moulds,
reassemble them and put them back on their bogie.   The bogie
is then shunted back to the furnace area, and the team of
strippers looks for more work.

    The batch of ingots is loaded into a soaking pit when one
becomes free.   The loading requires use of one of three
overhead cranes. Unloading also requires use of these
cranes, but in order to maintain their temperature, individual
ingots are left in their pit as long as possible. Thus once a
crane has been acquired for unloading, it is retained and is
used to unload the ingots one at a time at a pace dictated by
the rolling mill. Assume that the crane is released when the
last ingot in the batch has been unloaded.

Model data
==========

  Timings in minutes:
   furnace
    load and smelt   NORMAL:mean=165.0,st.dev.=20.0
    pour   CONSTANT:20 per batch

```
batch of ingots
  set                    CONSTANT:75
  load into pit          CONSTANT:15 per batch
  soak                   NORMAL:mean=160.0,st.dev.=30.0
  unload from pit        CONSTANT:1 per ingot
  roll                   CONSTANT:3 per ingot
strippers
  strip batch            UNIFORM:10.0->16.0
  clean moulds           UNIFORM:10.0->12.0
  reassemble moulds      UNIFORM:10.0->12.0

Resources:
  BOGIES                 BIN:initially 8
  CRANES                 RES:limit=3
  PITS                   RES:limit=10 batches
  MILL                   RES:limit=2
```

Assume that their are 4 furnaces and two teams of strippers. Assume further that all bogie movements take a negligible time. The furnaces start up at times 0, 40, 80, and 120 minutes respectively. Run your model for 1500 time units assuming a 'cold' start. Investigate the effect of priorities in the use of the soaking pit cranes and estimate a maximum value for the number of setting places required (the capacity of the siding).

4. Change the work cycle of a furnace in exercise 5.3 to the one detailed below. The furnace goes through the cycle

load; melt; refine; tap; clean;

The loading of scrap metal requires the use of a crane, C1. When loaded, the furnace melts its load using 3 units of electric power. Once melted, two units of electricity are returned, and one is retained. After melting, the metal is refined. Then the furnace is tapped (its contents are poured out). A tapping requires a set of moulds and another crane, C2. (In this case assume that the furnace discharges all of its load in one go.) After being tapped, the furnace relinquishes its last unit of electric power. Every ten such cycles, the furnace lining is inspected by a group of asbestos clad brickies who repair any cracks or faults. Use lower case letters to denote informally the activity durations.

5. A newspaper has an office for receiving advertisements placed by telephone. There are N telephone trunks, and M telephone operators. A call is accepted at once

should an operator be free. Otherwise, an incoming call is kept in a queuing system (FCFS). This consists of two arrays each with a capacity of K calls. The calls are always entered into a background queue, Q1. Whenever the foreground queue, Q2, is empty all the entries in Q1 are automatically transferred into Q2 (assume this takes zero time).

When a direct call has been accepted and completed, an operator spends a little time completing notes about it before looking for a fresh task. Then she is free to accept a call from Q2. The operator continues taking calls from Q2 in this manner until Q2 (and hence Q1) is empty. Not all calls can be accepted. If all N trunks are engaged, then an incoming call is rejected. A call must also be rejected if Q1 is full.

Model data
==========

```
        Timings in minutes:
          call inter-arrival   NEGEXP:mean=1/min
          advert placing       NORMAL:mean=4.0,st.dev.=1.0
          complete notes       NORMAL:mean=1.25,st.dev.=0.5
```

Let N (the number of trunks) be 15; K (the capacity of both Q1 and Q2) be 9; and M (the number of operators) be 6. Simulate for 8 hours.

6. The model of example 6, page 81, would be badly behaved if the request rate were low (it isn't in this case except right at the start). For then the scanner, which has a fine grain of time compared to other entities, would do much fruitless rotating and testing. It is instructive to modify the program in such a way that the scanner will go to sleep if there are no requests.

HINT: You will probably need to use the scheduling routine CANCEL which is an attribute of CLASS ENTITY. A call E.CANCEL (REF(ENTITY)E) removes E from the event list; it has no effect if E is not in the event list. (CURRENT.)CANCEL puts CURRENT to sleep out of the event list and resumes the actions of the new entity at the head of the event list. If, because of this, the event list becomes empty, then the call on CANCEL causes a run time error. DEMOS.CANCEL removes DEMOS from the event list; this may be useful in situations where the length of the simulation run is to be determined from internal conditions rather than predicted in advance.

5.2 FIND

A master entity attempting to locate a victim from a WAITQ by
a call on COOPT is always allotted the first available entity
without discrimination. Sometimes we would like the master
entity to be able to select and coopt a victim with specified
characteristics. For example, we may wish to select a lorry
whose external dimensions fit the space left on the ferry. To
do this, we need a more subtle routine than COOPT.

     This is provided by the routine FIND, also local to CLASS
WAITQ (see figure 5.2, page 78). FIND parallels COOPT in that
it locates a suitable victim and blocks the caller if need be
until one is located. FIND takes two parameters *3); a
user-defined reference variable V and a condition (boolean
expression) which usually involves V. This combination
enables arbitrarily complicated choices to be expressed, a
point which we now illustrate by an example.

     Suppose we are studying marriage bureau ploys. The class
of eligible men could have the outline

```
     [REF(WAITQ)READY;]

     ENTITY CLASS MAN;
     BEGIN
       BOOLEAN HANDSOME;
       INTEGER AGE, INCOME, WEALTH;
       ............
     ELIGIBLE:
     READY.WAIT;
       ............
     END***MAN***;
```

     When a man decides he is ready for marriage, he waits in
the WAITQ READY from which he hopes to be selected by a lady
in the model. It is up to each lady to find the beau of her
choice. CLASS LADY overleaf describes those who want a
husband who is at least rich.

---
*3). FIND has the heading

PROCEDURE FIND(V, C); NAME V, C; REF(ENTITY)V; BOOLEAN C;

Both V and C are called by NAME: (Jensen's device).

```
ENTITY CLASS LADY;
BEGIN REF(MAN)M;
    . . . . . . . . . . . . . .
CHOOSE:
    READY.FIND(M, M.WEALTH >= 500000);
FOUND:
    . . . . . . . . . . . . . .
END***LADY***;
```

At the label FOUND, the local variable M will reference a coopted man object whose wealth attribute is at least 500,000 (currency unspecified). Really selective ladies could try for a young, handsome, rich husband with a good income too! In their case

```
READY.FIND(M, M.HANDSOME AND M.AGE < 30
        AND M.WEALTH >= 500000 AND M.INCOME > 30000);
```

could be appropriate.

A call on FIND, say

```
Q.FIND(V, condition);                         [REF(WAITQ)Q;]
```

operates as follows. First the slaveq of Q is inspected. If it is not empty, then V is set to reference the entities in it in turn and the condition is tested against each. If a V is found for which the condition holds, then that V is extracted from the slaveq, coopted by the caller and control remains with the caller (CURRENT). Should the slaveq be empty or no such victim be found, the caller is put to sleep in the masterq of Q in order of its priority. Thereafter, each new slave arriving via a call on WAIT awakens the masters in turn who test to see if the newcomer satisfies their condition. The first master with a true FIND condition seizes the new slave and becomes unblocked. If no such master can be found, the new slave waits in the slaveq of Q in its priority order. Notice that V :- Q.COOPT is equivalent to Q.FIND(V, TRUE).

EXAMPLE 7:   TANKER SIMULATION

Tankers arrive periodically at a harbour and discharge their cargo into shore tanks. When a shore tank is full, or nearly so, its contents are automatically transferred to the refinery. While this transfer is taking place, a shore tank may not be filled by a tanker.

Model data
==========

Timings in hours:
 Tanker arrival rate   NEGEXP:0.125/hour
 Setup time for pump   CONSTANT:0.5 hours
 Pumping rate   CONSTANT:1000 tons/hour
 Discharge rate   CONSTANT:4000 tons/hour

Capacities in 1000 ton units:
 Tanker loads   15,20,25 equally likely
 Shore tank volume   70

Run the simulation for 1000 continuous hours with 5 shore
tanks. Take as initial conditions that two shore tanks are
empty and free, one is currently discharging and will be free
at 8 hours, and that the other two are currently being loaded
and will be freed at times 12 (with 45 units still free) and
3.5 (with 25 units free) respectively. The first tanker
arrives at time 0.0.

   We split the description of the model into two components
requiring entity declarations - TANKER and SHORETANK. Tankers
arrive, find a suitable shore tank from REF(WAITQ)TANKQ (that
is one with enough capacity left to take their load), pump
their load into the chosen shore tank and then depart.

```
ENTITY CLASS TANKER;
BEGIN
  REF(SHORETANK)ST; INTEGER LOAD;
  LOAD := ...;
AWAIT SHORETANK:
  TANKQ.FIND(ST, ST.FREE >= LOAD);
  HOLD(pumping time);
  ST.SCHEDULE(0.0);
END***TANKER***;
```

   Each shore tank waits passively in TANKQ until selected
by a tanker, and is then its slave whilst being loaded. After
each loading, a shore tank decides for itself what to do next.
If it has too little capacity left (taken fairly arbitrarily
as less than 20,000 tons) either to take another load or to
make it worthwhile waiting for another load, it discharges its
contents into the refinery. Then it returns empty to TANKQ.
If it has sufficient capacity left for another load, it
returns directly to TANKQ.

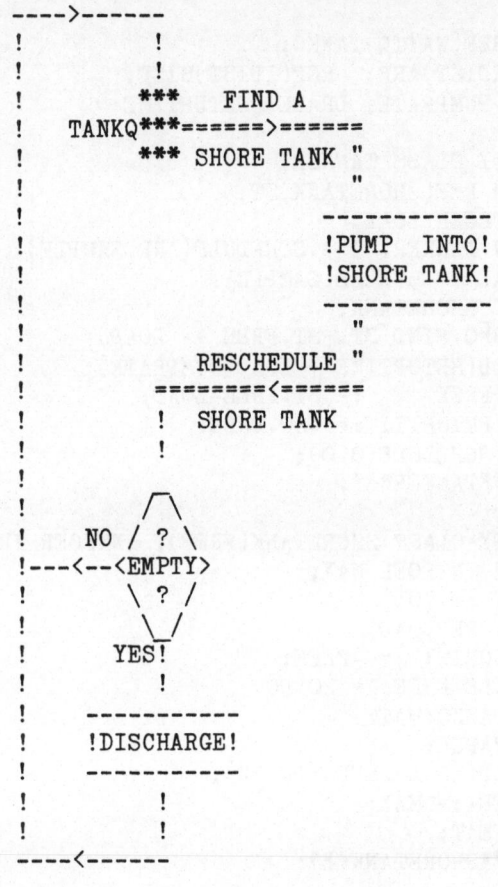

```
----->------
!         !
!         !
!            ***    FIND A
!     TANKQ***======>======
!            ***  SHORE TANK "
!                            "
!
!                      --------------
!                      !PUMP   INTO!
!                      !SHORE TANK!
!                      --------------
!                            "
!                 RESCHEDULE "
!                 ========<======
!                 !  SHORE TANK
!                 !
!
!                /\
!        NO /  ? \
!---<--<EMPTY>
!                \  ? /
!                 \/
!               YES!
!                 !
!           -----------
!           !DISCHARGE!
!           -----------
!                 !
!                 !
----<------
```

SHORETANK   TANKER

Figure 5.6 Tanker Simulation activity diagram.

```
ENTITY CLASS SHORETANK;
BEGIN
  ..........
LOOP: RE_LOAD:
  WHILE room for another load DO
    WAIT(TANKQ);
DISCHARGE:
  HOLD(time to empty);
  REPEAT;
END***SHORETANK***;
```

The complete program reads

```
DEMOS
  BEGIN REF(WAITQ)TANKQ;
    REF(RDIST)ARR;  REF(IDIST)SIZE;
    REAL PUMPRATE, DRATE, SETUPTIME;

    ENTITY CLASS TANKER;
    BEGIN REF(SHORETANK)ST;
      INTEGER LOAD;
      NEW TANKER("T").SCHEDULE(ARR.SAMPLE);
      LOAD := 5*SIZE.SAMPLE;
    AWAIT SHORETANK:
      TANKQ.FIND(ST, ST.FREE >= LOAD);
      HOLD(SETUPTIME + LOAD*PUMPRATE);
      ST.FREE     := ST.FREE-LOAD;
      ST.PRIORITY := -ST.FREE;
      ST.SCHEDULE(0.0);
    END***TANKER***;

    ENTITY CLASS SHORETANK(FREE); INTEGER FREE;
    BEGIN INTEGER MAX;
      MAX := 70;
    LOOP: RE_LOAD:
      PRIORITY := -FREE;
      WHILE FREE >= 20 DO
        TANKQ.WAIT;
    DISCHARGE:
      HOLD((MAX-FREE)*DRATE);
      FREE := MAX;
      REPEAT;
    END***SHORETANK***;

    TRACE;
    SETUPTIME := 0.5;
    PUMPRATE  := 1.0;
    DRATE     := 0.25;
    ARR       :- NEW NEGEXP("ARRIVALS", 0.125);
    SIZE      :- NEW RANDINT("LOAD", 3, 5);
    TANKQ     :- NEW WAITQ("SHORETANKS");
    NEW SHORETANK("S", 70).SCHEDULE(0.0);
    NEW SHORETANK("S", 70).SCHEDULE(0.0);
    NEW SHORETANK("S", 45).SCHEDULE(12.0);
    NEW SHORETANK("S", 25).SCHEDULE(3.5);
    NEW SHORETANK("S", 70).SCHEDULE(8.0);
    NEW TANKER("T").SCHEDULE(0.0);
    HOLD(1000.0);
  END;
```

***Output: Partial trace.
==========

```
 TIME/ CURRENT      AND ITS ACTIONS
                    ...................
21.259 T 2          SCHEDULES T 3 AT 26.493
                    FINDS S 4 IN SHORETANKS
                    HOLDS FOR 15.500, UNTIL 36.759
                    ...................
36.759 T 2          SCHEDULES S 4 NOW
                    ***TERMINATES
       S 4          HOLDS FOR 15.000, UNTIL 51.759
                    ...................
51.759 S 4          WAITS IN SHORETANKS
                    ...................
```

                              Partial report.

                    D I S T R I B U T I O N S
                    ****

```
TITLE      /   (RE)SET/ OBS/TYPE     /     A/     B/     SEED
ARRIVALS       0.000  128 NEGEXP      0.125            33427485
LOAD           0.000  128 RANDINT          3      5    22276755
```

                    W A I T   Q U E U E S
                    ****

```
TITLE        /   (RE)SET/ OBS/QMAX/QNOW/Q AVERAGE/ZEROS/ AV. WAIT
SHORETANKS       0.000  128    5    0    0.181    99      1.417
SHORETANKS *     0.000  128    5    2    1.849    30     14.230
```

REMARKS ON EXAMPLE 7

By using PRIORITY, we let the shore tanks wait in TANKQ
ordered according to their capacity remaining - least capacity
at the front. When the model was run with shore tank
priorities always zero, the average wait times rose slightly;
for tankers up to 1.417, and for shore tanks up to 14.230.

    There is a little interplay between the tanker and the
shore tank after the tanker has discharged its cargo. The
tanker sees to the updating of the shore tank's current
contents (ST.FREE := ST.FREE-LOAD) and of its priority
(ST.PRIORITY := -ST.FREE) before scheduling it.

In the models we have examined so far, we have been able to express the action histories of entities as sequences of activities, usually of the form

> acquire R1; acquire R2; ... acquire Rn;
> HOLD(activity duration);
> release R'1; release R'2; ... release R'm;

where the extra resources required (R1, R2, ..., Rn), be they modelled as RES, BIN or ENTITY objects, have been requested and acquired one at a time. In this chapter, we consider some models in which this is not possible. For example, an entity may not be able to start its next activity unless ALL the resources required for its commencement are available; or it may need to wait and see which resources turn up next before deciding what it should do. Such complications arise all the time in real life simulations. We now give several short, but illustrative, examples.

6.1 CONDITION QUEUES

EXAMPLE 8: PORT SYSTEM WITH TIDES

Consider an extension to the Port System of example 2, page 40, which takes account of the state of the tide. Boats arrive laden and depart empty. We now place the extra constraint that boats may only dock if the tide is not low. As before, they may leave whatever the state of the tide. It is still fair for a boat to request a jetty on arrival, but the following partial coding

```
ENTITY CLASS BOAT;
BEGIN
DOCK: JETTIES.ACQUIRE(1);
      TUGS.ACQUIRE(2);
      wait until the tide is not low;
      HOLD(2.0);
      TUGS.RELEASE(2);
      ..............
END***BOAT***;
```

is not satisfactory because a significant period of time may elapse before a boat actually uses the tugs if it acquires them while the tide is low. During this interval, one or other or both these tugs could perhaps be gainfully employed by boats wishing to leave the Port.

Notice that reversing the order of the tug and tide requests does not help because the tide may have gone out before two tugs are available. Boats wishing to leave their jetty must wait until such a time as two tugs are available AND it is not low tide.

Dealing with the periodic setting and resetting of the state of the tide is quite straightforward. Let low tides occur every 13 hours and last for 4 hours. We can represent the state of the tide by a global BOOLEAN LOWTIDE (initially FALSE) and arrange to set its value appropriately by an object of CLASS TIDE

```
[BOOLEAN LOWTIDE;]

ENTITY CLASS TIDE;
BEGIN
LOW_TIDE_ON:
   LOWTIDE := TRUE;
   HOLD(4.0);
   LOWTIDE := FALSE;
LOW_TIDE_NOW_OFF:
   HOLD(9.0);
   REPEAT;
END***TIDE***;
```

The statement

```
NEW TIDE("TIDE").SCHEDULE(1.0);
```

(when executed at simulation time zero) corresponds to low tides starting at TIME = 1.00, 14.00, 27.00, ...

We can now express the condition for docking in DEMOS by

```
TUGS.AVAIL >= 2 AND NOT LOWTIDE
```

Notice that we have not modelled low tide as a resource: in no sense will a boat wish to seize the tide!

```
-------------------------------
!          CONDQ              !<---REF(CONDQ)DOCKQ
-------------------------------
!TITLE              "DOCKQ"!
!condition queue           ! for entities w'until
!REF(ENTITY)PROCEDURE FIRST!
!REF(ENTITY)PROCEDURE LAST !
!INTEGER PROCEDURE LENGTH  !
!PROCEDURE WAITUNTIL(COND) !
!PROCEDURE SIGNAL          !
!BOOLEAN ALL        FALSE!
-------------------------------
```

Figure 6.1 Result of DOCKQ :- NEW CONDQ("DOCKQ").

DEMOS allows entities awaiting a particular condition to arise to be detained in a condition queue (of CLASS CONDQ, see figure 6.1) by a WAITUNTIL command. For example, the docking activity of CLASS BOAT will now read

```
[REF(CONDQ)DOCKQ;]

JETTIES.ACQUIRE(1);
DOCKQ.WAITUNTIL(TUGS.AVAIL >= 2 AND NOT LOWTIDE);
TUGS.ACQUIRE(2);
HOLD(2.0);
TUGS.RELEASE(2);
```

The synchronisation works as follows: let entity E (or indeed, the DEMOS block itself) issue the request

```
Q.WAITUNTIL(condition);              [REF(CONDQ)Q;]
```

(The condition can be any boolean valued expression and may thus be arbitrarily complicated. The condition is dynamically re-evaluated each time it is tested - it is called by NAME - and is best considered as being local to E the maker of the request rather than the condition queue Q.) The caller E continues straight on as CURRENT without delay should the condition evaluate to TRUE AND E have priority over entities waiting in the condition queue. If the condition evaluates to FALSE, then E is removed from the event list and passivated (put to sleep) in the condition queue of Q (in priority order, of course). There it remains until it is awakened, tested and its condition is found to be TRUE. Arranging to reawaken such dormant entities at the appropriate moment can be implemented in several ways and is the subject of much debate in the

discrete event world. In DEMOS, the responsibility is put
squarely on the shoulders of the programmer himself (an
aproach which follows the philosophy of the host language
SIMULA. See Nygaard and Dahl [41, section 2.3.5]).

In this example, several boats may be blocked at a given
time due to insufficient tugs and/or the state of the tide.
The only possible times at which they can be unblocked are a)
when another boat releases some tugs, and b) when the tide
turns from being low. Thus the programmer has to ensure that
DOCKQ is signalled (by a call DOCKQ.SIGNAL) whenever tugs are
released or LOWTIDE is reset to FALSE. A call on SIGNAL, e.g.

        Q.SIGNAL;   [REF(CONDQ)Q;]

operates as follows. If the condition queue of Q is empty, it
has no effect. Otherwise its intention is to unblock those
entities waiting until at the front end of Q that can now go
(there may be several). Denote the entities waiting until in
the condition queue of Q by E1(== Q.FIRST), E2, ..., En. Then
Q.SIGNAL enters E1 into the event list at the current clock
time, but as last entity at that time. When E1 becomes
CURRENT, it tests its own condition. If this evaluates to
FALSE, E1 drops out of the event list and falls asleep again
at the head of the condition queue. If the condition of E1
evaluates to TRUE, then E1 leaves the condition queue AND
promotes E2 into the event list IMMEDIATELY behind itself. E1
now continues on as CURRENT, usually acquiring resources whose
availability was tested in the condition, and thus diminishing
the total pool of resources. E.g.

        DOCKQ.WAITUNTIL(TUGS.AVAIL >= 2 AND NOT LOWTIDE);
        TUGS.ACQUIRE(2);

When E1 steps down as CURRENT, the new first entity in the
event list is E2. If E2's condition evaluates to TRUE, then
E3 is promoted into the event list directly behind E2, and E2
acquires the resources it wants; otherwise E2 is dropped from
the event list back to the head of the condition queue and E3
is not tested at all. Thus SIGNAL activates entities at the
head of the condition queue in turn either until the queue is
exhausted or else an entity condition fails. See page 160 for
semi-formal algorithms for WAITUNTIL and SIGNAL.

The complete program is given below. For added textual
prominence, we have starred the lines containing calls on
SIGNAL.

```
DEMOS
  BEGIN REF(RES)TUGS, JETTIES;
    REF(CONDQ)DOCKQ;
    REF(RDIST)NEXT, DISCHARGE;
    BOOLEAN LOWTIDE;

    ENTITY CLASS BOAT;
    BEGIN NEW BOAT("BOAT").SCHEDULE(NEXT.SAMPLE);
    DOCK:
      JETTIES.ACQUIRE(1);
      DOCKQ.WAITUNTIL(TUGS.AVAIL >= 2 AND NOT LOWTIDE);
      TUGS.ACQUIRE(2);
      HOLD(2.0);
      TUGS.RELEASE(2);
      DOCKQ.SIGNAL;                                          *
    UNLOAD:
      HOLD(DISCHARGE.SAMPLE);
    LEAVE:
      TUGS.ACQUIRE(1);
      HOLD(2.0);
      TUGS.RELEASE(1);   JETTIES.RELEASE(1);
      DOCKQ.SIGNAL;                                          *
    END***BOAT***;

    ENTITY CLASS TIDE;
    BEGIN
    LOW_TIDE_ON:
      LOWTIDE := TRUE;
      HOLD(4.0);
      LOWTIDE := FALSE;
      DOCKQ.SIGNAL;                                          *
    LOW_TIDE_NOW_OFF:
      HOLD(9.0);
      REPEAT;
    END***TIDE***;

    TRACE;
    TUGS      :- NEW RES("TUGS", 3);
    JETTIES   :- NEW RES("JETTIES", 2);
    DOCKQ     :- NEW CONDQ("DOCKQ");
    NEXT      :- NEW NEGEXP("NEXT BOAT", 0.1);
    DISCHARGE :- NEW NORMAL("DISCHARGE",14.0,3.0);
    NEW TIDE("TIDE").SCHEDULE(1.0);
    NEW BOAT("BOAT").SCHEDULE(0.0);
    HOLD(28.0*24.0);
  END;
```

***Output: (Partial Trace and Partial Report.)
==========

```
  TIME/  CURRENT     AND ITS ACTION(S)
         .....................
 53.000  TIDE 1      HOLDS FOR 4.000, UNTIL 57.000
 53.403  BOAT 3      RELEASES 1 TO TUGS
                     RELEASES 1 TO JETTIES
                     SIGNALS DOCKQ
                     ***TERMINATES
 56.849  BOAT 5      SCHEDULES BOAT 6 AT 61.864
                     SEIZES 1 OF JETTIES
                     W'UNTIL IN DOCKQ
 57.000  TIDE 1      SIGNALS DOCKQ
                     HOLDS FOR 9.000, UNTIL 66.000
         BOAT 5      LEAVES DOCKQ
                     SEIZES 2 OF TUGS
                     HOLDS FOR 2.000, UNTIL 59.000
         .....................
```

Partial report.

R E S O U R C E S
****

TITLE /	(RE)SET/	OBS/	LIM/	MIN/	NOW/	% USAGE/	AV.WAIT/	QMAX
TUGS	0.000	114	3	0	3	17.063	0.000	1
JETTIES	0.000	56	2	0	0	81.396	6.343	7

C O N D I T I O N   Q U E U E S
****

TITLE /	(RE)SET/	OBS/	QMAX/	QNOW/	Q AVERAGE/	ZEROS/	AV. WAIT
DOCKQ	0.000	58	2	0	7.683E-02	36	0.890

REMARKS ON EXAMPLE 8

We pick up the trace at time 53.0, when the fifth low tide period is setting in. The trace shows LOWTIDE being set at time 53.0 and reset at time 57.0. At time 56.849, BOAT 5 seizes 1 jetty and then enters DOCKQ to await its condition being set. At time 57.0, the tide is reset and a signal is sent to DOCKQ. This awakens BOAT 5 which continues on its way seizing two tugs.

The partial report shows that the extra constraint has caused a little more congestion (the average wait for a jetty is up to 6.343 from 5.498, and for a tug is 1.006 instead of 0.0285; compare with the results on page 43). The column headings in the condition queue reports have been explained in connection with WAITQs (see page 88) but this time we require only one line per queue as the master/slave situation does not obtain.

In this example, boats leaving and boats arriving compete for tugs. Boats arriving never actually queue for tugs on the resource TUGS itself: when they escape from DOCKQ two tugs are available. But boats leaving do queue on the resource TUGS and it is important to realise that the calls which release tugs and signal DOCKQ, e.g.

    TUGS.RELEASE(2);   DOCKQ.SIGNAL;

in effect give boats leaving priority because boats queueing on the resource TUGS (all of which are waiting to leave) are tested before SIGNAL has a chance to test any wait until conditions. Perhaps this is as it should be, but if not the priority can be changed simply by reversing the order of the calls

    DOCKQ.SIGNAL;   TUGS.RELEASE(2);

Make sure you understand why (follow through the examples using the semi-formal algorithms on page 160).

Another way of doing the same sort of thing is to introduce a second CONDQ (here OUTQ) for boats leaving. We create it by

    OUTQ :- NEW CONDQ("LEAVING");   [REF(CONDQ)OUTQ;]

The condition for boats leaving could be quite simple as

    OUTQ.WAITUNTIL(TUGS.AVAIL > 0);

We also need to signal OUTQ at appropriate times: times at which tugs are released. Thus the lines DOCKQ.SIGNAL; inside CLASS BOAT are to be replaced by

    DOCKQ.SIGNAL; OUTQ.SIGNAL;

(reverse the order of the calls if you wish boats leaving to have priority). Note that there is no point at all in signalling OUTQ when the tide turns - it is of no concern to entities waiting in that CONDQ. In general, when resources are released, some, but not all, CONDQs need to be be signalled. It is enough to signal only those CONDQs containing entities waiting on the freshly released resources.

EXAMPLE 9: TANKER SIMULATION AGAIN

As an extension to the basic model (example 7, page 95), we assume that tankers carry one of five types of oil. The grade of oil is indicated by INTEGER TYPE which takes values in the range 1 through 5, a higher value indicating a better grade of oil. In order to unload when docked, they need a shore tank which (in order of preference):

a) has the same type of fuel and sufficient capacity to take all that the tanker is carrying

b) has the same type of oil but not enough capacity to accept the full load

c) is empty and previously held either the same or a better type of fuel

d) is empty and previously held an inferior type of oil. In this case, the shore tank must first be cleaned. This takes a long time and is the last resort.

In this new situation it is much harder to express the search by using FIND, although it could perhaps be done by devious use of PRIORITY within shore tank. Even so it would lead to a non-transparent program text and in cases like this we really need another mechanism so that we can express the program logic clearly. It is best to have all the decisions at one point in the program instead of scattered over several entities. This is where the hitherto unexplained BOOLEAN PROCEDURE AVAIL local to WAITQ (see figure 5.2, page 78) comes into its own. A call

        Q.AVAIL(E, condition);   [REF(WAITQ)Q;]

tries to locate an entity E satisfying the condition (just like FIND), but does NOT coopt the entity E if found nor block the caller if an entity E satisfying the condition cannot be found. It returns TRUE and sets E to refer to the found

entity if one can be located; if not, it returns FALSE and
sets E to NONE.

In this variation of example 7, it is convenient to use
two WAITQs to hold available shore tanks. We place completely
empty shore tanks in EMPTYQ and partly full shore tanks in
TANKQ. Note that in this description, a shore tank will
discharge its contents into the refinery when less than 5
units of volume are available.

```
[REF(WAITQ)EMPTYQ, TANKQ;]

ENTITY CLASS SHORETANK(FREE); INTEGER FREE;
BEGIN INTEGER TYPE, MAX;
  TYPE := an appropriate type;
  MAX  := 70;
  IF FREE = MAX THEN GOTO EMPTY;
LOOP:  PART_FULL:
  WHILE FREE >= 5 DO
  BEGIN Q.SIGNAL;
    TANKQ.WAIT;
  END;
  HOLD(time to empty);
EMPTY:
  PRIORITY := -TYPE;
  Q.SIGNAL;
  EMPTYQ.WAIT;
  PRIORITY := O;
  REPEAT;
END***SHORETANK***;
```

The body of CLASS SHORETANK consists of an initialisation
(setting TYPE and MAX: FREE, as a parameter, is already set)
and then the main loop is entered at EMPTY if the initial
value of FREE = 70; otherwise at PART_FULL. We use PRIORITY
only in EMPTYQ where shore tanks are ranked with those
containing the least quality oil at the front. A shore tank
is coopted by several tankers in turn who part fill it (then
it returns to TANKQ). When the shore tank is full, or very
nearly so (less than 5 free units of capacity remain), then it
does not return to TANKQ, but discharges its contents into the
refinery and joins EMPTYQ. A shore tank coopted from EMPTYQ
under conditions c) or d) may have its TYPE reset; under
condition d), it will also have to be cleaned.

A tanker looks first for a shore tank in TANKQ of the
same type and with sufficient capacity

a)   TANKQ.AVAIL(ST, ST.TYPE = TYPE AND ST.FREE >= LOAD)

If this search fails, it then tries to locate a shore tank which is available for loading and contains the same type of oil

b)   TANKQ.AVAIL(ST, ST.TYPE = TYPE)

Notice that testing first on condition a) and then on condition b) implies two sweeps through TANKQ unless the shore tanks have been ideally sorted first (and they haven't - try to do so as an extra exercise). Further if a) fails then we need not express condition b) as

     ST.TYPE = TYPE AND ST.FREE < LOAD

If this second search fails, then the tanker turns its attention to EMPTYQ. It now tries to locate a shore tank in EMPTYQ which contained oil of the same or of a better quality.

c)   EMPTYQ.AVAIL(ST, ST.TYPE >= TYPE)

Since we have queued shore tanks in EMPTYQ ranked according to -TYPE, we automatically return the shore tank of least quality passing the test. Finally if all else fails, then any shore tank in EMPTYQ will do.

d)   EMPTYQ.AVAIL(ST, TRUE)

If all of these tests fail, then a tanker must wait until a suitable shore tank does appear in either TANKQ or EMPTYQ. We thus require a CONDQ (here Q) and make the request via a wait until statement of the form

          Q.WAITUNTIL(OR4(a, b, c, d));

where we have used our own BOOLEAN PROCEDURE OR4 (defined below; see also exercise 6.1).
ASIDE: the reader should be able to convince himself that the formulation

          Q.WAITUNTIL(a OR b OR c OR d);

does not work because each of the part conditions a, b, c, and d is called in turn before any OR operation is carried out. Each one not only returns TRUE or FALSE but also sets ST. Thus the test on b overwrites the assignment to ST in a, the test on c that in b, and the test on d that in c.

CLASS TANKER now has the form:

```
BOOLEAN PROCEDURE OR4(A,B,C,D);NAME A,B,C,D;BOOLEAN A,B,C,D;
  OR4 := IF A THEN TRUE ELSE IF B THEN TRUE ELSE
         IF C THEN TRUE ELSE D;

ENTITY CLASS TANKER;
BEGIN INTEGER TYPE, LOAD, L; REF(SHORETANK)ST;
  NEW TANKER("T").SCHEDULE(ARR.SAMPLE);
  TYPE := an appropriate type;
  LOAD := an appropriate load;
  WHILE LOAD > 0 DO
  BEGIN
GET_SHORE_TANK:
  Q.WAITUNTIL(OR4(TANK Q.AVAIL(ST, ST.TYPE = TYPE
                              AND ST.FREE >= LOAD),
                  TANKQ.AVAIL(ST, ST.TYPE = TYPE),
                  EMPTYQ.AVAIL(ST,ST.TYPE >=TYPE),
                  EMPTYQ.AVAIL(ST, TRUE)));
  ST.COOPT;
  IF ST.TYPE < TYPE THEN HOLD(CLEAN.SAMPLE);
  ST.TYPE := TYPE;
PUMP:
  L := IF ST.FREE >= LOAD THEN LOAD ELSE ST.FREE;
  HOLD(SETUPTIME + L*PUMPRATE);
RELEASE_SHORE_TANK:
  ST.FREE := ST.FREE - L;
  ST.SCHEDULE(0.0);
  LOAD := LOAD - L;
  PRIORITY := PRIORITY + 1;
  END;
END***TANKER***;
```

The main body of CLASS TANKER consists of a loop in which it remains until it has discharged all of its cargo (until LOAD = 0). While a tanker does try to discharge all of its cargo in one go (conditions a), c) and d)), a shore tank seized under condition b) has not enough capacity left and in this case the tanker will have to queue again in Q (it is given increased priority each time). When its wait until condition is TRUE, a tanker leaves Q with its local variable ST referencing the most suitable storage tank thanks to the call on AVAIL. But ST is still in its WAITQ and hasn't yet been coopted. To cater for this case (coopting an explicitly named entity) there is a PROCEDURE COOPT local to CLASS ENTITY. A call

ST.COOPT removes ST from its current queue (if any) and places
it under the bondage of CURRENT (in this case, a tanker). The
tanker then causes it to be cleaned if it was empty and
contained inferior quality oil is transferred. Then the type
of ST is reset, a quantity L of oil is transferred from the
tanker to the shore tank and ST is rescheduled. ST decides
for itself what to do next (join TANKQ or discharge). Finally
the tanker's own priority is incremented (it may loop again).

EXERCISES 6

1. In SIMULA and ALGOL 60, compound conditions, such as
A AND B and A OR B, are evaluated by first finding the value
of A, then the value of B, and then performing the AND or the
OR operation. If we wish to drop out of a compound evaluation
with a minimum of testing, we can CODE

```
        IF A THEN B ELSE FALSE     instead of    A AND B
        IF A THEN TRUE ELSE B      instead of    A OR  B
```

Write BOOLEAN PROCEDUREs AND2 and OR2 to perform these
optimisations.

2. Customers with a predetermined thirst - taken as 1 to
6 pints - arrive at a pub, queue for a beer, drink it, and
then either rejoin the beer queue or else (if their thirst has
been assuaged) leave the pub. A barmaid serves the customers
giving each a clean glass for his beer every time. Her other
task is to wash empty glasses (these are collected from the
customer and placed within her orbit by a waiter). While
neither of these tasks is interruptible once started, the task
of serving a customer naturally takes precedence. The waiter
enters the bar every 30 minutes, collects all the empties, and
places them on the bar top for the barmaid. He then retires
to perform his other duties. Run your model for 4 hours with
15 glasses, all initially clean.

3. Repeat the Port System of example 8, page 100, with
the following different tidal constraints: boats can dock
only at high tide and may leave only if it is not low tide.

Model data
==========

Timings in minutes:
    Customer arrival   NEGEXP:mean=0.2/min
    Waiter (re)entry   CONSTANT:30
    Pouring   CONSTANT:1
    Drinking   UNIFORM:15.0->25.0
    Washing   CONSTANT:0.5

4.   Consider the following (very simplified) model of a
single lane of cars at a four way traffic intersection in
which we ignore possible interference from other lanes.   Cars
arriving at the junction can turn left, continue straight on
or turn right when the lights ahead are green and the car
ahead is sufficiently clear.

Model data
==========

Timings in seconds:
    Car inter-arrival   NEGEXP:0.15/second
    Lights green   CONSTANT:20
    Lights red   CONSTANT:24
    Time to clear   NORMAL:mean=2.0,st.dev.=0.5

Simulate for two hours under the initial conditions that at
time 0.0 the lights are just turning green and the first car
arrives.

5.   Sketch a solution to the following problem. Consider
a junction consisting of a single lane side road joining a
main road. The main road has one lane in each direction.
Traffic is not allowed entry from the main road into the side
road. Traffic moving from the side road on to the main road
may filter right when the near lane is clear; or may turn left
on to the main road only when both the near lane and the far
lane of the main road are free.

6.   Boats arrive periodically at both ends of a long,
narrow canal. For this exercise, we ignore such complications
as tugs, storms, etc. (which can easily be added) and
concentrate on deciding which direction should have control of
the canal. The canal is narrow (so boats may not pass each
other in either direction), and long (so that several boats
are allowed to travel along it in the same direction).   Let
the time taken to pass through the canal be CTIME. To reduce

the risk of collision, boats travelling in the same direction
must be well separated. Once a boat has entered the canal, no
other boat may follow it until at least CTIME/3 has elapsed.
Model the system when the canal direction is switched
according to the fixed time slot rule. Here each direction
has a time slot of fixed length in rotation. When the time
slot is up, any boats currently in the canal are cleared, but
boats not actually in the canal are blocked. When all the
boats are clear, the direction of allowed travel is switched.

7. Repeat exercise 6.6 switching canal direction when
the length of the blocked queue has reached a certain limit,
say L. N.B. in conditions of overload, it is possible to get
at least L boats in queueing for each direction. To prevent
the switching mechanism from looping, give each direction a
certain minimum burst, say L*CTIME/3.

8. Repeat exercise 6.6 switching control of the canal
only when the queue for the direction in control is empty.
N.B. the switching mechanism may have to go into 'neutral' if
both queues are empty.

9. Repeat exercise 6.6 switching when the blocked queue
is longer than the queue in control.

10. Remind yourself of exercise 4.8, page 72. As
billets queue for a soaking pit they lose heat. Newcomers are
clearly warmer than those blocked earlier. Modify exercise
4.8 so that when a fourth billet joins the queue for the pits,
the FIRST billet in the queue is removed and deposited
outside. It will only be brought back when there are no
billets waiting for a pit and 5 pits are empty. Assume that
such billet movements also require the use of a soaking pit
crane.

6.2 CONDITION QUEUES WITH ALL SET

This section deals with the case when the entities in a
condition queue are waiting on different conditions. In this
case we want a call on SIGNAL to test each and every member of
the queue and not to drop out if one entity condition fails.

EXAMPLE 10: DINING PHILOSOPHERS

Five philosophers are seated round a circular table which

contains an inexhaustible supply of spaghetti within easy reach of all at its centre. Between each pair of adjacent philosophers is a fork. The philosophers have a simple life style

```
LOOP: think;
      eat;
      REPEAT;
```

In order to eat, a philosopher requires both the fork on his left and the fork on his right. Each thus competes for resources with his immediate neighbours. The orgy is to last for 3 hours.

Model data
==========

```
Timings in minutes:
 Think                 RANDINT:20->30
 Eat                   RANDINT:10->20
Resources:
 FORK         REF(RES)ARRAY FORK(1:5):limit=1 each
```

In this model we represent the forks by REF(RES)ARRAY FORK(1:5) and initialise by

```
FOR K := 1 STEP 1 UNTIL 5 DO            [INTEGER K;]
   FORK(K) :- NEW RES(EDIT("FORK", K), 1);
```

We number the forks so that philosopher n finds FORK(n) on his left and FORK(n+1) on his right (FORK(1) in the case of philosopher 5). Then CLASS PHILOSOPHER can be written

```
ENTITY CLASS PHILOSOPHER(N); INTEGER N;
BEGIN REF(RES)L, R;
  L :- FORK(N);
  R :- FORK(IF N=5 THEN 1 ELSE N+1);
LOOP:
  HOLD(THINK.SAMPLE);
  Q.WAITUNTIL(L.AVAIL > 0 AND R.AVAIL > 0);
  L.ACQUIRE(1);  R.ACQUIRE(1);
  HOLD(EAT.SAMPLE);
  L.RELEASE(1);  R.RELEASE(1);
  Q.SIGNAL;
  REPEAT;
END***PHILOSOPHER***;
```

The new facet of this example lies in the fact that each
philosopher has a different wait until condition (no two
philosophers await the availability of the same pair of forks)
and this causes some problems. If we let them all wait in the
same queue, then we must remember that SIGNAL is coded (as so
far revealed) to stop testing queue members when the condition
of one member (the current FIRST) fails. Thus if the
condition of an earlier queue member is FALSE, the remainder
will not be tested even though their conditions, being
different, may yield TRUE! Giving each philosopher his own
queue doesn't really help in this case either (although in
general it may be a useful idea) as we then have to decide
which queue gets priority.

To solve this and similar problems, we have given CONDQ
another attribute - BOOLEAN ALL - which is initially FALSE.
When ALL is FALSE, SIGNAL operates as previously explained.
When ALL is set to TRUE by such an assignment as

                C.ALL := TRUE;   [REF(CONDQ)C;]

a call on SIGNAL will test the condition of each and every
entity waiting until in the CONDQ. This gives us what we
want: by using a single CONDQ with ALL set, philosophers are
queued ranked according to their time of entry (their
priorities are all zero) and every member of the condition
queue will be tested. The complete program reads

```
DEMOS
  BEGIN INTEGER K;
    REF(RES)ARRAY FORK(1:5);
    REF(IDIST)THINK, EAT;
    REF(CONDQ)Q;

    ENTITY CLASS PHILOSOPHER(N);............;

    Q     :- NEW CONDQ("AWAIT EAT");
    Q.ALL := TRUE;
    THINK :- NEW RANDINT("THINK", 20, 30);
    EAT   :- NEW RANDINT("EAT"  , 10, 20);
    FOR K := 1 STEP 1 UNTIL 5 DO
      FORK(K) :- NEW RES(EDIT("FORK", K), 1);
    TRACE;
    FOR K := 1 STEP 1 UNTIL 5 DO
      NEW PHILOSOPHER("P", K).SCHEDULE(0.0);
    HOLD(180.0);
  END;
```

***Output:
==========

(At time 24.0 when we pick up the trace, P1 and P4 are eating,
P2, P3, and P5 are thinking.)

   TIME/ CURRENT   AND ITS ACTION(S)

   ....

24.000   P 3   W'UNTIL IN AWAIT EAT
25.000   P 2   W'UNTIL IN AWAIT EAT
26.000   P 5   W'UNTIL IN AWAIT EAT
34.000   P 4   RELEASES 1 TO FORK 4
                    RELEASES 1 TO FORK 5
                    SIGNALS AWAIT EAT
                    HOLDS FOR 23.000, UNTIL 57.000
         P 3   LEAVES AWAIT EAT
                    SEIZES 1 OF FORK 3
                    SEIZES 1 OF FORK 4
                    HOLDS FOR 18.000, UNTIL 52.000
37.000   P 1   RELEASES 1 OF FORK 1
                    RELEASES 1 OF FORK 2
                    SIGNALS AWAIT EAT
                    HOLDS FOR 27.000, UNTIL 64.000
         P 5   LEAVES AWAIT EAT
                    SEIZES 1 OF FORK 5
                    SEIZES 1 OF FORK 1
                    HOLDS FOR 12.000, UNTIL 49.000

   ....

                    CLOCK TIME = 180.000
****
*   *
*   R E P O R T   *
*   *
****

                    D I S T R I B U T I O N S
                    ****

TITLE /	(RE)SET/	OBS/	TYPE /	A/	B/	SEED
THINK	0.000	23	RANDINT	20	30	33427485
EAT	0.000	20	RANDINT	10	20	22276755

R E S O U R C E S
****

TITLE /	(RE)SET/	OBS/	LIM/	MIN/	NOW/	% USAGE/	AV.WAIT/	QMAX
FORK 1	0.000	7	1	0	0	62.778	0.000	1
FORK 2	0.000	7	1	0	0	60.556	0.000	1
FORK 3	0.000	7	1	0	0	67.222	0.000	1
FORK 4	0.000	8	1	0	1	68.333	0.000	1
FORK 5	0.000	7	1	0	0	62.222	0.000	1

C O N D I T I O N   Q U E U E S
****

TITLE /	(RE)SET/	OBS/	QMAX/	QNOW/	Q AVERAGE/	ZEROS/	AV.WAIT
AWAIT EAT *	0.000	20	3	1	0.489	8	4.400

REMARKS ON EXAMPLE 11

At time 26.0, P3, P2, and P5 (in that order) are waiting until
in Q. When P4 releases his forks at time 34.0, P3 can
proceed. When P1 releases his forks at time 37.000, P2 is
tested first but is still blocked. P5 is allowed to proceed.

The only other thing worth remarking on is that the
condition queues with ALL set are specially marked in reports
with an asterisk following their TITLE (see AWAIT EAT above).

EXERCISES 6 (continued)

11. Unsealed containers are placed on a conveyor belt
every CYCLE seconds. The belt moves with a regular but jerky
action past a row of N sealing machines. The movement of the
belt is such that the containers are stationary for PAUSE
seconds in front of each machine. The movement into the next
position takes MOVE seconds (CYCLE = MOVE+PAUSE). During each
pause, a fresh container is added at one end of the belt, and
the 'oldest' container is removed from the other. It is also
during part of this time interval that an unsealed container
may be sealed. Sealing takes SEAL seconds and a sealing is
not allowed to be started if the belt is moving or if less
than SEAL seconds remain of the current pause period.

The sealing is done by a complicated machine which has
two parts: a picker which dips into an inexhaustible supply
of seals and returns with one, and a capper which accepts a

seal from its picker partner (thus sending it off for another seal) and then waits its chance to seal. It will seal the next unsealed container that pauses in front given enough time to perform the operation. Then it collects a new seal from its picker.

Assume that each picker starts primed with a seal and at time 0.0 the first unsealed container is placed on the belt (it will be in position in front of the first sealing machine at TIME = CYCLE). Run your model for 8 simulated hours with N = 6 sealing machines, PAUSE = 5 seconds, MOVE = 3 seconds, SEAL = 2 seconds,and the time for a picker to fetch a seal at 7.0->11.0 seconds, UNIFORMly distributed. Report on the number of unsealed containers that get through. Experiment further with N.

12. Metal plates arrive periodically at a plate cutting yard to be cut into shape. The yard's cutting shop contains two cutters C1 and C2, each of which has its own buffer area for up to three uncut plates. Plates are typed on arrival into those requiring cutting by C1 and those by C2 (equally likely). If the appropriate buffer is full, freshly arriving plates are dumped on one side in the yard. They are brought in from the cold only when there is buffer space and the arrival area is empty. Plate movements are carried out by a crane which can handle one at a time.

Model data
==========

Timings in minutes:
Plate inter-arrival   NEGEXP:0.1 per minute
Cutting time   NORMAL:mean=8.0,st.dev.=2.0
Crane movement times
  arrival-buffer   CONSTANT:1
  arrival-dump   CONSTANT:0.5
  dump-buffer   CONSTANT:1

N.B. wherever plates are stacked they are picked up in last-come, first-served order since they are piled one on top of the other. Assume that when dumped outside the plates are sorted into 2 piles - one awaiting C1, the other C2.

6.3 WAITS UNTIL: SIGNAL VERSUS SNOOPY

There are two main approaches for dealing with entities which

are waiting until. One places the responsibility on the
programmer; the other leaves it to the system itself to do the
reawakenings. The second method was used in SIMON 75 (Hills
and Birtwistle [16]) and used a special entity object named
SNOOPY. Transferred to the context of DEMOS, a rough outline
of the SIMON 75 SNOOPY is

```
[REF(WATCHDOG)SNOOPY;]

ENTITY CLASS WATCHDOG;
BEGIN REF(CONDQ)Q;
  FOR each CONDQ Q DO
    Q.SIGNAL;
    HOLD until next event time;
  REPEAT;
END***WATCHDOG***;
```

SNOOPY is meant to operate as follows. When it becomes
CURRENT, it signals the user-created CONDQs in some
predetermined order (say, the order in which they were created
by NEW CONDQ ...). When all the CONDQs have been tested in
this manner, SNOOPY holds until the next event time,
reappearing as the last entry scheduled for that time. SNOOPY
thus becomes CURRENT again when all the resources to be freed
at that clock time have been released and can now set about
testing the conditions of any blocked entities.

Notice that the wait until routine associated with SNOOPY
differs from the one used in DEMOS in some details. An entity
E executing a wait until should now always be put to sleep in
the appropriate CONDQ and left to be awakened by SNOOPY.
Otherwise, some waiting entities may be by passed; for
example, those already waiting on the same condition as E.
Notice also that SNOOPY need only be active when it has work
to do (not all the CONDQs are empty). If SNOOPY is passive
when a wait until call is made, then that call is responsible
for activating it (a technique similar to that used in
awakening the scanner in exercise 5.6, page 93).

However this rough outline for SNOOPY is certainly not
fool proof. For an entity unblocked from a later CONDQ, Qm
say, may alter conditions which enable entities blocked in one
or more earlier CONDQs to go; indeed, these entities may even
test the value of Qm.LENGTH as a part of their condition. A
way round this is to force SNOOPY out of its depicted FOR-loop
and make it repeat again from the beginning whenever it
unblocks one entity from the current CONDQ that it is testing

(there are many simple variations on this theme).   This is
clearly a slower algorithm than the original one, and it is
less transparent.

Vaucher [39] also discusses a 'generalised wait until
statement' (read Franta [33, pages 188-194] for a more
accessible account).   Instead of having user-defined CONDQs,
Vaucher's algorithm makes use of a single system defined queue
in which all entities waiting until are queued.   Vaucher's
SNOOPY also reappears alternately in the event list which can
give rise to certain subtle differences in performance. It is
instructive   to   compare   Vaucher's   algorithm   and   its
corresponding wait until routine with the ones sketched in
this chapter and find ways in which they can be busted.

The decision to implement wait until with SIGNAL rather
than SNOOPY was based on the following points:

a) waits until usually cover complicated situations.   In
order to show that a program is correct, it is desirable to be
able to argue from the program text exactly what should happen
next.   The algorithm for SIGNAL is very simple and is under
direct user control; SNOOPY has a rather more complicated
algorithm and operates more remotely behind the scenes. It is
correspondingly more difficult to ensure that the correct
synchronisations   take   place.   See   Palme   [42]   for an
interesting paper on a similar theme.

b) because DEMOS contains RES, BIN, and WAITQ facilities
which automatically test and promote any waiting entities when
incremented, the number of CONDQs in DEMOS programs is quite
small.   (In SIMON 75 and ECSL programs, every non-bound
activity has an associated CONDQ.) Further the CONDQs to test
when resources are released, etc., are directly available from
the activity diagrams and so the calls on SIGNAL are not all
that difficult to get right. Remember that when a condition
is reset, only those CONDQs containing entities waiting on
that condition need be tested, and not all of them. It is
surprising that most compilers for activity based languages
simply throw away this information; otherwise they could be
quite competitive with event or process based discrete event
simulation languages.

c) SIGNAL is more efficient than SNOOPY; usually of the
order of 2 or 3 times, but in pathological cases this factor
can increase unboundedly.

   d) and last, but not least, it follows the approach of
the host language SIMULA (see Nygaard and Dahl [41]).

   So it is not just an argument about ease of use (SNOOPY)
against efficiency (SIGNAL). It should also be borne in mind
that waits until are often quite complicated and in these
situations there is no substitute for clear thought and
well-defined tools. One of the dangers of SNOOPY is that it
is all too easy to write down something that 'works' (in the
sense that it is not obviously wrong), and accept it without
proper checking.

EXERCISES 6 (continued)

13. Why is it usually preferable to code

a)   HOLD(T-TIME);
     Q.WAITUNTIL(condition);

instead of

b) Q.WAITUNTIL(TIME >= T AND condition); ?

7 INTERRUPTS

In this chapter, we investigate a few models in which the expected action history of an entity is not followed due, perhaps, to equipment failure or to interruptions by another entity.

In the very simplest cases, the disturbance merely imposes an unexpected delay on the victim. For example, should a machine part fail, then the machine operator may well be able to continue on with his current task as soon as a repair has been carried out. But all too often interrupts cannot be cast into such a simple mould. For an interrupt usually means: "Stop what you are doing now and get on with something else". For example, a hospital doctor doing his morning rounds may be interrupted to deal with an emergency case. While he is away, the rounds must go on under some one else's supervision, and will probably have been completed before he has finished dealing with the emergency. So there is no compunction for the specialist to return to his previous task.

The possibilities are many and various and instead of trying to be all things to all men, DEMOS provides a few simple tools which can be applied to cover a wide range of problems. As usual, these DEMOS tools are motivated by particular examples.

7.1 SIMPLE BREAKDOWNS

A stream of orders is processed on a lathe L. If we assume that there are always orders waiting, then we can describe the actions of the lathe by

```
[REF(COUNT)DONE;  REF(LATHE)L;]

ENTITY CLASS LATHE;
BEGIN
  HOLD(process time);
  DONE.UPDATE(1);
  REPEAT;
END***LATHE***;
```

We now throw in the complication that the lathe is subject to periodic breakdowns. Each breakdown requires a halt in the current job for a spare part to be fitted (by the lathe operator himself). Then the lathe continues on with the same order and from where it left off.

The most appealing way of accounting for breakdowns in the model is to mirror them the way they really are. As seen by the lathe, they are unpredictable, external events and accordingly we prepare a separate entity description

```
ENTITY CLASS BREAKDOWN;
BEGIN
LATHE_RUNNING:
  HOLD(time to next breakdown);
LATHE_DOWN:
  cause L to break down;
  HOLD(repair time for L);
  restart L;
  REPEAT;
END***BREAKDOWN***;
```

Let a breakdown occur at time t and the lathe's current job be timed to finish at time T (T >= t). At time t, L will be scheduled in the event list with an associated event time of T. (The event time of a scheduled entity E is accessible via a call E.EVTIME. REAL PROCEDURE EVTIME is an attribute of all entity objects.) The LSC of L will be pointing to the statement HOLD(process time). We have to ensure that this statement is not completed at time T, but at time 'T + repair time for L'. When a breakdown occurs, we will usually not be able to predict how long the repair will take as the resources required to effect the repair may not be available (although that is not the case here). Even worse, perhaps the repairman's gear may need a sudden repair!

The safest and most general way of handling the problem is to remove the victim from the event list when the breakdown occurs, and reschedule it after the repair has been carried out. Following this plan in CLASS BREAKDOWN below, we note how much of the lathe's current job remains to be done (TLEFT = T-t), remove L from the event list (L.CANCEL), carry out the repair, and then reschedule the lathe with a delay of TLEFT (L.SCHEDULE(TLEFT)). A semi-formal outline of CLASS BREAKDOWN is

```
ENTITY CLASS BREAKDOWN;
BEGIN REAL TLEFT;
LATHE_RUNNING:
  HOLD(time to next breakdown);
LATHE_DOWN:
  TLEFT := L.EVTIME-TIME;
  L.CANCEL;
  HOLD(repair time for L);
  L.SCHEDULE(TLEFT);
  REPEAT;
END***BREAKDOWN***;
```

EXERCISES 7

   1. Write a complete DEMOS program for the model described
in this section.

Model data
==========

Timings in minutes:
  lathe processing time   NORMAL:mean=15.0,st.dev.=3.0
  between breakdowns   NEGEXP:mean=1/300 mins
  repair time   NORMAL:mean=30.0,st.dev.=5.0

This time, after the lathe has been repaired it must be reset
before it can continue. Let the reset time be a constant 5
minutes. Run your model for four weeks of simulated time
assuming no discontinuities.

   2. Repeat exercise 7.1 above with the following twist:
when a breakdown occurs, the current order is spoiled. Keep
track in another COUNT 'SPOILED'.   Assume that it takes 6
minutes to reset the lathe and discard a spoiled order.

HINT: You may care to send a signal to the lathe and schedule
it immediately the repair has been carried out. The signal is
to indicate which alternative has cropped up and we then let
the lathe itself sort out which COUNT to update and which
extra delay is needed over and above TLEFT.

   3. A machine shop contains six identical lathes.   A
continous stream of orders arrives at the machine shop
carefully timed to ensure that there are always orders
waiting.   Each lathe is subject to periodic breakdown, but
this time the repairs are to be carried out by a specialist

repairman. The solitary repairman has other duties to perform when not repairing a lathe. Although these other duties are of a lower priority, they cannot be interrupted once started.

Model data
==========

     Timings in minutes:
       lathe processing time   NORMAL:mean=10.0,st.dev.=2.0
       between breakdowns   NEGEXP:mean=1/300 mins
       lathe reset time   CONSTANT:5
       repair time   CONSTANT:30
       other duty   CONSTANT:15

Run your model for 4 weeks assuming no discontinuities between shifts.

7.2 INTERRUPTS

It doesn't require many extra complications before the CANCEL/SCHEDULE mechanism of chapter 7.1 proves to be inadequate. But we have learned one important lesson - that of writing the interrupting agent as a separate entity.

    In the next example, the victim has to drop its resources when interrupted and try to regain control of them in competition with other entities. For security reasons, a share in a resource can only be released by the entity holding it, i.e. an interrupted victim has to be activated in order to relinquish its own resources. Thus we require quite a different technique from the CANCEL/SCHEDULE of chapter 7.1 where the victim lay passively out of the event list throughout the breakdown. In fact it turns out to be easiest to let the interrupt be sent across just as a signal and to let the victim sort out his own reaction to it (as in exercise 7.2) instead of being imposed upon from without.

EXAMPLE 11: COAL HOPPER

Consider a coal depot where coal is loaded by gravity from a hopper into one lorry at a time. If the lorries are served FCFS, then we can model CLASS LORRY by

       [REF(RES)HOPPER;]

```
ENTITY CLASS LORRY;
BEGIN
  HOPPER.ACQUIRE(1);
  HOLD(load time);
  HOPPER.RELEASE(1);
END***LORRY***;
```

We now alter the rule for who is to be loaded. Lorries are now allocated a priority in the range 1 through 4. A freshly arriving a lorry can interrupt the lorry currently being loaded if it has a greater priority than the latter. The interrupted entity has its priority increased by one each time it is interrupted - an attempt to see that a lorry with a low initial priority cannot be delayed too long. Then it rejoins the queue for the hopper and tries again.

Notice that this is not just a simple pushdown effect. For if Lp dispaces Lr, Lr does not necessarily acquire the hopper again when Lp quits. For in the mean time, a third lorry Lq may arrive with priority in between those of the other two (PRIORITYp >= PRIORITYq > PRIORITYr). When Lp quits, Lq seizes the hopper. When Lr is displaced, its incremented priority ensures that it becomes the first entity queueing for the hopper. But it will be pushed back down the queue by a later arrival with higher priority or should its own interrupter be interrupted. Notice that a lorry may be interrupted several times before being fully loaded.

The synchronisation is achieved in DEMOS as follows: at time t, let Lr be loading and Lp deliver an an interrupt. The key statements executed by Lp and Lr at time t are

```
        Lp                        Lr

1)   Lr.INTERRUPT(1);
2)   HOPPER.ACQUIRE(1);
3)                            HOPPER.RELEASE(1);
4)                            PRIORITY:=PRIORITY+1;
5)                            INTERRUPTED := 0;
6)                            HOPPER.ACQUIRE(1);
7)   HOLD(load time);
```

1) PROCEDURE INTERRUPT is local to CLASS ENTITY and takes an INTEGER parameter n (should there be several interrupts, each can be given a distinguishing number). A call E.INTERRUPT(n) operates as follows: first the routine saves the value of n in an INTEGER variable INTERRUPTED local to E

(INTEGER INTERRUPTED is another ENTITY attribute) and then E is placed in the event list, at the current clock time but as last entity scheduled for this time. When the ongoing active phase of CURRENT finishes (here with a HOPPER.ACQUIRE(1)), E is promoted to be the new CURRENT.

2) Lp attempts to gain control of the hopper, but must wait; by the nature of the problem, it will be inserted at the head of the queue for the hopper.

3) Lr is now CURRENT and finds its own local INTEGER variable INTERRUPTED set to n. It releases the hopper (which will be seized by Lp), and then

4, 5, 6) Lr increases its own priority, sets its own INTERRUPTED to zero, and then attempts to regain control of the hopper. It joins the hopper queue behind Lp.

7) Lp now gains control of the hopper and a fresh loading starts.

Model data
==========

```
Timings in minutes:
  lorry arrival rate     NEGEXP:mean=1/12 per minute
  loading rate           0.1 tons/min
Capacities:
  lorry load             5,10,15 tons,equally likely
Priority:                RANDINT:1->4
```

The complete program for an 2 hour run reads:

```
DEMOS
  BEGIN REAL RATE;
    REF(ENTITY)USER;   REF(RES)HOPPER;
    REF(IDIST)P, VOL;  REF(RDIST)NEXT;

    BOOLEAN PROCEDURE AND2(A, B); NAME A, B; BOOLEAN A, B;
      AND2 := IF A THEN B ELSE FALSE;

    ENTITY CLASS LORRY;
    BEGIN REAL TLEFT, LOAD, START;
      NEW LORRY("L").SCHEDULE(NEXT.SAMPLE);
      PRIORITY := P.SAMPLE;
      LOAD    := 5*VOL.SAMPLE;
      TLEFT   := LOAD/RATE;
```

```
          IF AND2(USER =/= NONE, PRIORITY > USER.PRIORITY)
            THEN USER.INTERRUPT(1);
          WHILE TLEFT > 0.0 DO
          BEGIN HOPPER.ACQUIRE(1);
       LOADING_STARTS:
              USER  :- CURRENT;
              START := TIME;
              HOLD(TLEFT);
       DONE OR INTERRUPTED:
              USER  :- NONE;
              HOPPER.RELEASE(1);
              IF INTERRUPTED = 0 THEN TLEFT := 0.0 ELSE
              BEGIN INTERRUPTED := 0;
                TLEFT    := TLEFT - (TIME-START);
                PRIORITY := PRIORITY + 1;
              END;
            END***OF WHILE LOOP***;
       END***LORRY***;

          TRACE;
          RATE    := 1.0;
          P       :- NEW RANDINT("PRIORITY", 1, 4);
          VOL     :- NEW RANDINT("LORRY LOAD", 1, 3);
          NEXT    :- NEW NEGEXP("NEXT LORRY", 1/12);
          HOPPER :- NEW RES("HOPPER", 1);
          NEW LORRY("L").SCHEDULE(0.0);
          HOLD(120.0);
       END;
```

***Output:
==========

```
  TIME/ CURRENT  AND ITS ACTION(S)

 0.000  DEMOS     SCHEDULES L 1 AT 0.000
                  HOLDS FOR 120.000, UNTIL 120.000
        L 1       SCHEDULES L 2 AT 7.358
                  SEIZES 1 OF HOPPER
                  HOLDS FOR 15.000, UNTIL 15.000
 7.358  L 2       SCHEDULES L 3 AT 88.690
                  INTERRUPTS L 1, WITH POWER = 1
                  CANCELS L 1
                  AWAITS 1 OF HOPPER
        L 1       RELEASES 1 TO HOPPER
                  AWAITS 1 OF HOPPER
        L 2       SEIZES 1 OF HOPPER
                  HOLDS FOR 5.000, UNTIL 12.358
```

```
12.358            RELEASES 1 TO HOPPER
                  ***TERMINATES
        L 1       SEIZES 1 OF HOPPER
                  HOLDS FOR 7.642, UNTIL 20.000
20.000            RELEASES 1 TO HOPPER
                  ***TERMINATES
        . . . . . . . . . . . . . . . . . . . . . .
```

```
                  CLOCK TIME =  120.000
*********************************************************************
*                                                                   *
*                        R E P O R T                                *
*                                                                   *
*********************************************************************
```

D I S T R I B U T I O N S
****

TITLE	/	(RE)SET/OBS/ TYPE	/	A/	B/	SEED
PRIORITY		0.000 44 RANDINT		1	4	33427485
LORRY LOAD		0.000 44 RANDINT		1	3	22276755
NEXT LORRY		0.000 44 NEGEXP	8.333E-02			46847980

R E S O U R C E S
****

TITLE	/	(RE)SET/	OBS/	LIM/	MIN/	NOW/	% USAGE/	AV. WAIT/	QMAX
HOPPER		0.000	51	1	0	0	82.252	17.978	8

REMARKS ON EXAMPLE 11

The trace shows L1 starting an expected 15 minute load at time
0.0.   When interrupted at time 7.358 by L2, L1 relinquishes
the hopper and tries again. When L1 eventually regains
control of the hopper at time 12.358, it has 15.0-7.358 =
7.642 minutes worth of loading left.   This time no
interruptions are made (L3 does not enter the system until
well after L2 has quit).

As to the program itself, the global variable USER always
references the current occupier of the hopper (or NONE). A
freshly arriving lorry sends an interrupt only if the hopper
is occupied (USER =/= NONE) and its priority is greater than
that of the hopper (PRIORITY > USER.PRIORITY). By writing the
interrupt in the form

        IF condition THEN INTERRUPT(1);

we only disturb the occupier when it has to give up the
hopper.

        The victim is at once rescheduled in the event list with
its local variable INTERRUPTED set to 1 signifying that an
interrupt has been made. N.B. After an interrupt has been
dealt with, remember to reset INTERRUPTED to zero (or some
other suitable neutral value) to signify that no interrupt is
now pending.

        It is up to the lorry concerned to remember how much
loading remains. This has been done in a rather special way
by computing the length of the loading time straight away and
recording it in TLEFT. Each time the lorry has a spell on the
hopper and is interrupted, TLEFT is decremented by the time
just spent (TIME-START). If no interrupt occurs, TLEFT is set
straight to zero. The next time the lorry gains control of
the hopper, it will try to retain it for the full expected
period, namely TLEFT.

EXAMPLE 12: QUARRY

A quarry contains a narrow seam of high quality stone on the
edge of a broad front of average quality stone. Early each
day the site is blasted producing sufficient rock of both
qualities to meet the days demand. Two types of truck arrive:
large trucks which take the average quality stone, and small
trucks for the high quality stone. The site has three
mechanical diggers: two large diggers, L1 and L2, are used to
load average quality stone on to the large trucks. They are
too large to manoeuvre near the narrow seam and can thus never
be used to load the high quality stone. The site geography
demands that the high quality stone be loaded by a third,
smaller digger S. The large diggers can load at a
considerably faster rate than the small digger S. When S has
no customer for high quality stone it is allowed to load a
large truck should L1 and L2 be busy. But should a high
quality customer then arrive, S stops loading average quality
stone and loads high quality stone. Meanwhile its previous
customer does not necessarily have to wait for the small
digger to become free again - it can be loaded by a large
digger if one becomes free first. S may also be interrupted
if it is loading a large truck with average quality stone when
a large digger becomes free. The large digger should take

over the job freeing the small digger as it loads at a   faster
rate.

Model data
==========

```
        Timings in hours:
          large truck inter-arrival  NEGEXP:mean=22/hour
          small truck inter-arrival  NEGEXP:mean=10/hour
        Capacities:
          large truck load              20 tons
          small truck load               5 tons
        Loading rates:
          large digger               240 tons/hour
          small digger                60 tons/hour
```

We first sketch a solution ignoring interrupts and then add in
the code for the interrupts. The initial solution has large
and small trucks arriving at their own rates. On arrival,
they signal their presence to the small digger S (by Q.SIGNAL)
and then wait for attention in WAITQs LTQ   and   STQ
respectively.

```
            [REF(WAITQ)LTQ, STQ;]

                ENTITY CLASS TRUCK;
                BEGIN
                  REAL LOAD;
                END***TRUCK***;

        TRUCK CLASS LTRUCK;          TRUCK CLASS STRUCK;
        BEGIN schedule next;         BEGIN schedule next;
          LOAD := 20.0;                LOAD := 5.0;
          Q.SIGNAL;                     Q.SIGNAL;
          LTQ.WAIT;                     STQ.WAIT;
        END***LTRUCK***;             END***STRUCK***;
```

The two digger classes are fairly obvious. The large diggers
deal only with trucks in LTQ

```
                ENTITY CLASS LDIGGER;
                BEGIN REF(TRUCK)T;
                  T :- LTQ.COOPT;
                  HOLD(load time);
                  T.SCHEDULE(0.0);
                  REPEAT;
                END***LDIGGER***;
```

The small digger can load trucks from either STQ or LTQ. We use a wait until condition to suspend it until the appropriate choice can be made.

```
ENTITY CLASS SDIGGER;
BEGIN REF(TRUCK)T;
  Q.WAITUNTIL(STQ.LENGTH > 0 OR LTQ.LENGTH > 0);
  IF STQ.LENGTH > 0 THEN
LOAD_SMALL_TRUCK:
  BEGIN T :- STQ.COOPT;
    HOLD(load time);
    T.SCHEDULE(0.0);
  END ELSE
LOAD_LARGE_TRUCK:
  BEGIN T :- LTQ.COOPT;
    HOLD(load time);
    T.SCHEDULE(0.0);
  END;
  T :- NONE;
  REPEAT;
END***SDIGGER***;
```

When the truck T has been loaded and sent on its way (by T.SCHEDULE), the local variable T of S is reset to NONE prior to S re-entering the CONDQ Q. Thus T.S == NONE is a sign that S is idle.

We now introduce the interrupts in turn. First consider the possible interrupt when a small truck arrives and finds the small digger loading a large truck (expressed by S.T IS LTRUCK; if S is idle or dealing with another small truck, then no interrupt is necessary). The newly arrived small truck has to force S to stop loading its large truck at once. S can then allow S.T to rejoin LTQ partly filled (and with higher priority?), and then S can start loading the interrupting small truck. The interruption is achieved by re-coding small truck as

```
TRUCK CLASS STRUCK;
BEGIN schedule next;
  LOAD := 5.0;
  IF S.T IS LTRUCK THEN S.INTERRUPT(1)
                   ELSE Q.SIGNAL;
  STQ.WAIT;
END***STRUCK***;
```

We now expand the ELSE branch of SDIGGER

```
      LOAD_LARGE_TRUCK:
        BEGIN T :- LTQ.COOPT;
          HOLD(load time);
        POSSIBLE_INTERRUPT:
          IF INTERRUPTED=0 THEN T.SCHEDULE(0.0) ELSE
          BEGIN
            note that T is partially filled;
            let T rejoin LTQ;
            INTERRUPTED := 0;
          END;
        END;
```

We can make this part somewhat tidier by recoding LTRUCK as

```
      TRUCK CLASS LTRUCK;
      BEGIN schedule next;
        LOAD := 20.0;
        WHILE LOAD > 0.0 DO
        BEGIN
          Q.SIGNAL;
          LTQ.WAIT;
        END;
      END***LTRUCK***;
```

and then the main ELSE branch of CLASS SDIGGER turns into

```
      LOAD LARGE TRUCK:
        BEGIN T :- LTQ.COOPT;
          HOLD(load time);
        POSSIBLE_INTERRUPT:
          IF INTERRUPTED = 0 THEN T.LOAD := 0.0 ELSE
          BEGIN
            T.LOAD       := partly filled;
            T.PRIORITY   := T.PRIORITY + 1;
            INTERRUPTED := 0;
          END;
        END;
```

When rescheduled, the large truck T quits if its LOAD = 0.0;
else it re-enters LTQ with increased priority.

The second type of interrupt occurs when a large digger
becomes free and the small digger is loading a large truck.
Since a large digger is so much faster than the small digger,
it seems only sensible that it should take over. Accordingly,
a large digger will issue an interrupt when that situation
arises. We tentatively code

```
          ENTITY CLASS LDIGGER;
          BEGIN REF(TRUCK)T;
            T :- LTQ.COOPT;
            HOLD(load time);
            T.LOAD := 0.0;
            T.SCHEDULE(0.0);
            IF LTQ.LENGTH = 0 AND S.T IS LTRUCK THEN
                S.INTERRUPT(2);
            REPEAT;
          END***LTRUCK***;
```

On the interrupt call, the issuer of the call continues
straight on and awaits the arrival of the large truck T in
LTQ. The interrupt stops S from working on its current large
truck.   S resets the current load of the truck T and sends it
off to LTQ where it will at once get service (a large digger
is waiting).   S then re-enters the CONDQ Q. The complete
program reads

```
  DEMOS
    BEGIN REF(SDIGGER)S;
      REF(CONDQ)Q;  REF(WAITQ)LTQ, STQ;
      REF(RDIST)NEXTL, NEXTS;

      COMMENT-----------------T R U C K S-----------------;

      ENTITY CLASS TRUCK;
      BEGIN
        REAL LOAD;
      END***TRUCK***;

      TRUCK CLASS LTRUCK;
      BEGIN LOAD := 20.0;
        NEW LTRUCK("L").SCHEDULE(NEXTL.SAMPLE);
        WHILE LOAD > 0.0 DO
        BEGIN Q.SIGNAL;
          LTQ.WAIT;
        END;
      END***LTRUCK***;

      TRUCK CLASS STRUCK;
      BEGIN LOAD := 5.0;
        NEW STRUCK("S").SCHEDULE(NEXTS.SAMPLE);
        IF S.T IS LTRUCK THEN S.INTERRUPT(1) ELSE Q.SIGNAL;
        STQ.WAIT;
      END***STRUCK***;
```

```
COMMENT-----------------D I G G E R S----------------;

ENTITY CLASS DIGGER;
BEGIN
  REF(TRUCK)T; REAL RATE;
END***DIGGER**;

DIGGER CLASS LDIGGER;
BEGIN RATE := 240.0;
LOOP:   T :- LTQ.COOPT;
  HOLD(T.LOAD/RATE);
  T.LOAD := 0.0;
  T.SCHEDULE(0.0);  T :- NONE;
  IF LTQ.LENGTH = 0 AND S.T IS LTRUCK THEN
     S.INTERRUPT(2);
  REPEAT;
END***LDIGGER***;

DIGGER CLASS SDIGGER;
BEGIN REAL START;
  RATE := 60.0;
LOOP:
  Q.WAITUNTIL(STQ.LENGTH > 0 OR LTQ.LENGTH > 0);
  IF STQ.LENGTH > 0 THEN
LOAD_SMALL_TRUCK:
  BEGIN T :- STQ.COOPT;
    HOLD(T.LOAD/RATE);
  END ELSE
LOAD_LARGE_TRUCK:
  BEGIN START := TIME;
    T :- LTQ.COOPT;
    HOLD(T.LOAD/RATE);
    IF INTERRUPTED = 0 THEN T.LOAD := 0.0 ELSE
    BEGIN
      T.LOAD       := T.LOAD-(TIME-START)*RATE;
      T.PRIORITY   := 1;
      INTERRUPTED := 0;
    END;
  END;
  T.SCHEDULE(0.0);
  T :- NONE;
  REPEAT;
END***SDIGGER***;

NEXTL :- NEW NEGEXP("NEXT LARGE", 22.0);
NEXTS :- NEW NEGEXP("NEXT SMALL", 10.0);
Q     :- NEW CONDQ("SQ");
```

```
      STQ   :- NEW WAITQ("STRUCKQ");
      LTQ   :- NEW WAITQ("LTRUCKQ");

      S     :- NEW SDIGGER("S DIGGER");
      S.SCHEDULE(0.0);
      NEW LDIGGER("L DIGGER").SCHEDULE(0.0);
      NEW LDIGGER("L DIGGER").SCHEDULE(0.0);
      NEW LTRUCK("L").SCHEDULE(0.0);
      NEW STRUCK("S").SCHEDULE(0.0);
      HOLD(10.0);
    END;
```

***Output:
==========

                    CLOCK TIME =   10.000
****
*   *
*   R E P O R T   *
*   *
****

                    D I S T R I B U T I O N S
                    ****

TITLE /	(RE)SET/	OBS/	TYPE /	A/	B/	SEED
NEXT LARGE	0.000	215	NEGEXP	22.000		33427485
NEXT SMALL	0.000	100	NEGEXP	10.000		22276755

                    W A I T   Q U E U E S
                    ****

TITLE /		(RE)SET/	OBS/	QMAX/	QNOW/	Q AVERAGE/	ZEROS/	AV. WAIT
STRUCKQ		0.000	97	1	0	0.000	97	0.000
STRUCKQ	*	0.000	97	4	3	0.796	25	8.082E-02
LTRUCKQ		0.000	224	2	0	0.319	185	1.422E-02
LTRUCKQ	*	0.000	224	13	8	3.296	48	0.136

                    C O N D I T I O N   Q U E U E S
                    ****

TITLE /	(RE)SET/	OBS/	QMAX/	QNOW/	Q AVERAGE/	ZEROS/	AV. WAIT
SQ	0.000	114	1	0	5.038E-02	99	4.149E-03
```
```

REMARKS ON EXAMPLE 12

In the final listing, just as (ENTITY CLASS) TRUCK was used to
define the common attribute LOAD, so have we also included
(ENTITY CLASS) DIGGER which contains attributes common to
LDIGGER and SDIGGER.   REAL RATE is set to the appropriate
loading rate for each type of digger at the next level;
REF(TRUCK)T references a digger's current customer or is NONE.

     Besides interrupting an active entity (i.e. one in the
event list), one may also interrupt an entity which is passive
(i.e. waiting (until) in a queue, blocked on a resource, or
passivated). In the latter cases, the interrupted entity will
depart from its current explicit or implicit queue (if any)
and be placed in the event list immediately behind its
interrupter CURRENT with INTERRUPTED set.

When a loading by S is interrupted we have to be able to
compute how much S has managed to load before the interrupt.
This we do by noting when an interruptible loading operation
starts in START. When an interrupt occurs, the amount loaded
during this operation is given by (TIME-START)*RATE.

                       Scheduling with NOW

The programmed strategy in example 12 is rather unfair in one
respect.   Suppose that S is currently loading a large truck
Tn, another large truck Tm (m > n) waits in LTQ and then a
large digger, L1 say, becomes free. Our coding directs L1 to
coopt Tm. As L1 loads faster than S, Tm could well be loaded
and away before Tn. It would be fairer to let L1 interrupt S
and take over responsibility for loading Tn.   S would then
naturally get on with Tm. If we alter the coding of the
interrupt inside CLASS LDIGGER to

     IF S.T IS LTRUCK THEN S.INTERRUPT(2);

then L1 will still coopt Tm and S picks up Tn again! This is
because the actions of L1, S and Tn, although all executed at
the same clock time, are threaded so

          L1   S   Tn

     1) S.INTERRUPT(2);
     2) T :- LTQ.COOPT;
     3) HOLD(........);

```
4)                      T.LOAD    := ..;
5)                      T.PRIORITY := ..;
6)                      T.SCHEDULE(0.0);
7)                      T :- NONE;
8)                      INTERRUPTED := 0;
9)                      Q.WAITUNTIL(...);
10)                                             LTQ.WAIT;
```

Action 2) means that L1 coopts Tm since Tn does not enter LTQ
until action 10). It is essential that S be given the
opportunity to release Tn and Tn be allowed to enter LTQ (with
its increased priority taking it to the front) before L1
attempts a coopt. This we can arrange by the insertion of
appropriate HOLDs and by using the rather special REAL
PROCEDURE NOW. NOW is intended to express urgency. Whereas
E.SCHEDULE(0.0) schedules E at the current clock time but as
the LAST entity at that time, E.SCHEDULE(NOW) is treated as a
priority request and E actually PREEMPTS CURRENT. When the
next phase of E is over, then the pushed-down previous CURRENT
will be restored. Thus the following alterations do trick.

```
        IF S.T IS LTRUCK THEN S.INTERRUPT(2);
        HOLD(0.0);
        REPEAT;
```

inside CLASS LDIGGER, and

```
        T.SCHEDULE(NOW);
        T :- NONE;
        T.INTERRUPTED := 0;
        HOLD(0.0);
        Q.WAITUNTIL(.....);
```

inside CLASS SDIGGER. These extra HOLDs produce the following
new threading of code

```
        L1                  S                   Tn

1)  S.INTERRUPT(2);
2)  HOLD(0.0);
3)                      T.LOAD    := ..;
4)                      T.PRIORITY := ..;
5)                      T.SCHEDULE(NOW);
6)                                          LTQ.WAIT;
7)                      T :- NONE;
8)                      T.INTERRUPTED := 0;
9)                      HOLD(0.0);
```

```
10) T :- LTQ.COOPT;
11) HOLD(........);
12)                    Q.WAITUNTIL(.....);
```

EXERCISES 7 (continued)

4. Cars are transported from a harbour and over the water by a fleet of ferries each with a capacity of 20 cars. The ferry service runs continuously round the clock and a departure is scheduled every hour on the hour. The ferry due to depart at n o'clock arrives at NORMAL (mean=20, standard deviation=5) minutes past (n-1) o'clock, unloads, and then takes on board as many cars as it can up until its scheduled departure time. At that time, the ferry will continue to load while the queue is not empty and it is not yet full.

Car arrivals at the ferry point are random (NEGEXP distributed) with different arrival rates according to the time of day. In daytime [06.00-18.00), they arrive at a mean rate of 15 per hour; at night time [18.00-06.00), they arrive at a mean rate of 9 per hour. Season ticket holders get priority in the queue. The percentage of season ticket holders is 40 in daytime and 25 at night. Find the mean waiting times of season ticket holders and other cars and also the mean delay of the ferry by running your model over a 28 day month. Take as your initial conditions that the first car arrives at time 5 minutes and the first ferry at time 20 minutes.

Model data
==========

```
     Timings in minutes:
       unload ferry          RANDINT:6->12
       load each car         CONSTANT:1
```

5. Customers queueing for service in a shop are characterised by their own individual impatience. They leave the queue after a certain time if not already being served or placed first in the queue. Model the system given that customers arrive at a mean rate of one per minute (NEGEXP distributed) and that each service lasts for 40-60 seconds (UNIFORMly distributed). A customer quits the shop after RANDINT 120-300 seconds if not already being served, or else he is not the first in the queue.

Run your model for 4 simulated hours assuming that the first customer arrives at time 0.0.

6. In example 12, page 130, the validity of an interrupt was tested by the interrupter instead of by the recipient. Another way is to make the interrupt and let the recipient decide for himself whether to accept it, ignore it, or reserve it for later attention. For example, in our formulation of the small digger S if we altered the interrupt calls to

> INTERRUPT(n);

instead of

> IF condition THEN INTERRUPT(n);

then S would receive interrupts when

a) waiting until in Q (always accepted),

b) loading a small truck (always ignored),

c) loading a large truck (always accepted if n = 1, always ignored if n = 2).

Recode the whole problem according to this suggestion. (No solution is given to this exercise.)

8.1 SOME LOOSE ENDS

This primer has introduced the DEMOS facilities (resource types, queues, distributions, etc.) by a sequence of examples which usually illustrate the point at hand but not much more. Here we spend a little extra time on periodic reporting, starting up simulations and closing them down.

Periodic reports can be issued rather neatly using an object of such a class as REPORTER below.

```
ENTITY CLASS REPORTER(T); REAL T;
BEGIN
  HOLD(T);
  REPORT;
  RESET;
  REPEAT;
END***REPORTER***;

REF(REPORTER)R;

R :- NEW REPORTER("DAILY REPORT", 24.0);
R.SCHEDULE(0.0);
```

Working in hourly units, R will issue a full report on the last day's facility usage every 24 hours. REPORT is a global DEMOS procedure which prints standard reports on the usage of all the DEMOS facilities created by the user. The report covers their usage since the object's creation (if not reset) or since its last reset. (The DEMOS system itself calls this procedure at the end of each simulation run.) RESET is another global DEMOS procedure which resets all DEMOS facilities created by the user so that they now collect afresh over the next time period.

PROCEDURE RESET is also useful in the warm start situation. We have usually started up our models by letting the first arrivals fall due at time 0.0. It takes some time before enough entities have worked their ways through the system for it to have settled down to approximately normal working conditions. The cold start naturally biases the facility reports as initially there will be little interference between entities. Using RESET it is easy to let the system settle down and then gather data over the desired time slot. We merely change code in the DEMOS block from the usual

        HOLD(simulation period);

into

        HOLD(warm up period);
        RESET;
        HOLD(time slot);

The final report covers a period of duration 'time slot'. The length of the warm up period is usually chosen by some rule of thumb rather than by a precise method. Shannon [37, pages 183-186] is particularly informative on this topic and gives several further references.

      Closing down a simulation is less of a problem in DEMOS as the DEMOS block can itself be treated as an entity and acquire resources, wait until in queues, etc. This neat and very effective idea was borrowed directly from SIMULA; it was used in example 5 (pages 67 through 71), and exercises 3-13 (page 53), 4.5 (page 65), and 4.12 (page 74). See further remarks on page 159.

DEMOS facilities not covered

Besides the global procedures REPORT and RESET mentioned above, there are also procedures REPORT and RESET local to classes RES, BIN, and the various queues - CONDQ, QUEUE, and WAITQ. We are able to report and reset all user created facilities, select those of one class (e.g. all RES objects) and even select single items (e.g. a single BIN).

      There is a class EMPIRICAL which can be used to represent empirical data tabulated as a cumulative probability function.

      In connection with the design of experiments, the default values for distribution seeds can be overridden (useful for antithetic drawings) and the DEMOS-defined first seed value (33427485 - and hence all the other seeds) can be changed. In fact, even the random number generators can be replaced.

There are also several snapshot routines which can be called to detail individual entities either waiting (until) in queues, awaiting resources, or scheduled in the event list.

There is a CLASS ACCUMULATE which parallels CLASS TALLY, but for time dependent variables. And there is a CLASS REGRESSION too.

Finally, CLASS ENTITY contains certain additional attributes. BOOLEAN PROCEDURE AVAIL (which returns TRUE if the entity is not coopted); BOOLEAN PROCEDURE IDLE (which returns TRUE if the entity is not in the event list); REF(ENTITY)PROCEDURE NEXTEV (which returns NONE if the entity is idle or last in the event list, otherwise a reference to the next entity in the event list); and REAL PROCEDURE EVTIME (which returns the entity's scheduled time if it lies in the event list. Otherwise, a call on EVTIME causes a run time error: if in doubt, check using IF NOT E.IDLE THEN .....).

8.2 THE SIMULA IMPLEMENTATION

It is worth remarking on how much DEMOS owes to SIMULA. Although we have certainly borrowed ideas from other languages (resource types and reporting from GPSS, conditions and activity diagrams from CSL and ECSL), DEMOS would not exist without the inspiration of its host language which positively invites the user to write his programs in process (= entity) style. All we have done is add a few user-oriented bells and whistles.

DEMOS is implemented as a SIMULA context (prefixed by SIMSET, but not by SIMULATION) and extends over roughly 2000 cards. Along with suitable documentation and testing, DEMOS was approximately a 9 man-month project. The resulting system is portable and has proved easy to extend, alter and maintain.

Implementing a DEMOS compiler from scratch was out of the question because DEMOS is SIMULA plus, and SIMULA is itself a 15 man-year project. However a DEMOS compiler would have certain advantages. It could, for example, give error messages written in DEMOS (rather than SIMULA) terminology (although it must be admitted that SIMULA compilers are pretty good in this respect anyway), detect the possibility of deadlock at compile time, accept a DEMOS program written with waits until and itself insert the correct calls on SIGNAL, give resource usage cross-reference lists, do away with the

need for explicitly titling every DEMOS object (as in NEW
BOAT("BOAT"), etc.). Without a compiler, the same effect can
be achieved by using a pre-processor, which is much easier to
write but more expensive to run.

    Clementson [21] and Matthewson [26] have gone further
than this and written PROGRAM GENERATORS; inter-active
programs which ask the user about his model and then actually
write the code for him! Clementson's system produces code for
ECSL, but Matthewson's stores the structure of the model and
can then be persuaded to produce code for several different
languages - GASP, ECSL, SIMULA, DEMOS ... Thus he can develop
a program in SIMULA, say, on a large machine, and run it in
GASP on a small machine. It also reinforces the point that
activity diagrams can be used as bases for writing simulations
in any simulation programming language. Both a program
generator and a pre-processor for DEMOS are under
consideration.

    There are many advantages to coding DEMOS in SIMULA.
Firstly, SIMULA is widely implemented and to a good standard.
The implementors of SIMULA systems meet regularly in the
SIMULA STANDARDS GROUP. The hope being that this would ensure
that SIMULA systems are compatible now and will remain so in
the future. Experience with porting DEMOS has been fairly
trouble free, only the CDC implementation [3] giving rise to
non-trivial problems. DEMOS was implemented on DEC System 10
hardware [6] and has been ported to DEC System 20 [also 6],
IBM 360/370 [8], and ICL System 4 [9], and ICL 2900 hardware
with no modifications at all. The UNIVAC 1100 implementation
[7] does not yet support virtual labels, so that version of
DEMOS has to make do without REPEAT. Both the NDRE [4] and
CDC [3] SIMULA implementations quote key words. Once that
hurdle has been accounted for, the NDRE version supports
neither virtual labels nor functions returning references, so
that REPEAT is out, and the function REF(ENTITY)PROCEDURE
NEXTEV has had to be rewritten as a procedure. The CDC [3]
SIMULA compiler still does not treat virtual quantities
correctly, and the DEMOS code for the reset and report
routines had to be 'bent' to fit. Altogether, the experience
has not been too bad (have you tried porting FORTRAN programs
from one machine to another?). The situation should improve
in the very near future when the Norwegian Computing Center's
portable SIMULA implementations [10] are released, making
identical SIMULA compilers available on an even wider range of
hardware.

Secondly, SIMULA's object and context features are considerably ahead of anything offered by other languages. It is easy to 'see' how to implement DEMOS facilities as SIMULA objects. The context feature enables an implementation to progress in an orderly fashion layer by layer, each new step adding in a few new interrelated ideas. SIMULA has very strict security and consistency checks so that many mistakes are picked up as soon as possible at compile time.

Thirdly, any ideas not built into DEMOS can be added straightforwardly (which eases the designer's dilemma - if in doubt, leave it out!). One easy addition (should the arguments of chapter 6.3, page 120, fail to be convincing) would be to put in one's own SNOOPY. But the area in which advanced users will most probably want to make changes is in the REPORT routines. Here it is sufficient to extend the facility concerned and define one's own REPORT routine, e.g.

```
RES CLASS MY_RES;
BEGIN
   PROCEDURE REPORT;..........;
END***MY_REPORT***;
```

and then work with MY_RES objects instead of RES objects. The newly written REPORT replaces the standard DEMOS report thanks to SIMULA's VIRTUAL mechanism. For further detail on VIRTUAL, see [11, chapter 4] or [15].

Finally, DEMOS is not the end of the road. The user should proceed in standard SIMULA fashion to develop his own more specialised contexts for his own areas of interest, e.g.

```
DEMOS CLASS STEEL(N_MILLS, N_PITS);
          INTEGER N_MILLS, N_PITS;
BEGIN
   ENTITY CLASS FURNACE;.....;
   ........................
   REF(RES)MILLS, PITS;
   .................
   MILLS :- NEW RES("MILLS", N_MILLS);
   PITS  :- NEW RES("PITS",  N_PITS;
END***STEEL***;
```

For examples of other contexts on SIMULA, study Lie's SIMWAP [17], Rogeberg's TETRASIM [18], and Vaucher's GPSSS [19].

Several other simulation packages have been implemented as extensions to general programming languages. The two best known to the author are SIMONE and ALGOLSIM. SIMONE (see Kaubisch et al. [24]) is an extension to PASCAL produced by extending a PASCAL compiler. Its design was heavily influenced by SIMULA. ALGOLSIM (Shearn [30]) is an extension to ALGOL 68. Both papers are well written, and it is interesting to compare ALGOL 68, PASCAL and SIMULA as extendible languages.

Virjo [40] gives a very thorough comparison of GPSS, SIMSCRIPT, and SIMULA. The paper includes several examples coded in all three languages and run on a variety of machines.

The distribution of DEMOS

As stated in the preface, DEMOS is an ordinary SIMULA program and will run on any computer that supports SIMULA (see references [3-10]). The DEMOS Reference Manual ([14]) gives full documentation of the complete DEMOS system, and includes a SIMULA source listing of DEMOS as an appendix. It is the author's hope that this will lead to DEMOS being read and improved by others, and to its being used in education to show what the components of a discrete event simulation language are and how they fit together. The DEMOS system is maintained by the author who will be pleased (?) to receive constructive criticisms and error reports.

The DEMOS system (both source code and reference manual) are distributed in machine readable form as unlabelled files on IBM standard, 9 track tapes. In North America, the system is available from the author:

> Graham Birtwistle,
> Computer Science Department,
> University of Calgary,
> Calgary, Alberta, Canada T2N 1N4.
> Tlf: (403) 284 6055

Otherwise, write to:

> Henk Sol,
> Information Systems Research Group,
> Faculty of Economics,
> University of Groningen,
> PO Box 800, 97 AV Groningen,
> The Netherlands.

Tail piece

There is still much to learn and this primer has merely scratched the surface. Fishman [32] and/or Shannon [37] (which both contain many further references) are ways into the important topics of experimental design and input/output analysis. Franta [33] combines an explanation of SIMULA together with an introduction to the statistical aspects of simulation. Note especially his treatment of the regenerative method. Poole and Szymankiewicz [27], Pritsker and Kiviat [28] and Schribner [29] contain many simulation examples which can be used to build up modelling experience if you are not on an actual project. Reference [28] in particular contains a good selection of examples and exercises.

Finally, note that when you have managed to work your way through this book and complete the exercises then ... then you can keep it on your bookshelf. For it is intended as an introductory teaching text and not as a reference manual. Once a certain competence in DEMOS has been reached, then the DEMOS Reference Manual [14] and the appropriate SIMULA User's Manual [3-9] should prove more useful.

REFERENCES

SIMULA DEFINITION

1) O-J.Dahl, B.Myhrhaug, and K.Nygaard
    "SIMULA 67 Common Base Language"
    NCC Publication S-52
    Norwegian Computing Center, Oslo, 1970.

2) P.Naur (Editor)
    "Revised Report on the Algorithmic Language ALGOL 60"
    CACM, 6(1), 1963, pp.1-17.

SIMULA MANUALS

3) "Control Data 6400/6500/6600 Computer Systems
    SIMULA Reference Manual"
    Control Data Corporation, 1969.

4) "NDRE Simula Implementation User's Manual"
    NDRE Publication S-370 (3rd. Edition)
    Norwegian Defence Research Establishment, Kjeller, 1977.
    (This is another implementation for CDC.)

5) "TPH SIMULA Reference Manual (NORD 10)"
    Norsk Data A.S., Oslo, Norway, 1977.

6) "DEC System 10 SIMULA Language Handbook
    Part 1: User's Guide"
    Swedish Defense Research Establishment, Stockholm, 1975.
    This compiler has been modified to run on the DEC 20.

7) "EXEC-8 SIMULA User's Guide"
    NCC Publication S-36
    Norwegian Computing Center, Oslo, 1971.

8) "SIMULA for IBM 360/370: User's Guide"
    NCC Publication S-24
    Norwegian Computing Center, Oslo, 1971.

9) "System 4 Multijob SIMULA Programmer's Manual"
    (ICL System 4)
    Program Library Unit, Edinburgh University.

10) S-PORT - the portable Simula project.
     Implementations by the Norwegian Computing Center and
     others for UNIVAC, HONEYWELL, VAX, and PRIME computers
     are now underway. Contact NCC for details.

SIMULA TEXTS

11) G.M.Birtwistle, O-J.Dahl, B.Myhrhaug, and K.Nygaard
     "SIMULA BEGIN"
     Studentlitteratur, Lund, Sweden, 1973.

12) H.Rohlfing
     "SIMULA: Eine Einfuhrung"
     Bibliographisches Institut AG, Mannheim, 1973.

13) P.R.Hills
     "An introduction to simulation using SIMULA"
     NCC Publication S-55
     Norwegian Computing Center, Oslo, 1973.

SIMULA USAGE

14) G.M.Birtwistle
     "DEMOS Reference Manual"
     278 pp. 2nd. Edition, July, 1981.

15) G.M.Birtwistle
     "The design and implementation of DEMOS"
     In preparation.

16) P.R.Hills and G.M.Birtwistle
     "SIMON 75 Reference Manual"
     P.R.Hills, Shaldon, Devon, England, 1976.

17) A.Lie, K.Elgsaas, and J.Evensmo
     "SIMWAP a computer package for warehouse planning"
     NCC Publication S-42
     Norwegian Computing Center, Oslo, 1972.

18) T.Rogeberg
     "Simulation and Simula as applied to the design
     and analysis of telephone systems"
     NCC Publication S-30
     Norwegian Computing Center, Oslo, 1970.

19) J.Vaucher
    "Simulation data structures using Simula 67"
    Proc. Winter Simulation Conference, 1971, pp.255-260.

OTHER SIMULATION LANGUAGES

20) J.N.Buxton and J.G.Laski
    "Control and Simulation Language"
    Computer Journal, 5(3), 1962.

21) A.Clementson
    "Extended Control and Simulation Language"
    University of Birmingham, England, 1973.

22) P.R.Hills
    "SIMON - a simulation language in ALGOL"
    in S.M.Hollingdale(Editor), "Simulation in OR",
    English Universities Press, London, 1965.

23) P.R.Hills
    "HOCUS - Basic and Advanced Manuals"
    PE Group, Egham, Surrey, England, 1971.

24) W.H.Kaubisch, R.H.Perrott, and C.A.R.Hoare
    "Quasi-parallel programming"
    Software Practice and Experience, 6(4), 1976, pp.341-356

25) P.J.Kiviat, R.Villanueva, and H.M.Markowitz
    "The SIMSCRIPT II.5 Programming Language"
    Prentice-Hall, 1968.

26) S.C.Matthewson
    "Simulation Program Generators"
    Simulation, 23(6), December 1974, pp.181-189.

27) T.Poole and J.Szymankiewicz
    "Using Simulation to solve problems"
    McGraw-Hill, 1977.

28) A.A.B.Pritsker and P.J.Kiviat
    "Simulation with GASP II"
    Prentice-Hall, 1969.

29) T.Schribner
    "Simulation using GPSS"
    Wiley, 1974.

30) D.C.S.Shearn
"Discrete Event Simulation in ALGOL 68"
Software Practice and Experience, 5(4), 1975, pp.279-293.

THEORY OF SIMULATION

31) D.Y.Downham and F.D.K.Roberts
"Multiplicative congruential pseudo-random number
generators"
Computer Journal, 10(1), 1967, pp.74-77.

32) G.S.Fishman
"Concepts and Methods in Discrete Event Digital
Simulation"
Wiley, 1973.

33) W.R.Franta
"The process view of simulation"
North Holland, 1978.

34) A.T.Fuller
"The period of pseudo-random numbers generated by
Lehmer's congruential method"
Computer Journal, 19(2), 1976, pp.173-177.

35) D.E.Knuth
"The art of computer programming"
Addison-Wesley, 1969.

36) M.Ohlin
"Next Random - a method of fast access to any number in
the random generator cycle"
Simula Newsletter, 6(2), 1977, pp.18-20.

37) R.E.Shannon
"Systems Simulation: the art and science"
Prentice-Hall, 1975.

38) A.C.Shaw
"The Logical Design of Operating Systems"
Prentice-Hall, 1974.

39) J.Vaucher
"A generalised wait until algorithm for general purpose
simulation languages"
Proc. Winter Simulation Conference, 1973, pp.177-183.

40) A. Virjo
    "A comparison of some discrete event simulation languages"
    NORDDATA 72 Conference, Helsinki, 1972.
    Republished by the Norwegian Computing Center.

OTHER TOPICS

41) K.Nygaard and O-J.Dahl
    "The development of the SIMULA languages"
    ACM Conference "A history of programming languages",
    Proceedings edited by A. Wexelblatt, Academic Press, 1981.

42) J.Palme
    "How I fought with hardware and software and succeeded"
    Software Practice and Experience, 8(1), 1978, pp.77-81.

APPENDIX A: OUTLINE OF SIMULA

SIMULA STATEMENTS

```
block
  DEMOS BEGIN declarations;
        statements;
      END

  BEGIN INTEGER K, S;
    FOR K := 1 STEP 1 UNTIL N DO
      S := S + X(K)**2;
  END

compound_statement
  BEGIN SUM := SUM + X;
    N := N + 1;
  END

procedure_statement
  REPEAT
  HOLD(0.0)
  TUGS.ACQUIRE(2)

goto_statement
  GOTO EXIT

assignment
  M := M + 1
  P :- Q :- NONE
  T.LOAD := 16.0

object_generator
  NEW BOAT("BOAT")

for_statement
  FOR K := 1 STEP 1 UNTIL N DO X(K) := TRUE

  FOR K := 3, 1, 4, 1, 5, 9 DO FREQ(K) := FREQ(K)+1

  FOR Q :- Q1, Q2, Q3, Q4 DO Q.SIGNAL
```

```
if_statement
  IF TUGS.AVAIL = O THEN TUGQ.WAIT

  IF FREE < 5 THEN
    BEGIN HOLD(10.0);
      E.WAIT;
    END ELSE T.WAIT
```

```
while_statement
  WHILE Q.LENGTH > O DO Q.FIRST.SCHEDULE(NOW)
```

```
inspect_statement (not used in this book)
  INSPECT T WHEN TRUCK DO LOAD := 16.0
```

```
dummy_statement
```

SIMULA DECLARATIONS

```
type_declaration
  INTEGER A, B, C

  REF(BOAT)B1, QE2
```

```
array_declaration
  REF(RES)ARRAY INNERS, OUTERS(1:N)

  INTEGER ARRAY BOARD(1:8, 1:8)
```

```
external declaration
  EXTERNAL CLASS DEMOS
```

```
procedure_declaration
  PROCEDURE TOWIN(V); REF(VEHICLE)V;
  BEGIN
    IF V == NONE THEN ERROR("NO VEHICLE") ELSE
    IF V.BROKENDOWN THEN FALSEALARM ELSE
      VICTIM :- V;
  END***TOWIN***

  INTEGER PROCEDURE SUM(M, N); INTEGER M, N;
  BEGIN
    SUM := M + N;
  END***SUM***;
```

PROCEDURE PARAMETERS
=====================

PARAMETER SPECIFICATION	VALUE	REF	NAME
REAL/INTEGER/CHARACTER/BOOLEAN	d	*	o
REF(any class)	*	d	o
TEXT	o	d	o
REAL/INTEGER/CHARACTER/BOOLEAN ARRAY	o	d	o
REF(any class)/TEXT ARRAY	*	d	o
PROCEDURE/LABEL/SWITCH	*	d	o

d: default *: illegal o: optional

class_declaration (somewhat restricted)
  CLASS POINT(X, Y); REAL X, Y;
  BEGIN REAL R;
    R := SQRT(X**2 + Y**2);
  END***POINT***

  POINT CLASS POLAR;
  BEGIN REAL ANGLE;
    ANGLE := IF R = 0.0 THEN 0.0 ELSE ARCTAN(X, Y);
  END***POLAR***

CLASS PARAMETERS
================

PARAMETER SPECIFICATION	VALUE	REF
REAL/INTEGER/CHARACTER/BOOLEAN	d	*
REF(any class)	*	d
TEXT	o	d
REAL/INTEGER/CHARACTER/BOOLEAN ARRAY	o	d
REF(any class)/TEXT ARRAY	*	d

d: default *:illegal o: optional

Resource declarations

```
CLASS RES(TITLE,AVAIL); VALUE TITLE;                    33
 TEXT TITLE; INTEGER AVAIL;
BEGIN
 PROCEDURE ACQUIRE(N); INTEGER N;                       33
 PROCEDURE RELEASE(N); INTEGER N;                       33
 PROCEDURE REPORT;                                      43
END***RES***;


CLASS BIN(TITLE,AVAIL); VALUE TITLE;
 TEXT TITLE; INTEGER AVAIL;                             65
BEGIN
 PROCEDURE TAKE(N); INTEGER N;                          66
 PROCEDURE GIVE(N); INTEGER N;                          67
 PROCEDURE REPORT;                                      71
END***BIN***;
```

Queue declarations

```
CLASS QUEUE(TITLE); VALUE TITLE; TEXT TITLE;            80
BEGIN
 REF(ENTITY)PROCEDURE FIRST;                            80
 REF(ENTITY)PROCEDURE LAST;                             80
 INTEGER LENGTH;                                        80
 PROCEDURE REPORT;                                   as 105
END***QUEUE***;


CLASS WAITQ(TITLE); VALUE TITLE; TEXT TITLE;            78
BEGIN
 REF(QUEUE)MASTERQ, SLAVEQ;                             78
 REF(ENTITY)PROCEDURE FIRST;                            79
 REF(ENTITY)PROCEDURE LAST;                             79
 INTEGER LENGTH;                                        79
 REF(ENTITY)PROCEDURE COOPT;                            79
 PROCEDURE FIND(E, COND); NAME E, COND;
  REF(ENTITY)E; BOOLEAN COND;                           95
 BOOLEAN PROCEDURE AVAIL(E,COND);NAME E,COND;
  REF(ENTITY)E; BOOLEAN COND;                          107
 PROCEDURE WAIT;                                        79
 PROCEDURE REPORT;                                      88
END***WAITQ***;
```

```
CLASS CONDQ(TITLE); VALUE TITLE; TEXT TITLE;              107
BEGIN
 BOOLEAN ALL;                                             115
 REF(ENTITY)PROCEDURE FIRST;                              102
 REF(ENTITY)PROCEDURE LAST;                               102
 INTEGER LENGTH;                                          102
 PROCEDURE WAITUNTIL(C); NAME C; BOOLEAN C;               102
 PROCEDURE SIGNAL;                                        103
 PROCEDURE REPORT;                                        105
END***CONDQ***;
```

                     The main program impersonator

```
ENTITY CLASS MAINPROGRAM;
BEGIN
   DETACH;
   REPEAT;
END***MAINPROGRAM***;

REF(ENTITY)DEMOS;
```

                     ... and the various routines
                 N.B. the random number generators are
                    given separately in Appendix C.

```
PROCEDURE READDIST(D, TITLE); NAME D;                      49
 VALUE TITLE; REF(DIST)D; TEXT TITLE;
PROCEDURE TRACE;                                           44
PROCEDURE NOTRACE;                                         44
PROCEDURE HOLD(T); REAL T;                                 36
REAL PROCEDURE TIME;                                       36
REAL PROCEDURE NOW;                                       138
REF(ENTITY)PROCEDURE CURRENT;                             36
PROCEDURE REPORT;                                         143
PROCEDURE RESET;                                          143
TEXT PROCEDURE EDIT(T,N); VALUE T; TEXT T; INTEGER N;      53

DEMOS :- NEW MAIN("DEMOS");
DEMOS.SCHEDULE(0.0);
INNER;
HOLD(0.0);
REPORT;
END***DEMOS***;
```

The MAIN PROGRAM

It is desirable to have the DEMOS block entering into the simulation as an entity, but this cannot be managed directly as context blocks may not be referenced. The same effect is achieved by having an entity of CLASS MAINPROGRAM. REF(ENTITY)DEMOS is a reference to a special 'impersonating' object. It can be scheduled, held, and cancelled just like any other entity. But every time it becomes CURRENT, it transfers control back to the DEMOS context block (that is the effect of the SIMULA routine DETACH in this case) whose user-written main program actions are thereby continued. Thus a HOLD(T) written in the program block causes the DEMOS object to be rescheduled at 'TIME+T' and the actions of (the new) CURRENT to be resumed. Thus the DEMOS context block will not be active again until the DEMOS object becomes CURRENT.

A simulation run ends when an exit is made through the END of the user-written part of the DEMOS context block. It is usually desirable that the DEMOS context block itself decides the length of the run, but it is possible to cancel the DEMOS object and leave the decision to other entities.

DEMOS synchronisations

The DEMOS synchronisation pairs ACQUIRE/RELEASE, TAKE/GIVE, COOPT/SCHEDULE, WAITUNTIL/SIGNAL can be expressed in terms of calls on a more primitive procedure pair GET/PUT. This helps to ensure their consistency and once the underlying GET/PUT pair are understood it makes it easier to write synchronisations correctly. GET and PUT are (informally) listed below.

```
PROCEDURE GET(Q, AVAIL, SEIZE); NAME AVAIL; REF(QUEUE)Q;
                         BOOLEAN AVAIL; statement SEIZE;
BEGIN CURRENT.INTO(Q);
  WHILE NOT(Q.FIRST == CURRENT AND AVAIL) DO
    CURRENT.CANCEL;
  CURRENT.OUT;
  enter Q.FIRST into event list immediately after CURRENT;
  SEIZE;
END***GET***;
```

```
    PROCEDURE PUT(Q, RETURN); REF(QUEUE)Q; statement RETURN;
    BEGIN
      IF Q.FIRST =/= NONE THEN Q.FIRST.SCHEDULE(0.0);
      RETURN;
    END***PUT***;
```

In terms of this pair, the DEMOS routines are

                            REF(RES)R;

```
R.ACQUIRE(n);
    GET(R.q, R.AVAIL >= n, R.AVAIL := R.AVAIL - n);
R.RELEASE(n);
    PUT(R.q,  R.AVAIL := R.AVAIL + n);
```


                            REF(BIN)B;

```
B.TAKE(n);
    GET(B.q, B.AVAIL >= n, B.AVAIL := B.AVAIL - n);
B.GIVE(n);
    PUT(B.q, B.AVAIL := B.AVAIL + n);
```


                            REF(CONDQ)Q;

```
Q.WAITUNTIL(c);
    GET(Q.condition queue, c, null);
Q.SIGNAL;
    PUT(Q.condition queue, null);
```


                            REF(WAITQ)W;

```
W.COOPT;
    GET(Q.MASTERQ, Q.SLAVEQ.LENGTH > 0,
            COOPT :- Q.SLAVEQ.FIRST.COOPT);
W.WAIT;
    PUT(Q.MASTERQ, BEGIN IF Q.MASTERQ.LENGTH > 0 THEN
                        Q.MASTERQ.FIRST.SCHEDULE(0.0);
                    CURRENT.CANCEL;
                END;)
```

Two cases do not quite fit into this general pattern: FIND and
SIGNAL with ALL set. The reader is encouraged to modify GET
and PUT himself so that these routines can be accommodated.

APPENDIX C: DEMOS RANDOM NUMBER GENERATORS

There are 9 random drawing facilities in DEMOS which are
categorised according to the type of distribution they sample
from. RDISTs return REAL values (CONSTANT, EMPIRICAL, NEGEXP,
NORMAL, UNIFORM, ERLANG); IDISTs return INTEGER values
(RANDINT, POISSON); and the one BDIST (DRAW) returns a BOOLEAN
value. Their common portion is defined in CLASS DIST which is
then used as prefix to the other three.

```
      CLASS DIST(TITLE); VALUE TITLE; TEXT TITLE;
      BEGIN
         INTEGER U;
         PROCEDURE REPORT;
         U := some suitable seed;
      END***DIST***;
```

Note that we can override the initial value given to U (a
necessary feature for designed experiments. Negative U values
produce antithetic drawings).

```
      DIST CLASS RDIST; VIRTUAL: REAL PROCEDURE SAMPLE;;
      DIST CLASS IDIST; VIRTUAL: INTEGER PROCEDURE SAMPLE;;
      DIST CLASS BDIST; VIRTUAL: BOOLEAN PROCEDURE SAMPLE;;
```

In practice, the virtual part means that we can reference any
sub-class of RDIST with a REF(RDIST) variable and still access
its appropriate procedure SAMPLE. Similarly with IDIST and
BDIST.

```
      RDIST CLASS CONSTANT(A); REAL A;
      BEGIN
         REAL PROCEDURE SAMPLE;
      END***CONSTANT***;
```

A call on SAMPLE ALWAYS returns A.

```
      RDIST CLASS NORMAL(A, B); REAL A, B;
      BEGIN
         REAL PROCEDURE SAMPLE;
         IF B < 0 THEN B := -B;
      END***NORMAL***;
```

A call on SAMPLE returns a drawing from a normal distribution
with mean A and standard deviation B.

```
        RDIST CLASS NEGEXP(A); REAL A;
        BEGIN
          REAL PROCEDURE SAMPLE;
          A := ABS(A);
          IF A = 0.0 THEN A := 0.0001;
        END***NEGEXP***;
```

A call on SAMPLE returns a drawing from a negexp distribution
with mean time between arrivals of 1/A.

```
        RDIST CLASS UNIFORM(A, B); REAL A, B;
        BEGIN
          REAL PROCEDURE SAMPLE;
          IF A > B THEN swap A<->B;
        END***UNIFORM***;
```

A call on SAMPLE returns a drawing from a uniform distribution
with lower bound A and upper bound B.

```
        RDIST CLASS ERLANG(A, B); REAL A, B;
        BEGIN
          REAL PROCEDURE SAMPLE;
          IF A <= 0.0 THEN A := -A;
          IF B <= 0.0 THEN B := -B;
        END***ERLANG***;
```

A call on SAMPLE returns a drawing from an ERLANG distribution
with mean A and standard deviation $1/(A*sqrt(B))$.

```
        RDIST CLASS EMPIRICAL(N); INTEGER N;
        BEGIN REAL ARRAY P, X(1:N);
          REAL PROCEDURE SAMPLE;
          read in the values p1,x1: p2,x2: ...: pn,xn
          which represent a cumulative  distribution.
          (p1=0.0, pn=1.0, pm>pr, xm>xr for m>r);
        END***EMPIRICAL***;
```

A call on SAMPLE returns a drawing from the cumulative
probability function represented by the P and X tables, x1 <=
SAMPLE <= xn. Linear interpolation is used.

```
      IDIST CLASS RANDINT(A, B); INTEGER A, B;
      BEGIN
        INTEGER PROCEDURE SAMPLE;
        IF A > B THEN swap A<->B;
      END***RANDINT***;
```

A call on SAMPLE returns an integer randomly distributed
between A and B.

```
      IDIST CLASS POISSON(A); REAL A;
      BEGIN
        INTEGER PROCEDURE SAMPLE;
      END***POISSON***;
```

A call on SAMPLE returns a drawing from a POISSON distribution
with mean A.

And finally

```
      BDIST CLASS DRAW(P); REAL P;
      BEGIN
        BOOLEAN PROCEDURE SAMPLE;
      END***DRAW***;
```

A call on SAMPLE returns TRUE with probability P (always FALSE
if P <= 0.0, and always TRUE if P >= 1.0).

ANSWERS TO EXERCISES

CHAPTER 2
=========

2.1 CLASS LORRY;
    BEGIN INTEGER REG, LOAD;
      load;
      deliver;
    END***LORRY***;

2.2

    CLASS CUSTOMER;   !   CUSTOMER   !
    BEGIN   ------------------
      enter shop;   !enter shop;   !
      wait if barber   !wait if barber!
        not free;   ! not free;   !
      get haircut;   ->!get haircut; !
      pay barber;   !pay barber;   !
      leave shop;   !leave shop;   !
    END***CUSTOMER***;   ------------------

2.3 CLASS CAR(REGISTERED, WEIGHT, MAXSPEED, SEATS);
      INTEGER REGISTERED, MAXSPEED, SEATS; REAL WEIGHT;
    BEGIN BOOLEAN BROKENDOWN;
      IF REGISTERED < 1885 OR WEIGHT <= 0.0
        OR MAXSPEED < 50   OR SEATS < 1 THEN error;
    END***CAR***;

    REF(CAR)JAG;
    JAG :- NEW CAR(1970, 1.2, 240, 2);
    JAG.BROKENDOWN := TRUE;

    !   CAR   !<--REF(CAR)JAG

    ! REGISTERED   1970 !
    ! WEIGHT   1.2 !
    ! MAXSPEED   240 !
    ! SEATS   2 !
    ! BROKENDOWN   TRUE !

    ! IF REGISTERED < 1885   !
    !   OR WEIGHT <= 0.0   !
    !   OR MAXSPEED < 50   !
    !   OR SEATS < 1 THEN error; !

```
2.4 CLASS BOAT(TONNAGE); INTEGER TONNAGE;
    BEGIN INTEGER LOAD, CREW;
      IF TONNAGE < 1000 THEN error;
      CREW := 5 + TONNAGE/200;
    END***BOAT***;

    REF(BOAT)B;

    B       :- NEW BOAT(2600);
    B.LOAD := 1600;
```

```
-------------------------------------
!              BOAT             !<--REF(BOAT)B
-------------------------------------
! TONNAGE                  2600 !
! LOAD                     1600 !
! CREW                       18 !
-------------------------------------
! IF TONNAGE < 1000 THEN error; !
! CREW := 5 + TONNAGE/200;      !
-------------------------------------
```

2.5 A straightforward example is one's address. When asked
    the question "Where do you live?", "No. 12" is an
    adequate answer if already on that particular street; "No.
    12, Main Street", if in one's home town, "No. 12 Main
    Street, Bingley" if out of town, etc., etc.

```
2.6 CLASS ORDER;
    BEGIN INTEGER NUMBER, ARRIVAL;
      REAL SETUP_TIME, PROCESSING_TIME;
    END***ORDER***;

    ORDER CLASS BATCH;
    BEGIN
      INTEGER SIZE;
    END***BATCH***;

    ORDER CLASS SINGLE;
    BEGIN
      REAL WEIGHT, FINISHING_TIME;
    END***SINGLE***;

    SINGLE CLASS PLATE;
    BEGIN
      REAL LENGTH, WIDTH;
    END***PLATE***;
```

2.7 There is, of course, a variety of 'solutions' to this
    problem depending upon what you have in mind.   A typical
    skeleton context could be

```
        CLASS HARBOUR;
        BEGIN
          CLASS CRANE.............;
          CLASS BOAT..............;
          BOAT CLASS CARGO........;
          BOAT CLASS PASSENGER....;
          BOAT CLASS TANKER.......;
          BOAT CLASS TUG..........;
          CLASS CONTAINER.........;
          CLASS TIDE..............;
          ........................
        END***HARBOUR***;
```

which we would use to prefix a user program thus

```
        HARBOUR
          BEGIN
            REF(CRANE)C1, C2;
            REF(TUG)T1, T2, T3;
            .................
          END;
```


CHAPTER 3
=========

3.1 The Macbeth analogy allows one player per role,   but in a
    play with a chorus we can have several actors with the
    same lines.

        In the world of music, only the conductor has the
    complete score for a symphony (which corresponds to a full
    DEMOS trace). Different part scores are produced for 1st.
    violins, 2nd. violins, etc. Each such score gives only
    the one part and a count of the bars when its players are
    silent (which corresponds to a 'HOLD'). Note that in this
    case, we have several players per role playing in unison.
    In simulation models, several objects may well have the
    same class declaration, but they can be executed at
    different speeds and start at different times.

3.2 TRACE

TIME	CUSTOMER	CURRENT ACTION	NEXT EVENT
0.0	C1	arrive	
	C1	request 1 barber	
	C1	seize 1 barber	
	C1	start haircut	15.0
15.0	C1	release 1 barber	
	C1	quit	****
20.0	C2	arrive	
	C2	request 1 barber	
	C2	seize 1 barber	
	C2	start haircut	35.0
35.0	C3	arrive	
	C3	request 1 barber	
	C2	release 1 barber	
	C2	quit	****
	C3	seize 1 barber	
	C3	start haircut	50.0
40.0	C4	arrive	
	C4	request 1 barber	
50.0	C3	release 1 barber	
	C3	quit	****
	C4	seize 1 barber	
	C4	start haircut	65.0
65.0	C4	release 1 barber	
	C4	quit	****

ACTIVITY DIAGRAM   CUSTOMER

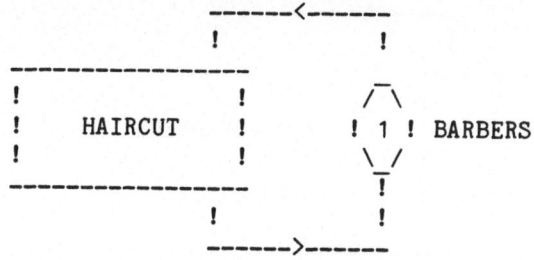

```
DECLARATION   CLASS CUSTOMER;
              BEGIN acquire 1 barber;
                get haircut;
                release 1 barber;
              END***CUSTOMER***;
```

3.3 TRACE

TIME	CUSTOMER	CURRENT ACTION	NEXT EVENT
0.0	C1	arrive	
	C1	request 1 barber	
	C1	seize 1 barber	
	C1	start haircut	15.0
15.0	C1	release 1 barber	
	C1	quit	****
20.0	C2	arrive	
	C2	request 1 barber	
	C2	seize 1 barber	
	C2	start haircut	35.0
35.0	C3	arrive	
	C3	request 1 barber	
	C3	seize 1 barber	
	C3	start haircut	50.0
	C2	release 1 barber	
	C2	quit	****
40.0	C4	arrive	
	C4	request 1 barber	
	C4	seize 1 barber	
	C4	start haircut	55.0
50.0	C3	release 1 barber	
	C3	quit	****
55.0	C4	release 1 barber	
	C4	quit	****

ACTIVITY DIAGRAM   CUSTOMER

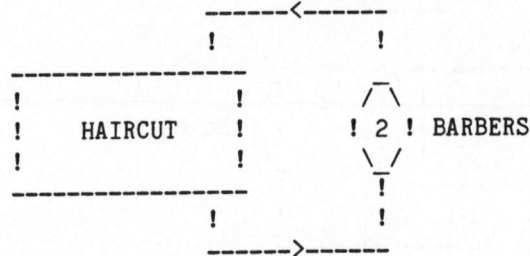

DECLARATION Exactly as in exercise 3.2 above.

3.4 TRACE

TIME	VAN	CURRENT ACTION	NEXT EVENT
0.0	V1	arrive	
	V1	request w'bridge	
	V1	seize w'bridge	3.0
	V1	start weighing	
1.0	V2	arrive	
	V2	request w'bridge	
3.0	V1	release w'bridge	
	V1	start unloading	23.0
	V2	seize w'bridge	
	V2	start weighing	6.0
6.0	V2	release w'bridge	
	V2	start unloading	26.0
23.0	V1	request w'bridge	
	V1	seize w'bridge	
	V1	start weighing	26.0
24.0	V3	arrive	
	V3	request w'bridge	
25.0	V4	arrive	
	V4	request w'bridge	
26.0	V2	request w'bridge	
	V1	release w'bridge	
	V1	quit	****
	V3	seize w'bridge	
	V3	start weighing	29.0
29.0	V3	release w'bridge	
	V3	start unloading	49.0
	V4	seize w'bridge	
	V4	start weighing	32.0
32.0	V4	release w'bridge	
	V4	start unloading	52.0
	V2	seize w'bridge	
	V2	start weighing	35.0
35.0	V2	release w'bridge	
	V2	quit	****

(V3 and V4 are currently unloading.)

```
DECLARATION  CLASS VAN;
             BEGIN acquire 1 w'bridge;
               weigh in;
               release 1 w'bridge;
               unload;
               acquire 1 w'bridge;
               weigh out;
               release 1 w'bridge;
             END***VAN***;
```

ACTIVITY DIAGRAM   VAN

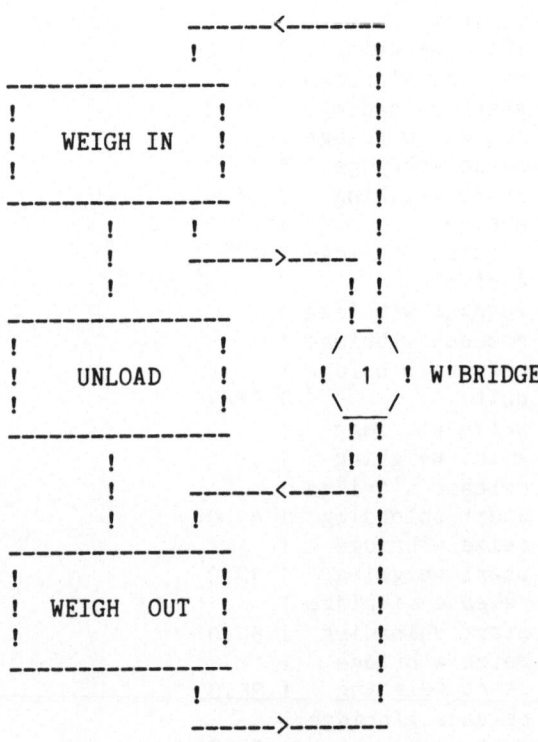

In our model, vans are served on the first-come, first-served principle (FCFS). See particularly at time = 26.0 when V3 heads the waiting queue for the weighbridge. V2 and V4 are also blocked at the weighbridge when V1 releases it. If vans moving out were given priority, V2 would be the next to acquire the weighbridge.

```
3.5 BEGIN EXTERNAL CLASS DEMOS;
      DEMOS
        BEGIN REF(RES)BARBERS;

          ENTITY CLASS CUSTOMER;
          BEGIN BARBERS.ACQUIRE(1);
            HOLD(15.0);
            BARBERS.RELEASE(1);
          END***CUSTOMER***;

          BARBERS :- NEW RES("BARBERS", 1);
          NEW CUSTOMER("C").SCHEDULE(0.0);
          NEW CUSTOMER("C").SCHEDULE(20.0);
          NEW CUSTOMER("C").SCHEDULE(35.0);
          NEW CUSTOMER("C").SCHEDULE(40.0);
          HOLD(65.0);
        END;
    END;

3.6 BEGIN EXTERNAL CLASS DEMOS;
      DEMOS
        BEGIN REF(RES)WEIGHBRIDGE;

          ENTITY CLASS VAN;
          BEGIN
          ENTER:
            WEIGHBRIDGE.ACQUIRE(1);
            HOLD(3.0);
            WEIGHBRIDGE.RELEASE(1);
          UNLOAD:
            HOLD(20.0);
          LEAVE:
            WEIGHBRIDGE.ACQUIRE(1);
            HOLD(3.0);
            WEIGHBRIDGE.RELEASE(1);
          END***VAN***;

          WEIGHBRIDGE :- NEW RES("W'BRIDGE", 1);
          NEW VAN("V").SCHEDULE(0.0);
          NEW VAN("V").SCHEDULE(1.0);
          NEW VAN("V").SCHEDULE(24.0);
          NEW VAN("V").SCHEDULE(25.0);
          HOLD(40.0);
        END;
    END;
```

```
3.7 TIME ! EVENT LIST                              ! W'BRIDGE
    --------------------------------------------------------
     0 ! D(0)                                      !
     0 ! D(0),V1(0)                                !
     0 ! D(0),V1(0),V2(1)                          !
     0 ! D(0),V1(0),V2(1),V3(24)                   !
     0 ! D(0),V1(0),V2(1),V3(24),V4(25)            !
     0 ! V1(0),V2(1),V3(24),V4(25),D(40)           !
     1 ! V2(1),V1(3),V3(24),V4(25),D(40)           !
     3 ! V1(3),V3(24),V4(25),D(40)                 ! V2
     3 ! V1(3),V2(3),V3(24),V4(25),D(40)           !
     3 ! V2(3),V1(23),V3(24),V4(25),D(40)          !
     6 ! V2(6),V1(23),V3(24),V4(25),D(40)          !
    23 ! V1(23),V3(24),V4(25),V2(26),D(40)         !
    24 ! V3(24),V4(25),V2(26),V1(26),D(40)         !
    25 ! V4(25),V2(26),V1(26),D(40)                ! V3
    26 ! V2(26),V1(26),D(40)                       ! V3,V4
    26 ! V1(26),D(40)                              ! V3,V4,V2
    26 ! V1(26),V3(26),D(40)                       ! V4,V2
    26 ! V3(26),D(40)                              ! V4,V2
    29 ! V3(29),D(40)                              ! V4,V2
    29 ! V3(29),V4(29),D(40)                       ! V2
    29 ! V4(29),D(40),V3(49)                       ! V2
    32 ! V4(32),D(40),V3(49)                       ! V2
    32 ! V4(32),V2(32),D(40),V3(49)                !
    32 ! V2(32),D(40),V3(49),V4(52)                !
    35 ! V2(35),D(40),V3(49),V4(52)                !
    40 ! D(40),V3(49),V4(52)                       !
    ..........................................
```

N.B. Here, space considerations have forced us tc represent event times by integers.

3.8 See example 2, page 40.

3.9 RANDOM CLASS NORMAL(MEAN, SIG); REAL MEAN, SIG;
    BEGIN
      REAL PROCEDURE SAMPLE;
      BEGIN REAL SUM; INTEGER K;
        FOR K := 1 STEP 1 UNTIL 12 DO
          SUM := SUM + NEXT;
        SAMPLE := MEAN + (SUM-6.0)*SIG;
      END***SAMPLE***;

      IF SIG < 0.0 THEN error;
    END***NORMAL***;

This algorithm is based upon the Central Limit Theorem. For better methods, see Fishman [33, p.128] or Shannon [37, p.362].

3.10 ACTIVITY DIAGRAM

```
        ---<---- ---->---
        !     !_!     !
-------------   / \    ------------------
! HAIR CUT !   ! 1 !   ! CUT AND SHAVE !
-------------   \_/    ------------------
        !     !_!     !
        --->---- ----<---


     C1         BARBERS        C2
```

```
DEMOS
  BEGIN REF(RES)BARBERS;
    REF(RDIST)C1, C2, S1, S2;

    ENTITY CLASS CUT;
    BEGIN NEW CUT("CUT").SCHEDULE(C1.SAMPLE);
      BARBERS.ACQUIRE(1);
      HOLD(S1.SAMPLE);
      BARBERS.RELEASE(1);
    END***CUT***;

    ENTITY CLASS BOTH;
    BEGIN NEW BOTH("BOTH").SCHEDULE(C2.SAMPLE);
      BARBERS.ACQUIRE(1);
      HOLD(S2.SAMPLE);
      BARBERS.RELEASE(1);
    END***BOTH***;

    READDIST(C1, "C1");  READDIST(C2, "C2");
    READDIST(S1, "S1");  READDIST(S2, "S2");
    BARBERS :- NEW RES("BARBERS", 1);
    NEW CUT("CUT").SCHEDULE(0.0);
    NEW BOTH("BOTH").SCHEDULE(10.0);
    HOLD(480.0);
  END;
```

```
***Input:
=========

C1  NEGEXP          0.025 C2  NEGEXP   0.01666667
S1  UNIFORM  12.0  24.0 S2  UNIFORM  20.0  36.0
```

3.11 ACTIVITY DIAGRAM

```
            ----<--- --->----
            !    ! !      !
    -----------   /‾\   -----------
    ! SERVE 1 !  ! 2 !  ! SERVE 2 !
    -----------   \_/   -----------
            !    ! !      !
            ---->--- ---<----


    MECH 1        CLERK        MECH 2
```

```
DEMOS
  BEGIN REF(RES)CLERK;
    REF(RDIST)NEXTM1, NEXTM2, SERVE1, SERVE2;

    ENTITY CLASS MECH1;
    BEGIN
      NEW MECH1("M1:").SCHEDULE(NEXTM1.SAMPLE);
      CLERK.ACQUIRE(1);
      HOLD(SERVE1.SAMPLE);
      CLERK.RELEASE(1);
    END***MECH1***;

    ENTITY CLASS MECH2;
    BEGIN
      NEW MECH2("M2:").SCHEDULE(NEXTM2.SAMPLE);
      CLERK.ACQUIRE(1);
      HOLD(SERVE2.SAMPLE);
      CLERK.RELEASE(1);
    END***MECH2***;

    READDIST(NEXTM1, "NEXT M1");
    READDIST(NEXTM2, "NEXT M2");
    READDIST(SERVE1, "SERVE 1");
    READDIST(SERVE2, "SERVE 2");
    CLERK :- NEW RES("CLERK", 2);
    NEW MECH1("M1:").SCHEDULE(0.0);
    NEW MECH2("M2:").SCHEDULE(0.0);
    HOLD(480.0*60.0);
  END;

***Input:
=========

NEXT M1  NEGEXP     0.005
NEXT M2  NEGEXP     0.008
```

```
SERVE 1  UNIFORM  100.0  200.0
SERVE 2  UNIFORM   75.0  150.0
```

Notice that this model is structurally identical to that of exercise 3.10.

3.12 ACTIVITY DIAGRAM

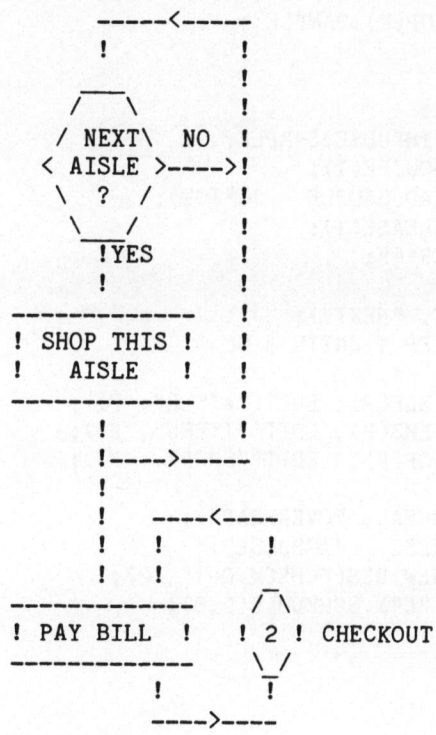

CUSTOMER

```
DEMOS
  BEGIN
    REF(RES)CHECKOUT;
    REF(RDIST)ARRAY SHOP(1:3);
    REF(BDIST)ARRAY AISLE(1:3);
    REF(IDIST)ARRAY ITEMS(1:3);
    REF(RDIST)NEXT, OVERHEAD;  INTEGER P;
    REF(IDIST)IMPULSE;
```

```
      ENTITY CLASS CUSTOMER;
      BEGIN INTEGER K, TOT;
        NEW CUSTOMER("C").SCHEDULE(NEXT.SAMPLE);
      DO_SHOPPING:
        FOR K := 1 STEP 1 UNTIL 3 DO
        BEGIN
          IF AISLE(K).SAMPLE THEN
          BEGIN TOT := TOT+ITEMS(K).SAMPLE;
            HOLD(SHOP(K).SAMPLE);
          END;
        END;
      PAY_AND_LEAVE:
        TOT := TOT+IMPULSE.SAMPLE;
        CHECKOUT.ACQUIRE(1);
        HOLD(OVERHEAD.SAMPLE + 10*TOT);
        CHECKOUT.RELEASE(1);
      END***CUSTOMER***;

      READDIST(NEXT, "NEXT");
      FOR P := 1 STEP 1 UNTIL 3 DO
      BEGIN
        READDIST(AISLE(P), EDIT("AISLE", P));
        READDIST(ITEMS(P), EDIT("ITEMS", P));
        READDIST(SHOP(P),  EDIT("SHOP",  P));
      END;
      READDIST(OVERHEAD, "OVERHEAD");
      READDIST(IMPULSE,  "IMPULSE");
      CHECKOUT :- NEW RES("CHECK OUT", 2);
      NEW CUSTOMER("C").SCHEDULE(0.0);
      HOLD(8*3600);
    END;

***Input:
=========

NEXT      NEGEXP    0.01
AISLE 1   DRAW      0.75
ITEMS 1   RANDINT   2       4
SHOP  1   UNIFORM   60.0   180.0
AISLE 2   DRAW      0.55
ITEMS 2   RANDINT   3       5
SHOP  2   UNIFORM   120.0  190.0
AISLE 3   DRAW      0.82
ITEMS 3   RANDINT   6       8
SHOP  3   UNIFORM   75.0   165.0
OVERHEAD  UNIFORM   15.0    35.0
IMPULSE   RANDINT   1       3
```

3.13 First cut off the arrival stream by an 'IF ... THEN'
      test. CLASS PATIENT becomes

```
ENTITY CLASS PATIENT;
BEGIN
  IF TIME <= 630.0 THEN
  BEGIN NEW PATIENT("P").SCHEDULE(next);
    DOCTOR.ACQUIRE(1);
    HOLD(consultation);
    DOCTOR.RELEASE(1);
  END;
END***PATIENT***;
```

Each patient thus checks for himself whether or not the
door is closed (TIME <= 10.30 o'clock). The first arrival
after that time exits at once and no further patients are
generated. To make sure that the doctor sees all the
patients, we can queue the DEMOS block itself behind the
last patient (if any) by replacing the statement
HOLD(90.0) in the DEMOS block by

```
HOLD(90.0);
DOCTOR.ACQUIRE(1);
```

When the DEMOS block is re-entered, all waiting patients
have been consulted.

3.14 In this situation, we cannot allow the n'th. patient
      object to generate patient the n+1'st. regardless. A
      simple, yet powerful, way out is to declare a completely
      separate object whose sole purpose is to generate patient
      objects, and remove the generating statement 'NEW
      PATIENT...' from the body of CLASS PATIENT. The new
      entity declaration is:

```
ENTITY CLASS GEN;
BEGIN HOLD(next);
  NEW PATIENT("P").SCHEDULE(0.0);
  REPEAT;
END***GEN***;
```

We also alter CLASS PATIENT by deleting

```
NEW PATIENT("P").SCHEDULE(next);
```

and the statement generating the first patient object (in
the DEMOS block) is replaced by

```
        FOR K := 1 STEP 1 UNTIL n DO              [INTEGER K;]
          NEW PATIENT("P").SCHEDULE(0.0);
        NEW GEN("G").SCHEDULE(0.0);
```

3.15
```
    Exercise 3.10
      C1        :- NEW NEGEXP("C1", 0.025);
      C2        :- NEW NEGEXP("C2", 0.01666667);
      S1        :- NEW UNIFORM("S1", 12.0, 24.0);
      S2        :- NEW UNIFORM("S2", 20.0, 36.0);
    Exercise 3.11
      NEXTM1    :- NEW NEGEXP("NEXTM1", 0.005);
      NEXTM2    :- NEW NEGEXP("NEXTM2", 0.008);
      SERVE1    :- NEW UNIFORM("SERVE1", 200.0, 400.0);
      SERVE2    :- NEW UNIFORM("SERVE2",  75.0, 150.0);
    Exercise 3.12
      NEXT      :- NEW NEGEXP("NEXT", 0.0125);
      AISLE(1)  :- NEW DRAW("AISLE 1", 0.75);
      AISLE(2)  :- NEW DRAW("AISLE 2", 0.55);
      AISLE(3)  :- NEW DRAW("AISLE 3", 0.82);
      ITEMS(1)  :- NEW RANDINT("ITEMS 1", 2, 4);
      ITEMS(2)  :- NEW RANDINT("ITEMS 2", 3, 5);
      ITEMS(3)  :- NEW RANDINT("ITEMS 3", 6, 8);
      SHOP(1)   :- NEW UNIFORM("SHOP 1",  60.0, 180.0);
      SHOP(2)   :- NEW UNIFORM("SHOP 2", 120.0, 180.0);
      SHOP(3)   :- NEW UNIFORM("SHOP 3",  75.0, 165.0);
      OVERHEAD  :- NEW UNIFORM("OVERHEAD",15.0,  35.0);
      IMPULSE   :- NEW RANDINT("IMPULSE", 1, 3);
```

CHAPTER 4
=========

4.1 DEMOS
```
    BEGIN INTEGER K;
      REF(RES)OVEN;
      REF(RDIST)ASSEMBLY, FIRE;
      REF(COUNT)WIDGETS;

      ENTITY CLASS ASSEMBLER;
      BEGIN HOLD(ASSEMBLY.SAMPLE);
        OVEN.ACQUIRE(1);
        HOLD(FIRE.SAMPLE);
        OVEN.RELEASE(1);
        WIDGETS.UPDATE(1);
        REPEAT;
      END***ASSEMBLER***;
```

```
      ASSEMBLY :- NEW UNIFORM("ASSEMBLY", 25.0, 35.0);
      FIRE     :- NEW NORMAL("FIRE", 8, 2);
      WIDGETS  :- NEW COUNT("WIDGETS");
      OVEN     :- NEW RES("OVEN", 1);
      FOR K := 1 STEP 1 UNTIL 3 DO
        NEW ASSEMBLER("ASSEMBLER").SCHEDULE(0.0);
      HOLD(40.0*60.0);
    END;

4.2 DEMOS
    BEGIN
      REF(RES)CRANE;  REF(COUNT)JOBS;
      REF(RDIST)LOAD, POLISH1, REPOS, POLISH2,
                REMOVE, NEXT, USE;

      ENTITY CLASS MACHINE;
      BEGIN
        CRANE.ACQUIRE(1);
      LOOP: FETCH_AND_LIFT:
        HOLD(LOAD.SAMPLE);
        CRANE.RELEASE(1);
      POLISH:
        HOLD(POLISH1.SAMPLE);
      RE_POSITION:
        CRANE.ACQUIRE(1);
        HOLD(REPOS.SAMPLE);
        CRANE.RELEASE(1);
      RE_POLISH:
        HOLD(POLISH2.SAMPLE);
      REMOVE_AND_STORE:
        CRANE.ACQUIRE(1);
        HOLD(REMOVE.SAMPLE);
        JOBS.UPDATE(1);
        REPEAT;
      END***MACHINE***;

      ENTITY CLASS OTHER;
      BEGIN
        NEW OTHER("OTHER").SCHEDULE(NEXT.SAMPLE);
        CRANE.ACQUIRE(1);
        HOLD(USE.SAMPLE);
        CRANE.RELEASE(1);
      END***OTHER***;

      CRANE   :- NEW RES("CRANE", 1);
      JOBS    :- NEW COUNT("JOBS DONE");
      LOAD    :- NEW UNIFORM("LOAD",  15.0, 29.0);
```

```
      POLISH1 :-  NEW UNIFORM("POLISH 1", 60.0, 100.0);
      REPOS   :-  NEW UNIFORM("REPOS", 8.0, 22.0);
      POLISH2 :-  NEW UNIFORM("POLISH 2", 80.0, 140.0);
      REMOVE  :-  NEW UNIFORM("REMOVE", 15.0, 30.0);
      NEXT    :-  NEW NEGEXP("NEXT O'JOB", 0.020);
      USE     :-  NEW NORMAL("USE", 25.0, 5.0);
      NEW OTHER("OTHER").SCHEDULE(20.0);
      NEW MACHINE("M").SCHEDULE(0.0);
      HOLD(24000.0);
    END;
```

Notice how we let the machine retain the crane through the remove and then the fetch and lift phases.

4.3 DEMOS

```
    BEGIN
      REF(RES)ADJUSTERS, INSPECTORS;
      REF(RDIST)NEXT, INSPECTION, READJUST;
      REF(BDIST)FAULTY;

      ENTITY CLASS TVSET;
      BEGIN
        NEW TVSET("TV").SCHEDULE(NEXT.SAMPLE);
      LOOP:
        INSPECTORS.ACQUIRE(1);
        HOLD(INSPECTION.SAMPLE);
        INSPECTORS.RELEASE(1);
      TEST_FOR_FAULT:
        IF FAULTY.SAMPLE THEN
        BEGIN
          ADJUSTERS.ACQUIRE(1);
          HOLD(READJUST.SAMPLE);
          ADJUSTERS.RELEASE(1);
          PRIORITY := PRIORITY + 1;
          REPEAT;
        END;
      END***TVSET***;

      ADJUSTERS   :- NEW RES("ADJUSTERS", 1);
      INSPECTORS  :- NEW RES("INSPECTORS", 2);
      NEXT        :- NEW NEGEXP("NEXT", 0.2);
      INSPECTION  :- NEW UNIFORM("INSPECTION", 6.0, 10.0);
      FAULTY      :- NEW DRAW("FAULTY", 0.10);
      READJUST    :- NEW NORMAL("READJUST", 30.0, 5.0);
      NEW TVSET("TVSET").SCHEDULE(0.0);
      HOLD(5*8*60);
    END;
```

The staging spaces may be roughly estimated from the QMAX
value reported for the RES objects.

4.4 DEMOS

```
    BEGIN REF(RES)WS1, WS2, SP2;
      REF(RDIST)ARRIVALS, STRIP, REBUILD;
      REF(COUNT)SUB; INTEGER L1, K;

      ENTITY CLASS UNIT;
      BEGIN
        IF L1=4 THEN SUB.UPDATE(1) ELSE
        BEGIN
        STRIPPING:
          L1 := L1+1;
          WS1.ACQUIRE(1);
          L1 := L1-1;
          HOLD(STRIP.SAMPLE);
        GET_WORK_SPACE_2:
          SP2.ACQUIRE(1);
          WS1.RELEASE(1);
          HOLD(IF SP2.AVAIL=1 THEN 0.2 ELSE 0.1);
        RE_BUILD:
          WS2.ACQUIRE(1);
          SP2.RELEASE(1);
          HOLD(REBUILD.SAMPLE);
          WS2.RELEASE(1);
        END;
      END***UNIT***;

      ENTITY CLASS NEXT;
      BEGIN NEW UNIT("UNIT").SCHEDULE(0.0);
        HOLD(ARRIVALS.SAMPLE);
        REPEAT;
      END***NEXT***;

      ARRIVALS :- NEW NEGEXP("ARR", 4.0);
      STRIP    :- NEW NORMAL("STRIP", 0.50, 0.05);
      REBUILD  :- NEW NORMAL("BUILD", 0.25, 0.1);
      WS1      :- NEW RES("WORK ST. 1", 2);
      WS2      :- NEW RES("WORK ST. 2", 1);
      SP2      :- NEW RES("AREA 2", 2);
      SUB      :- NEW COUNT("SUBCONTRACTS");
      FOR  K := 1 STEP 1 UNTIL 2 DO
        NEW UNIT("UNIT").SCHEDULE(0.0);
      NEW NEXT("NEXT").SCHEDULE(0.5);
      HOLD(136.0);
    END;
```

4.5 To stop the simulation run at the appropriate time, replace the HOLD(136.0) in the DEMOS block by

```
HOLD(134.0);
WS1.ACQUIRE(2);
SP2.ACQUIRE(2);
WS2.ACQUIRE(1);
```

Any units arriving after time 134.0 will be blocked requesting WS1.

4.6 DEMOS

```
   BEGIN REF(RES)ARRAY SERVER(1:5);
     REF(RDIST)ARR, SERVE;
     REF(COUNT)AGAIN, DONE;
     INTEGER K;

     ENTITY CLASS ITEM;
     BEGIN INTEGER K;
       NEW ITEM("ITEM").SCHEDULE(ARR.SAMPLE);
     LOOP:
       FOR K := 1 STEP 1 UNTIL 5 DO
       BEGIN
         HOLD(1.0);
         IF SERVER(K).AVAIL = 1 THEN
         BEGIN
           SERVER(K).ACQUIRE(1);
           HOLD(SERVE.SAMPLE);
           SERVER(K).RELEASE(1);
           DONE.UPDATE(1);
           GOTO L;
         END;
       END;
       HOLD(4.0);
       AGAIN.UPDATE(1);
       REPEAT;
   L:END***ITEM***;

     ARR   :- NEW NEGEXP("ARRIVALS", 4.0);
     SERVE :- NEW UNIFORM("SERVICE", 0.8, 1.2);
     AGAIN :- NEW COUNT("RE-CYCLES");
     DONE  :- NEW COUNT("ITEMS DONE");
     FOR K := 1 STEP 1 UNTIL 5 DO
       SERVER(K) :- NEW RES(EDIT("SERVER",K),1);
     NEW ITEM("ITEM").SCHEDULE(0.0);
     HOLD(480.0);
   END;
```

4.7 As in Exercise 4.6 above, except delete all references
    to the COUNT 'AGAIN' and alter the declaration of CLASS
    ITEM to

```
        ENTITY CLASS ITEM;
        BEGIN INTEGER K;
           NEW ITEM("ITEM").SCHEDULE(ARR.SAMPLE);
           FOR K := 1 STEP 1 UNTIL 4 DO
           BEGIN
             HOLD(1.0);
             IF SERVER(K).AVAIL = 1 THEN
             BEGIN SERVER(K).ACQUIRE(1);
               HOLD(SERVE.SAMPLE);
               SERVER(K).RELEASE(1);
               GOTO L;
             END;
           END;
           HOLD(1.0);
           SERVER(5).ACQUIRE(1);
           HOLD(SERVE.SAMPLE);
           SERVER(5).RELEASE(1);
         L:DONE.UPDATE(1);
        END***ITEM***;
```

The storage space required in front of server 5 can be
roughly estimated from the QMAX statistic of the
corresponding RES object. By declaring an appropriate
procedure local to CLASS ITEM, the declaration can be made
neater

```
        ENTITY CLASS ITEM;
        BEGIN INTEGER K;
          PROCEDURE SERVICE(N); INTEGER N;
          BEGIN SERVER(N).ACQUIRE(1);
            HOLD(SERVE.SAMPLE);
            SERVER(N).RELEASE(1);
            GOTO L;
          END***SERVICE***;

          NEW ITEM("ITEM").SCHEDULE(ARR.SAMPLE);
          FOR K := 1 STEP 1 UNTIL 4 DO
            IF SERVER(K).AVAIL THEN SERVICE(K);
          SERVICE(5);
        L:DONE.UPDATE(1);
        END***ITEM***;
```

4.8 DEMOS

```
    BEGIN REF(BIN)BOGIES;
      REF(RES)MILLS, PITS, CRANES;

      ENTITY CLASS FURNACE;
      BEGIN
        HOLD(heat billet time);
        BOGIES.TAKE(1);
        NEW BILLET("BILLET").SCHEDULE(0.0);
        REPEAT;
      END***FURNACE***;

      ENTITY CLASS BILLET;
      BEGIN
      UNLOAD:
        CRANES.ACQUIRE(1);
        IF PITS.AVAIL = 0 THEN
        BEGIN
        NO_PITS_FREE:
          HOLD(unload from bogie time);
          CRANES.RELEASE(1);
          BOGIES.GIVE(1);
        AWAIT_PIT:
          PITS.ACQUIRE(1); CRANES.ACQUIRE(1);
          HOLD(load into pit time);
          CRANES.RELEASE(1);
        END ELSE
        BEGIN
        STRAIGHT_IN:
          PITS.ACQUIRE(1);
          HOLD(from bogie into pit time);
          CRANES.RELEASE(1); BOGIES.GIVE(1);
        END;
      SOAKING:
        HOLD(soak time);
      ROLLING:
        MILLS.ACQUIRE(1); CRANES.ACQUIRE(1);
        HOLD(unload from pit time);
        CRANES.RELEASE(1); PITS.RELEASE(1);
        HOLD(roll time);
        MILLS.RELEASE(1);
      END***BILLET***;

      CRANES :- NEW RES("CRANES", 2);
      MILLS  :- NEW RES("MILLS",  1);
      PITS   :- NEW RES("PITS",  12);
      BOGIES :- NEW BIN("BOGIES", 9);
```

```
      NEW FURNACE("FURNACE").SCHEDULE(0.0);
      HOLD(simulation period);
    END;

4.9 DEMOS
    BEGIN REF(COUNT)DONE;  INTEGER K;
      REF(BIN)ASSEMBLED, GREASED, PACKED, INNERS, OUTERS;
      REF(RDIST)NEXTI, NEXTO, ASSEMBLE, GREASE, PACK;

      ENTITY CLASS IRING;
      BEGIN INNERS.GIVE(1);
        HOLD(NEXTI.SAMPLE);
        REPEAT;
      END***IRING***;

      ENTITY CLASS ORING;
      BEGIN OUTERS.GIVE(1);
        HOLD(NEXTO.SAMPLE);
        REPEAT;
      END***OUTER RINGS***;

      ENTITY CLASS ASSEMBLER;
      BEGIN INNERS.TAKE(1);  OUTERS.TAKE(1);
        HOLD(ASSEMBLE.SAMPLE);
        ASSEMBLED.GIVE(1);
        REPEAT;
      END***ASSEMBLER***;

      ENTITY CLASS GREASER;
      BEGIN ASSEMBLED.TAKE(1);
        HOLD(GREASE.SAMPLE);
        GREASED.GIVE(1);
        REPEAT;
      END***GREASER***;

      ENTITY CLASS PACKER;
      BEGIN GREASED.TAKE(2);
        HOLD(PACK.SAMPLE);
        DONE.UPDATE(1);
        REPEAT;
      END***PACKER***;

      ASSEMBLED :-  NEW BIN("ASSEMBLED", 0);
      GREASED   :-  NEW BIN("GREASED",   0);
      PACKED    :-  NEW BIN("PACKED",    0);
      INNERS    :-  NEW BIN("INNERS",   10);
      OUTERS    :-  NEW BIN("OUTERS",   10);
```

```
DONE       :-  NEW COUNT("JOBS DONE");
NEXTI      :-  NEW NEGEXP("INNER", 6.0);
NEXTO      :-  NEW NEGEXP("OUTER", 6.0);
ASSEMBLE   :-  NEW NORMAL("ASSEMBLE", 0.5, 0.1);
GREASE     :-  NEW CONSTANT("GREASE", 0.16);
PACK       :-  NEW NORMAL("PACK", 0.6, 0.1);

NEW IRING("I-RING").SCHEDULE(0.0);
NEW ORING("O-RING").SCHEDULE(0.0);

FOR K := 1 STEP 1 UNTIL 3 DO
  NEW ASSEMBLER("ASSEMBLER").SCHEDULE(0.0);
NEW GREASER("GREASER").SCHEDULE(0.0);
FOR K := 1 STEP 1 UNTIL 2 DO
  NEW PACKER("PACKER").SCHEDULE(0.0);
  HOLD(480.0);
END;
```

4.10 DEMOS

```
BEGIN REF(BIN)FAULTY, GOOD;  INTEGER K;
  REF(RDIST)RUN, REPAIR, OTHER;

  ENTITY CLASS OPERATOR;
  BEGIN      HOLD(0.4);
             FAULTY.GIVE(1);
  REPLACE:   GOOD.TAKE(1);
             HOLD(0.4);
  OK_TO_RUN:HOLD(RUN.SAMPLE);
             REPEAT;
  END***OPERATOR***;

  ENTITY CLASS REPAIRMAN;
  BEGIN
  DO_REPAIRS:
    WHILE FAULTY.AVAIL > 0 DO
    BEGIN FAULTY.TAKE(1);
      HOLD(REPAIR.SAMPLE);
      GOOD.GIVE(1);
    END;
  OTHER_WORK:
    HOLD(OTHER.SAMPLE);
    REPEAT;
  END***REPAIR***;

  RUN    :- NEW NORMAL("RUN", 36.0, 7.0);
  REPAIR :- NEW NORMAL("REPAIR", 2.0, 0.5);
  OTHER  :- NEW UNIFORM("OTHER", 0.5, 1.5);
```

```
      FAULTY :- NEW BIN("FAULTY", 1);
      GOOD   :- NEW BIN("GOOD", 0);
      FOR K := 1 STEP 1 UNTIL 3 DO
        NEW OPERATOR("O").SCHEDULE((2*K-1)*RUN.SAMPLE/6);
      NEW REPAIRMAN("R").SCHEDULE(0.0);
      HOLD(672.0);
    END;
```

4.11   a) INFINITE BUFFER
            ====================

```
DEMOS
  BEGIN REF(RES)ACCESS;  REF(BIN)MESSAGES;
    REF(RDIST)NEXTM, DECODE;

    ENTITY CLASS SENDER;
    BEGIN HOLD(NEXTM.SAMPLE);
      ACCESS.ACQUIRE(1);
      HOLD(0.05);
      ACCESS.RELEASE(1);
      MESSAGES.GIVE(1);
      REPEAT;
    END***SENDER***;

    ENTITY CLASS RECEIVER;
    BEGIN MESSAGES.TAKE(1);
      ACCESS.ACQUIRE(1);
      HOLD(0.05);
      ACCESS.RELEASE(1);
      HOLD(DECODE.SAMPLE);
      REPEAT;
    END***RECEIVER***;

    NEXTM     :- NEW NEGEXP("NEXTM", 1.0);
    DECODE    :- NEW UNIFORM("DECODE", 0.6, 1.4);
    ACCESS    :- NEW RES("ACCESS", 1);
    MESSAGES :- NEW BIN("MESSAGES",0);
    NEW SENDER("S").SCHEDULE(0.0);
    NEW RECEIVER("R").SCHEDULE(0.0);
    HOLD(100.0);
  END;
```

            b) BUFFER OF CAPACITY L
            ========================

In a) above, ACCESS is used to guarantee single access to
the buffer slots, and MESSAGES holds the number of

messages sent by S but not yet extracted by R. In b), S
may not be more than L slots ahead of R or else it starts
overwriting a previous message. This can be controlled by
a further BIN 'LEAD' which is used to block S should R be
L messages behind. To a) we add the declaration
REF(BIN)LEAD; and the initialising statement

```
    LEAD :- NEW BIN("LEAD", L);
```

The synchronisation is completed by altering the sequence

```
    HOLD(NEXTM.SAMPLE);
    ACCESS.ACQUIRE(1);
```

in CLASS SENDER to

```
    HOLD(NEXTM.SAMPLE);
    LEAD.TAKE(1);
    ACCESS.ACQUIRE(1);
```

which makes sure that S is not too far ahead before
attempting to place the next message in the buffer; and by
altering the sequence

```
    ACCESS.RELEASE(1);
```

inside CLASS RECEIVER to

```
    ACCESS.RELEASE(1);
    LEAD.GIVE(1);
```

This lets S know each time a slot has been freed.   We
must, of course, also declare and initialise L or else use
a constant.

4.12 DEMOS

```
    BEGIN INTEGER WEEK, DAY, K, N; REAL T;
    REF(RES)BAYS;
    REF(RDIST)PSERVICE,CSERVICE,NEXTP; REF(IDIST)GROUP;

    ENTITY CLASS PCAR;
    BEGIN PRIORITY := 1;
      NEW PCAR("P").SCHEDULE(NEXTP.SAMPLE);
      BAYS.ACQUIRE(1);
      HOLD(PSERVICE.SAMPLE);
      BAYS.RELEASE(1);
    END***POLICE CAR***;
```

```
ENTITY CLASS CAR;
BEGIN BAYS.ACQUIRE(1);
  HOLD(CSERVICE.SAMPLE);
  BAYS.RELEASE(1);
END***CAR***;


BAYS     :- NEW RES("BAYS", 5);
PSERVICE :- NEW NORMAL("PSERVICE", 2.5, 1.0);
NEXTP    :- NEW NEGEXP("NEXT P", 0.08333333);
GROUP    :- NEW RANDINT("GROUP", 12, 20);
CSERVICE :- NEW UNIFORM("CSERVICE", 1.5, 2.5);

DEMOS.PRIORITY := 2;
BAYS.ACQUIRE(5);
NEW PCAR("P").SCHEDULE(NEXTP.SAMPLE);

FOR WEEK := 1 STEP 1 UNTIL 4 DO
BEGIN
WEEKDAY:
  FOR DAY := 1 STEP 1 UNTIL 5 DO
  BEGIN HOLD(9.0);
    N := GROUP.SAMPLE;
    FOR K := 1 STEP 1 UNTIL N DO
      NEW CAR("C").SCHEDULE(0.0);
    BAYS.RELEASE(5);
    HOLD(8.0);
    T := TIME;
    BAYS.ACQUIRE(5);
    HOLD(7.0-(TIME-T));
  END;
SATURDAY:
  HOLD(9.0);
  N := GROUP.SAMPLE/2;
  FOR K := 1 STEP 1 UNTIL N DO
    NEW CAR("C").SCHEDULE(0.0);
  BAYS.RELEASE(5);
  HOLD(4.0);
  T := TIME;
  DEMOS.PRIORITY := 0;
  BAYS.ACQUIRE(5);
  DEMOS.PRIORITY := 2;
  HOLD(11.0-(TIME-T));
SUNDAY:
  HOLD(24.0);
END;
END;
```

CHAPTER 5
=========

5.1 DEMOS

```
    BEGIN REF(WAITQ)DESK;  INTEGER P;
      REF(RDIST)NEXTR, THERE, BACK, ST;
      REF(HISTOGRAM)THRU;

      ENTITY CLASS LIBRARIAN(N); INTEGER N;
      BEGIN INTEGER K, R; REF(QUEUE)Q;
        REF(ENTITY)C; REF(COUNT)SLIPS;
        Q     :- NEW QUEUE(EDIT("Q", N));
        SLIPS :- NEW COUNT(EDIT("SLIPS", N));
      LOOP: C :- DESK.COOPT;  R := 1;
        C.INTO(Q);
        HOLD(0.1);
      ANY_MORE:
        WHILE DESK.LENGTH > 0 AND R < 5 DO
        BEGIN C :- DESK.COOPT;  R := R + 1;
          C.INTO(Q);
          HOLD(0.1);
        END;
        SLIPS.UPDATE(R);
      GET_REQUESTS:
        HOLD(THERE.SAMPLE);
        HOLD(R*(1.0+ST.SAMPLE/5.0));
        HOLD(BACK.SAMPLE);
      SIGN_OUT:
        WHILE Q.LENGTH > 0 DO
        BEGIN HOLD(0.5);
          Q.FIRST.SCHEDULE(0.0);
        END;
        REPEAT;
      END***LIBRARIAN***;

      ENTITY CLASS REQUEST;
      BEGIN REAL ARRTIME;
       ARRTIME := TIME;
       NEW REQUEST("R").SCHEDULE(NEXTR.SAMPLE);
       DESK.WAIT;

      QUIT:
       THRU.UPDATE(TIME-ARRTIME);
      END***REQUEST***;

      NEXTR :- NEW NEGEXP("NEXT R", 0.5);
      THERE :- NEW UNIFORM("THERE", 0.5, 1.5);
```

```
    ST    :- NEW NORMAL("ST", 0.0, 1.0);
    BACK  :- NEW UNIFORM("BACK", 0.5, 2.0);
    DESK  :- NEW WAITQ("DESK");
    THRU  :- NEW HISTOGRAM("THRU",0,3,10);
    FOR P := 1 STEP 1 UNTIL 3 DO
      NEW LIBRARIAN("L", P).SCHEDULE(0.0);
    NEW REQUEST("R").SCHEDULE(0.0);
    HOLD(480.0);
  END;
```

5.2 The essence is to allow only one librarian to be attending
    to the desk queue at once. In our solution to Exercise
    5.1 whilst one librarian is signing in a request, another
    may poach the next in line. This we can avoid by using a
    RES   object   ACCESS   of   limit   1   and   inserting
    ACCESS.ACQUIRE(1)   after   the   label   LOOP   and
    ACCESS.RELEASE(1)   immediately   before   the   label
    GET_REQUESTS in the body of CLASS LIBRARIAN.

5.3 DEMOS

```
    BEGIN
      REF(RDIST)SMELT, STRIP, CLEAN_ASS, SOAK;
      REF(RES)PITS, CRANES, MILLS;
      REF(BIN)BOGIES;
      REF(WAITQ)STRIPQ;
      INTEGER K;

      ENTITY CLASS FURNACE;
      BEGIN INTEGER P;
      LOAD_AND_SMELT:
        HOLD(SMELT.SAMPLE);
      POUR:
        FOR P := 1 STEP 1 UNTIL 2 DO
        BEGIN BOGIES.TAKE(1);
          HOLD(20.0);
          NEW BATCH("B").SCHEDULE(0.0);
        END;
        REPEAT;
      END***FURNACE***;

      ENTITY CLASS STRIPPERS;
      BEGIN
        REF(BATCH)B;
      AWAIT_BATCH:
        B :- STRIPQ.COOPT;
        HOLD(STRIP.SAMPLE);
        B.SCHEDULE(0.0);
```

```
     CLEAN_AND_RE_ASSEMBLE:
       HOLD(CLEAN_ASS.SAMPLE);
       BOGIES.GIVE(1);
       REPEAT;
     END***STRIPPERS***;

     ENTITY CLASS BATCH;
     BEGIN
       HOLD(75.0);
       STRIPQ.WAIT;
     LOAD:
       PITS.ACQUIRE(1);  CRANES.ACQUIRE(1);
       HOLD(15.0);
       CRANES.RELEASE(1);
     SOAKING:
       HOLD(SOAK.SAMPLE);
     UNLOAD_15_AND_ROLL_14:
       MILLS.ACQUIRE(1);  CRANES.ACQUIRE(1);
       HOLD(1.0 + 14*3.0);
       CRANES.RELEASE(1);
       PITS.RELEASE(1);
     ROLL_THE_LAST:
       HOLD(3.0);
       MILLS.RELEASE(1);
     END***BATCH***;

     SMELT     :- NEW NORMAL("SMELT", 165.0, 20.0);
     STRIP     :- NEW UNIFORM("STRIP", 10.0, 16.0);
     CLEAN_ASS :- NEW UNIFORM("CLEAN ASS", 20.0, 24.0);
     SOAK      :- NEW NORMAL("SOAK", 160.0, 30.0);
     PITS      :- NEW RES("PITS",  10);
     CRANES    :- NEW RES("CRANES", 3);
     MILLS     :- NEW RES("MILLS",  2);
     BOGIES    :- NEW BIN("BOGIES", 8);
     STRIPQ    :- NEW WAITQ("AWAIT STRIP");

     FOR K := 1 STEP 1 UNTIL 4 DO
       NEW FURNACE("F").SCHEDULE(40*(K-1));

     FOR K := 1 STEP 1 UNTIL 2 DO
       NEW STRIPPERS("S").SCHEDULE(0.0);

     HOLD(1500.0);
   END;

5.4 REF(RES)POWER, BRICKIES, C1, C2;
   REF(BIN)BOGIES;
```

```
    ENTITY CLASS FURNACE;
    BEGIN INTEGER K;
      FOR K := 1 STEP 1 UNTIL 10 DO
      BEGIN
      LOAD:
        C1.ACQUIRE(1);
        HOLD(load);
        C1.RELEASE(1);
      MELT:
        POWER.ACQUIRE(3);
        HOLD(melt);
        POWER.RELEASE(2);
      REFINE:
        HOLD(refine);
      TAP:
        BOGIES.TAKE(1);  C2.ACQUIRE(1);
        HOLD(tap);
        NEW BATCH("B").SCHEDULE(0.0).
        C2.RELEASE(1); POWER.RELEASE(1);
      END;
    CLEAN:
      BRICKIES.ACQUIRE(1);
      HOLD(clean);
      BRICKIES.RELEASE(1);
      REPEAT;
    END***FURNACE***;

5.5 DEMOS
    BEGIN REF(WAITQ)Q1, Q2;  REF(RES)TRUNKS;
      REF(COUNT)CALLS, ACCEPTED, REJ, COMPLETED,
                OVERFLOWS, DIRECT, INDIRECT;
      REF(RDIST)ARR, NOTES, ADVERT;
      REF(HISTOGRAM)WAITTIMES, THRUTIMES;

      ENTITY CLASS CALL;
      BEGIN REAL ARRTIME;
        NEW CALL("CALL").SCHEDULE(ARR.SAMPLE);
        ARRTIME := TIME;
        CALLS.UPDATE(1);
        IF TRUNKS.AVAIL=0 THEN REJ.UPDATE(1)ELSE
        IF Q1.LENGTH=K THEN OVERFLOWS.UPDATE(1)ELSE
        BEGIN ACCEPTED.UPDATE(1);
          TRUNKS.ACQUIRE(1);
          IF Q2.MASTERQ.LENGTH > 0 THEN
          BEGIN DIRECT.UPDATE(1);
           Q2.WAIT;
          END ELSE
```

```
     BEGIN INDIRECT.UPDATE(1);
      IF Q2.LENGTH=0 THEN Q2.WAIT ELSE Q1.WAIT;
     END;
   AWAIT_END_OF_CONVERSATION:
     TRUNKS.RELEASE(1);
     THRUTIMES.UPDATE(TIME-ARRTIME);
     COMPLETED.UPDATE(1);
   END;
END***CALL***;

ENTITY CLASS OPERATOR;
BEGIN REF(CALL)C;
  C :- Q2.COOPT;
  IF Q2.LENGTH = 0 THEN Q1INTOQ2;
  WAITTIMES.UPDATE(TIME-C.ARRTIME);
  HOLD(ADVERT.SAMPLE);
  C.SCHEDULE(0.0);
  HOLD(NOTES.SAMPLE);
  REPEAT;
END***OPERATOR***;

PROCEDURE Q1INTOQ2;
BEGIN REF(ENTITY)C;
  WHILE Q1LENGTH > 0 DO
  BEGIN C :- Q1.FIRST;
    C.OUT;  C.INTO(Q2);
  END;
END***Q1 INTO Q2***;

INTEGER K, M, N, J;

K := 9;  M := 6;  N := 15;
ARR       :-  NEW NEGEXP("ARR", 1.0);
NOTES     :-  NEW NORMAL("NOTES", 4.0, 1.0);
ADVERT    :-  NEW NORMAL("ADVERT", 1.25, 0.5);
CALLS     :-  NEW COUNT("CALLS");
REJ       :-  NEW COUNT("REJ");
OVERFLOWS :-  NEW COUNT("OVERFLOWS");
COMPLETED :-  NEW COUNT("COMPLETED");
DIRECT    :-  NEW COUNT("DIRECT");
INDIRECT  :-  NEW COUNT("INDIRECT");
ACCEPTED  :-  NEW COUNT("ACCEPTED");
WAITTIMES :-  NEW HISTOGRAM("WAITS", 0.0, 10.0, 10);
THRUTIMES :-  NEW HISTOGRAM("THRUS", 0.0, 10.0, 10);
TRUNKS    :-  NEW RES("TRUNKS", N);
Q1        :-  NEW WAITQ("Q 1");
Q2        :-  NEW WAITQ("Q 2");
```

```
        FOR J := 1 STEP 1 UNTIL M DO
          NEW OPERATOR("O").SCHEDULE(0.0);

        NEW CALL("C").SCHEDULE(0.0);
        HOLD(480.0);
    END;
```

5.6 (Sketch only.) Maintain a BIN - PENDING - on the number
of as yet untreated requests in the various request
queues. Now a query places itself in a request queue by:

```
        PENDING.GIVE(1);
        REQUESTQ(N).WAIT;
```

The scanner executes a PENDING.TAKE(1) to await the next
query when the request queues are all empty. This keeps
the scanner asleep while no queries are currently pending.
When the scanner is woken up again, it has to compute
where it should be (quite tricky), HOLD until it is time
to lock onto the next station (careful as it will be in
mid-rotation or in mid-test). Then we let it rotate, test
and transmit while PENDING.AVAIL > 0. Then the scanner
saves its current status (time and position) and hangs
itself up with a PENDING.TAKE(1).

                       CHAPTER 6
                       =========
```

6.1 BOOLEAN PROCEDURE AND2(A, B); NAME A, B; BOOLEAN A, B;
    AND2 := IF A THEN B ELSE FALSE;

BOOLEAN PROCEDURE OR2(A, B); NAME A, B; BOOLEAN A, B;
    OR2  := IF A THEN TRUE ELSE B;

6.2 DEMOS
    BEGIN
      REF(RDIST)DRINK, POUR, WASH, NEXT;
      REF(IDIST)THIRST;
      REF(BIN)CLEAN, DIRTY, EMPTY;
      REF(CONDQ)IDLEQ;
      REF(WAITQ)BAR;

      ENTITY CLASS CUSTOMER;
      BEGIN INTEGER K, N;
        NEW CUSTOMER("C").SCHEDULE(NEXT.SAMPLE);
        N := THIRST.SAMPLE;
```

```
    FOR K := 1 STEP 1 UNTIL N DO
    BEGIN IDLEQ.SIGNAL;
      BAR.WAIT;
    DRINKING:
      HOLD(DRINK.SAMPLE);
      EMPTY.GIVE(1);
    END;
END***CUSTOMER***;

ENTITY CLASS WAITER;
BEGIN INTEGER N;
  N := 0;
  WHILE EMPTY.AVAIL > 0 DO
  BEGIN EMPTY.TAKE(1);
    HOLD(0.2);
    N := N+1;
  END;
  DIRTY.GIVE(N);  IDLEQ.SIGNAL;
  HOLD(30.0 - N*0.2);
  REPEAT;
END***WAITER***;

ENTITY CLASS BARMAID;
BEGIN
  REF(ENTITY)C;
  IDLEQ.WAITUNTIL(DIRTY.AVAIL > 0
       OR (BAR.LENGTH > 0 AND CLEAN.AVAIL > 0));
  IF (BAR.LENGTH > 0 AND CLEAN.AVAIL > 0) THEN
  BEGIN C :- BAR.COOPT;
    CLEAN.TAKE(1);
    HOLD(POUR.SAMPLE);
    C.SCHEDULE(0.0);
  END ELSE
  BEGIN DIRTY.TAKE(1);
    HOLD(WASH.SAMPLE);
    CLEAN.GIVE(1);  IDLEQ.SIGNAL;
  END;
  REPEAT;
END***BARMAID***;

CLEAN  :- NEW BIN("CLEAN", 15);
DIRTY  :- NEW BIN("DIRTY", 0);
EMPTY  :- NEW BIN("EMPTY", 0);
IDLEQ  :- NEW CONDQ("IDLE");
BAR    :- NEW WAITQ("BAR");
THIRST :- NEW RANDINT("THIRST", 1, 6);
DRINK  :- NEW UNIFORM("DRINK", 15.0, 25.0);
```

```
      POUR    :- NEW CONSTANT("POUR", 1.0);
      WASH    :- NEW CONSTANT("WASH", 0.5);
      NEXT    :- NEW NEGEXP("NEXT", 0.2);
      NEW BARMAID("B").SCHEDULE(0.0);
      NEW CUSTOMER("C").SCHEDULE(0.0);
      NEW WAITER("W").SCHEDULEY(0.0);
      HOLD(180.0);
    END;

6.3 DEMOS
      BEGIN REF(RES)TUGS, JETTIES;
        REF(CONDQ)DOCKQ, OUTQ;
        REF(RDIST)NEXT, DISCHARGE;
        BOOLEAN LOWTIDE, HIGHTIDE;

        ENTITY CLASS BOAT;
        BEGIN NEW BOAT("B").SCHEDULE(NEXT.SAMPLE);
        DOCK:
          JETTIES.ACQUIRE(1);
          DOCKQ.WAITUNTIL(TUGS.AVAIL >= 2 AND HIGHTIDE);
          TUGS.ACQUIRE(2);
          HOLD(2.0);
          TUGS.RELEASE(2);
          DOCKQ.SIGNAL;  OUTQ.SIGNAL;
        UNLOAD:
          HOLD(DISCHARGE.SAMPLE);
        LEAVE:
          OUTQ.WAITUNTIL(TUGS.AVAIL > 0 AND NOT LOWTIDE);
          TUGS.ACQUIRE(1);
          HOLD(2.0);
          TUGS.RELEASE(1);  JETTIES.RELEASE(1);
          DOCKQ.SIGNAL;  OUTQ.SIGNAL;
        END***BOAT***;

        ENTITY CLASS TIDE;
        BEGIN LOWTIDE := TRUE;
          HOLD(4.0);
          LOWTIDE := FALSE;
          OUTQ.SIGNAL;
          HOLD(2.5);
          HIGHTIDE := TRUE;
          DOCKQ.SIGNAL;
          HOLD(4.0);
          HIGHTIDE := FALSE;
          HOLD(2.5);
          REPEAT;
        END***TIDE***;
```

```
        TUGS    :- NEW RES("TUGS",    3);
        JETTIES :- NEW RES("JETTIES", 2);
        DOCKQ   :- NEW CONDQ("DOCK");
        OUTQ    :- NEW CONDQ("LEAVING");
        READDIST(NEXT,       "NEXT BOAT");
        READDIST(DISCHARGE, "DISCHARGE");
        NEW TIDE("TIDE").SCHEDULE(1.0);
        NEW BOAT("B").SCHEDULE(0.0);
        HOLD(28.0*24.0);
      END;
```

6.4 DEMOS

```
      BEGIN REF(CONDQ)LIGHTS;
        BOOLEAN OK, GREEN;
        REF(RDIST)NEXT, CLEAR;

        ENTITY CLASS CAR;
        BEGIN NEW CAR("C").SCHEDULE(NEXT.SAMPLE);
          LIGHTS.WAITUNTIL(OK AND GREEN);
          OK := FALSE;
          HOLD(CLEAR.SAMPLE);
          OK := TRUE;
          LIGHTS.SIGNAL;
        END***CAR***;

        ENTITY CLASS TLIGHTS;
        BEGIN
          GREEN := TRUE;
          LIGHTS.SIGNAL;
          HOLD(20.0);
          GREEN := FALSE;
          HOLD(24.0);
          REPEAT;
        END***TLIGHTS***;

        OK      := TRUE;
        LIGHTS :- NEW CONDQ("TRAFF.LIGHTS");
        NEXT   :- NEW NEGEXP("NEXT CAR", 0.03);
        CLEAR  :- NEW NORMAL("CLEAR TIME", 2.0, 0.5);
        NEW TLIGHTS("LIGHTS").SCHEDULE(0.0);
        NEW CAR("C").SCHEDULE(0.0);
        HOLD(7200.0);
      END;
```

6.5 We use RES objects NEAR and FAR to indicate whether or
    not the near and far lanes are currently free. They are
    switched by objects of CLASS CONVOY (representing a line

of cars with no break in between). There is a convoy for each direction. We declare

```
REF(RES)NEAR, FAR;

ENTITY CLASS CONVOY(LANE); REF(RES)LANE;
BEGIN
LANE_BLOCKED:
  LANE.ACQUIRE(1);
  HOLD(time for convoy to pass);
  LANE.RELEASE(1);
  LIGHTS.SIGNAL;
GAP:
  HOLD(safe to cross time);
  REPEAT;
END***CONVOY***;
```

and issue the initialising statements:

```
NEAR :- NEW RES("NEAR LANE", 1);
FAR  :- NEW RES("FAR LANE",  1);
NEW CONVOY("NEAR",NEAR).SCHEDULE(...);
NEW CONVOY("FAR",  FAR).SCHEDULE(...);
```

The cars elect to filter onto the main road (acquiring NEAR) or to cross the main road (acquiring both NEAR and FAR). In both cases, they need to be at the front of the queue and are delayed a little by the car in front (as in exercise 6.4).

```
ENTITY CLASS CAR;
BEGIN BOOLEAN FILTER;
  NEW CAR("C").SCHEDULE(NEXT);
  FILTER := probability of filtering;
  LIGHTS.WAITUNTIL(OK AND NEAR.AVAIL > 0
                   AND (FILTER OR FAR.AVAIL > 0));
  OK := FALSE;
  HOLD(time to clear);
  OK := TRUE;
  LIGHTS.SIGNAL;
END***CAR***;
```

6.6 In this answer, and in the answers to exercises 6.7–6.8 as well, we assume (without loss of generality) that the canal runs from east to west. We use Booleans SAIL(E) and SAIL(W) to indicate the prevailing direction. The prevailing direction is switched periodically by an object

of CLASS SWITCHER. Notice how it acquires 3 units of the
RES CANAL prior to doing the direction switching. This
gives any boats in the canal time to clear it.

```
DEMOS
  BEGIN REF(RDIST)NEXT;
    BOOLEAN ARRAY SAIL(1:2); REF(RES)CANAL;
    REF(CONDQ)ARRAY Q(1:2);  BOOLEAN ENTRY;
    INTEGER E, W;  REAL TIMESLOT, CTIME;

    ENTITY CLASS BOAT(D); INTEGER D;
    BEGIN
       NEW BOAT("B", D).SCHEDULE(NEXT.SAMPLE);
    AWAIT ENTRY_PERMISSION:
      Q(D).WAITUNTIL(SAIL(D) AND ENTRY);
      CANAL.ACQUIRE(1);
      ENTRY := FALSE;
    FIRST_PART_OF_CANAL:
      HOLD(CTIME/3.0);
      ENTRY := TRUE;
      Q(D).SIGNAL;
    REST_OF_CANAL:
      HOLD(2.0*CTIME/3.0);
      CANAL.RELEASE(1);
    END***BOAT***;

    ENTITY CLASS SWITCHER;
    BEGIN INTEGER D;
      PRIORITY := 1;
      CANAL.ACQUIRE(3);
    LOOP:
      FOR D := E, W DO
      BEGIN CANAL.RELEASE(3);
        SAIL(D) := TRUE;
        Q(D).SIGNAL;
        HOLD(TIMESLOT);
        SAIL(D) := FALSE;
        CANAL.ACQUIRE(3);
      END;
      REPEAT;
    END***SWITCHER***;

    CTIME := ...;  TIMESLOT := ...;
    E := 1;  W := 2;
    Q(E) :- NEW CONDQ("GOING EAST");
    Q(W) :- NEW CONDQ("GOING WEST");
    READDIST(NEXT, "NEXT");
```

```
      ENTRY := TRUE;
      CANAL :- NEW RES("CANAL", 3);

      NEW SWITCHER("S").SCHEDULE(0.0);
      NEW BOAT("W BOAT:", W).SCHEDULE(...);
      NEW BOAT("E BOAT:", E).SCHEDULE(...);
      HOLD(simulation period);
    END;
```

6.7 Declare globally, and suitably initialise

```
    REF(CONDQ)SQ;   INTEGER L;
```

and alter the definition of SWITCHER in exercise 6.6 to

```
    ENTITY CLASS SWITCHER;
    BEGIN INTEGER D;
      CANAL.ACQUIRE(3);
    LOOP:
      FOR D := E, W DO
      BEGIN CANAL.RELEASE(3);
        SAIL(D) := TRUE;
        Q(D).SIGNAL;
        HOLD(L*CTIME/3.0);
        SQ.WAITUNTIL(Q(3-D).LENGTH = L);
        SAIL(D) := FALSE;
        CANAL.ACQUIRE(3);
      END;
      REPEAT;
    END***SWITCHER***;
```

SQ is a third CONDQ specially for the SWITCHER object.
The value of 3-D is E if D=W, and W if D=E, i.e. if D is
the prevailing direction, 3-D returns the blocked
direction. Also, alter CLASS BOAT in 6.6 by including an
SQ.SIGNAL before the call on Q(D).WAITUNTIL.

6.8 As in 6.7, except alter the declaration of SWITCHER to

```
    ENTITY CLASS SWITCHER;
    BEGIN INTEGER D;
      PRIORITY := -1;
    LOOP:
      SQ.WAITUNTIL(Q(E).LENGTH > 0 OR Q(W).LENGTH > 0);
      D := IF Q(E).LENGTH > 0 AND Q(W).LENGTH > 0 THEN
            choose E or W, 50% each ELSE
          IF Q(E).LENGTH > 0 THEN E ELSE W;
```

```
    SAIL(D) := TRUE;
    Q(D).SIGNAL;
    CANAL.ACQUIRE(3);
    SAIL(D) := FALSE;
    CANAL.RELEASE(3);
    REPEAT;
END***SWITCHER***;
```

By giving the SWITCHER a low priority, when it queues for
the canal, it can be overtaken by any boat arriving for
the prevailing direction.

6.9 As in 6.7, but amend the declaration of SWITCHER to

```
ENTITY CLASS SWITCHER;
BEGIN INTEGER D;
  PRIORITY := 1;
  CANAL.ACQUIRE(3);
LOOP:
  FOR D := E, W DO
  BEGIN CANAL.RELEASE(3);
    SAIL(D) := TRUE;  SAIL(3-D) := FALSE;
    Q(D).SIGNAL;
    SQ.WAITUNTIL(Q(3-D).LENGTH > Q(D).LENGTH);
    SAIL(D) := FALSE;
    CANAL.ACQUIRE(3);
  END;
  REPEAT;
END***SWITCHER***;
```

6.10 Add to 4.8 the declarations and appropriate initialisati-
   ons of REF(CONDQ)PITS,OUTSIDE; and alter CLASS BILLET to:

```
ENTITY CLASS BILLET;
BEGIN BOOLEAN COLD;
AWAIT_PIT:
  CRANES.ACQUIRE(1);
  PITQ.WAITUNTIL(PITS.AVAIL > 0 OR PITQ.LENGTH >= 4);
  IF PITS.AVAIL = 0 THEN
  BEGIN
MOVED_OUTSIDE:
    HOLD(outside time);
    CRANES.RELEASE(1); OUTSIDE.SIGNAL;
    COLD := TRUE;
RETURNED:
    OUTSIDE.WAITUNTIL(CRANES.AVAIL > 0 AND
            PITS.AVAIL > 5 AND PITQ.LENGTH = 0);
```

```
      CRANES.ACQUIRE(1);
      PITS.ACQUIRE(1);
      HOLD(inside time);
    END ELSE PITS.ACQUIRE(1);
  INTO_PIT:
    HOLD(load time);
    CRANES.RELEASE(1);  OUTSIDE.SIGNAL;
  SOAK:
    HOLD(IF COLD THEN longer ELSE shorter);
  UNLOAD:
    MILLS.ACQUIRE(1);
    CRANES.ACQUIRE(1);
    HOLD(unload time);
    CRANES.RELEASE(1);
    PITS.RELEASE(1);  PITQ.SIGNAL;  OUTSIDE.SIGNAL;
  ROLL:
    HOLD(roll time);
    MILLS.RELEASE(1);
  END***BILLET***;

6.11 BEGIN INTEGER N, M, K;
     N := 6;
     M := N + 1;
     DEMOS
       BEGIN REF(COUNT)ARRAY DONE(1:N);
         BOOLEAN ARRAY POS(0:M); BOOLEAN CAPPING;
         REAL PAUSE, MOVE, SEAL;
         REF(COUNT)OK, FAIL;
         REF(CONDQ)CQ;  REF(WAITQ)PQ;
         REF(RDIST)FETCH;

         ENTITY CLASS BELT;
         BEGIN INTEGER K;
         LOOP: MOVING:
           HOLD(MOVE);
         IN_POSITION:
           FOR K := M STEP -1 UNTIL 1 DO
             POS(K) := POS(K-1);
           IF POS(M) THEN OK.UPDATE(1) ELSE FAIL.UPDATE(1);
           CAPPING := TRUE;
           CQ.SIGNAL;
           HOLD(PAUSE-SEAL);
         TOO_LATE:
           CAPPING := FALSE;
           HOLD(SEAL);
           REPEAT;
         END***BELT***;
```

```
        ENTITY CLASS PICKER(N); INTEGER N;
        BEGIN
        FETCHING:LOOP:
          HOLD(FETCH.SAMPLE);
        WAIT_UNTIL_SEAL_IS_PASSED:
          PQ.WAIT;
          REPEAT;
        END***PICKER***;

        ENTITY CLASS CAPPER(N); INTEGER N;
        BEGIN REF(PICKER)P;
        AWAIT_CONTAINER:
          CQ.WAITUNTIL(NOT POS(N) AND CAPPING);
          HOLD(SEAL);
          POS(N) := TRUE;
        FIND_PARTNER:
          PQ.FIND(P, P.N = N);
          P.SCHEDULE(0.0);
          REPEAT;
        END***CAPPER***;

        PAUSE := 5.0;  MOVE := 3.0;  SEAL := 2.0;
        OK    :- NEW COUNT("SEALED");
        FAIL  :- NEW COUNT("NOT SEALED");
        CQ    :- NEW CONDQ("CAPPERQ");
        CQ.ALL:= TRUE;
        PQ    :- NEW WAITQ("PICKERQ");
        FETCH :- NEW UNIFORM("GET SEAL", 7.0, 11.0);
        NEW BELT("BELT").SCHEDULE(0.0);
        FOR K := 1 STEP 1 UNTIL N DO
        BEGIN
          NEW PICKER("P", K).SCHEDULE(0.0);
          NEW CAPPER("C", K).SCHEDULE(0.0);
        END;
        HOLD(8.0*3600.0);
       END;
     END;
```

6.12 DEMOS

```
     BEGIN
      REF(IDIST)TYPE;
      REF(RDIST)NEXT, CUTTING;
      REF(RES)ARRAY C(1:2);
      REF(CONDQ)CQ; REF(WAITQ)ARRQ;
      REF(WAITQ)ARRAY OUTQ(1:2);
      INTEGER ARRAY L(1:2);
```

```
ENTITY CLASS PLATE;
BEGIN INTEGER N;
  NEW PLATE("P").SCHEDULE(NEXT.SAMPLE);
  N := TYPE.SAMPLE;
  CQ.SIGNAL;
JOIN_ARRIVAL_Q_AS_LAST:
  ARRQ.WAIT;

RESUME_WHEN_JOINING_CUTTER_Q:
  L(N) := L(N)+1;
  C(N).ACQUIRE(1);
  L(N) := L(N)-1;
  HOLD(CUTTING.SAMPLE);
  C(N).RELEASE(1);
  CQ.SIGNAL;
END***PLATE***;

ENTITY CLASS CRANE;
BEGIN REF(PLATE)P;
AWAIT_NEXT_TASK_BY_ARRIVAL_AREA:
  CQ.WAITUNTIL(ARRQ.LENGTH > 0
            OR L(1) < 3 AND OUTQ(1).LENGTH > 0
            OR L(2) < 3 AND OUTQ(2).LENGTH > 0);
MOVE_FROM_ARRIVAL_AREA:
  WHILE ARRQ.LENGTH > 0 DO
  BEGIN P :- ARRQ.LAST.COOPT;
    IF L(P.N)<3 THEN
    STRAIGHT_TO_CUTTER:
    BEGIN HOLD(1.0);
      P.SCHEDULE(0.0);
      HOLD(1.0);
    END ELSE
    STRAIGHT_OUTSIDE:
    BEGIN HOLD(0.5);
      P.INTO(OUTQ(P.N));
      HOLD(0.5);
    END;
  END;
MOVE_IN_FROM_OUTSIDE:
  IF L(1) < 3 AND OUTQ(1).LENGTH > 0 OR
    L(2) < 3 AND OUTQ(2).LENGTH > 0 THEN
  BEGIN HOLD(1.0);
    P :- IF L(1) < 3 AND OUTQ(1).LENGTH > 0 THEN
           OUTQ(1).LAST ELSE OUTQ(2).LAST;
    P.COOPT;
    HOLD(1.0);
    P.SCHEDULE(0.0);
```

```
         HOLD(1.0);
       END;
       REPEAT;
     END***CRANE***;

     NEXT    :- NEW NEGEXP("PLATE", 0.1);
     CUTTING :- NEW NORMAL("CUTTING", 8.0, 2.0);
     TYPE    :- NEW RANDINT("TYPE", 1, 2);
     C(1)    :- NEW RES("CUTTER", 1);
     C(2)    :- NEW RES("CUTTER", 1);
     ARRQ    :- NEW WAITQ("ARRIVALS");
     OUTQ(1) :- NEW WAITQ("OUTSIDE DUMP");
     OUTQ(2) :- NEW WAITQ("OUTSIDE DUMP");
     CQ      :- NEW CONDQ("IDLE CRANE");
     NEW PLATE("P").SCHEDULE(0.0);
     NEW CRANE("C").SCHEDULE(0.0);
     HOLD(480.0);
   END;
```

6.13 Because with b) you have to remember to signal Q at TIME
     = T. a) is also more efficient. Why?

                    CHAPTER 7
                    =========

7.1 DEMOS
     BEGIN REF(LATHE)L; REF(COUNT)DONE;
       REF(RDIST)P, UP, REPAIR;

```
       ENTITY CLASS LATHE;
       BEGIN HOLD(P.SAMPLE);
         DONE.UPDATE(1);
         REPEAT;
       END***LATHE***;

       ENTITY CLASS BREAKDOWN;
       BEGIN REAL TLEFT;
       LATHE_RUNNING:
         HOLD(UP.SAMPLE);
       LATHE_DOWN:
         L.CANCEL;
         TLEFT := L.EVTIME-TIME;
         HOLD(REPAIR.SAMPLE);
         L.SCHEDULE(TLEFT+5.0);
         REPEAT;
       END***BREAKDOWN***;
```

```
      DONE   :- NEW COUNT("DONE");
      P      :- NEW NORMAL("PROCESS",15.0,3.0);
      UP     :- NEW NEGEXP("RUNNING", 1/300);
      REPAIR :- NEW NORMAL("REPAIR", 30.0, 5.0);
      L :- NEW LATHE("L");  L.SCHEDULE(0.0);
      NEW BREAKDOWN("B_DOWN").SCHEDULE(0.0);
      HOLD(60*24*28);
    END;

7.2 DEMOS
    BEGIN
      REF(COUNT)DONE, SPOILED;
      REF(RDIST)P, UP, REPAIR;
      REF(LATHE)L;

      ENTITY CLASS LATHE;
      BEGIN INTEGER INTERRUPTED;
        HOLD(P.SAMPLE);
        IF INTERRUPTED > 0 THEN
        BEGIN INTERRUPTED := 0;
          SPOILED.UPDATE(1);
          HOLD(6.0);
        END ELSE DONE.UPDATE(1);
        REPEAT;
      END***LATHE***;

      ENTITY CLASS BREAKDOWN;
      BEGIN
      LATHE_RUNNING:
        HOLD(UP.SAMPLE);
      LATHE_DOWN:
        L.CANCEL;
        HOLD(REPAIR.SAMPLE);
        L.INTERRUPTED := 1;
        L.SCHEDULE(0.0);
        REPEAT;
      END***BREAKDOWN***;

      DONE    :- NEW COUNT("DONE");
      SPOILED :- NEW COUNT("REPAIR");
      UP      :- NEW NEGEXP("RUNNING", 1/300);
      REPAIR  :- NEW NORMAL("REPAIR", 30.0, 5.0);
      P       :- NEW NORMAL("PROCESS", 15.0, 3.0);
      L :- NEW LATHE("L");  L.SCHEDULE(0.0);
      NEW BREAKDOWN("B_DOWN").SCHEDULE(0.0);
      HOLD(60*24*28);
    END;
```

7.3 DEMOS

```
    BEGIN
      REF(RES)R;
      INTEGER K;
      REF(COUNT)DONE;
      REF(RDIST)P, UP, REPAIR;

      ENTITY CLASS LATHE;
      BEGIN
        NEW B_DOWN("B", CURRENT).SCHEDULE(0.0);
      LOOP:
        HOLD(P.SAMPLE);
        DONE.UPDATE(1);
        REPEAT;
      END***LATHE***;

      ENTITY CLASS B_DOWN(L); REF(LATHE)L;
      BEGIN REAL TLEFT;
        HOLD(UP.SAMPLE);
        TLEFT := L.EVTIME-TIME;
        L.CANCEL;
        R.ACQUIRE(1);
        HOLD(30.0);
        R.RELEASE(1);
        L.SCHEDULE(TLEFT+5.0);
        REPEAT;
      END***B_DOWN***;

      ENTITY CLASS OTHER;
      BEGIN PRIORITY := -1;
      LOOP:
        R.ACQUIRE(1);
        HOLD(15.0);
        R.RELEASE(1);
        REPEAT;
      END***OTHER***;

      FOR K := 1 STEP 1 UNTIL 6 DO
        NEW LATHE("L").SCHEDULE(0.0);
      NEW OTHER("O").SCHEDULE(0.0);
      R       :- NEW RES("REPAIRMAN", 1);
      DONE    :- NEW COUNT("DONE");
      P       :- NEW NORMAL("PROCESS",30.0,5.0);
      UP      :- NEW NEGEXP("RUNNING", 1/300);
      HOLD(60*24*28);
    END;
```

7.4 DEMOS

```
    BEGIN REF(FERRY)CF;
      INTEGER DAY, HOUR;
      REF(CONDQ)DOCKQ;
      REF(WAITQ)ARRQ;
      REF(BDIST)DAYS, NIGHTS;
      REF(IDIST)UNLOAD;
      REF(RDIST)NEXTF, NEXTD, NEXTN;
      REF(HISTOGRAM)ARRAY THRU(1:2);
      REF(RES)QUAY;

      BOOLEAN PROCEDURE DAYTIME;
       DAYTIME := HOUR >= 6 AND HOUR < 18;

      ENTITY CLASS CLOCK;
      BEGIN
        FOR DAY := 1 STEP 1 UNTIL 28 DO
        BEGIN
          FOR HOUR := 0 STEP 1 UNTIL 23 DO
          BEGIN
            NEW FERRY("F").SCHEDULE(NEXTF.SAMPLE);
            IF CF.IDLE THEN CF.INTERRUPT(1) ELSE
                CF.INTERRUPTED := 1;
            HOLD(1.0);
          END;
        END;
      END***CLOCK***;

      ENTITY CLASS CAR;
      BEGIN REF(CAR)N;  BOOLEAN SEASON;
        REAL ARRTIME;
        N :- NEW CAR("C");
        IF DAYTIME THEN
        BEGIN N.SCHEDULE(NEXTD.SAMPLE);
          SEASON := DAYS.SAMPLE;
        END ELSE
        BEGIN N.SCHEDULE(NEXTN.SAMPLE);
          SEASON := NIGHTS.SAMPLE;
        END;
        PRIORITY := IF SEASON THEN 2 ELSE 1;
        ARRTIME  := TIME;
        DOCKQ.SIGNAL;
        ARRQ.WAIT;
      ON_BOARD:
        THRU(PRIORITY).UPDATE(TIME-ARRTIME);
      END***CAR***;
```

```
        ENTITY CLASS FERRY;
        BEGIN INTEGER N;
        UNLOADING:
          QUAY.ACQUIRE(1);
          CF :- CURRENT;
          HOLD(UNLOAD.SAMPLE);
        LOAD:
          DOCKQ.WAITUNTIL(ARRQ.LENGTH > 0 AND N > 20 OR
                          INTERRUPTED > 0);
          WHILE ARRQ.LENGTH > 0 AND N < 20 DO
          BEGIN N := N+1;
            ARRQ.FIRST.SCHEDULE(0.0);
            HOLD(1/60);
          END;
          IF INTERRUPTED = 0 THEN GOTO LOAD;
          CF :- NONE;
          QUAY.RELEASE(1);
        END***FERRY***;

        UNLOAD :- NEW RANDINT("UNLOAD", 0.1, 0.2);
        DAYS   :- NEW DRAW("SEASON:DAY", 0.4);
        NIGHTS :- NEW DRAW("SEASON:NIGHT", 0.25);
        NEXTF  :- NEW NORMAL("FERRY", 1/3, 1/12);
        NEXTD  :- NEW NEGEXP("DAY RATE", 15.0);
        NEXTN  :- NEW NEGEXP("NIGHT RATE", 9.0);
        QUAY   :- NEW RES("QUAY", 1);
        DOCKQ  :- NEW CONDQ("FERRY LOAD Q");
        ARRQ   :- NEW WAITQ("DOCKSIDE Q");
        THRU(1):- NEW HISTOGRAM("NORMAL", 0.0, 1.0, 10);
        THRU(2):- NEW HISTOGRAM("SEASON", 0.0, 1.0, 10);
        NEW CAR("C").SCHEDULE(0.0);
        NEW CLOCK("CLOCK").SCHEDULE(0.0);
        HOLD(24.0*28.0);
      END;
```

7.5 DEMOS

```
      BEGIN REF(CONDQ)LINE;
        REF(RES)SERVER;
        REF(RDIST)NEXT, SERVE, P;

        ENTITY CLASS CUS;
        BEGIN
          INTEGER IMP;
          NEW CUS("C").SCHEDULE(NEXT.SAMPLE);
          IMP := P.SAMPLE;
          NEW ALARM("A", CURRENT).SCHEDULE(IMP);
          LINE.WAITUNTIL(SERVER.AVAIL>0 OR INTERRUPTED>0)
```

```
      IF INTERRUPTED = O THEN
      BEGIN SERVER.ACQUIRE(1);
        HOLD(SERVE.SAMPLE);
        SERVER.RELEASE(1);
        LINE.SIGNAL;
      END;
    END***CUS***;

    ENTITY CLASS ALARM(E); REF(ENTITY)E;
    BEGIN
      IF E.IDLE AND E=/=LINE.FIRST THEN E.INTERRUPT(1);
    END***ALARM***;

    LINE   :- NEW CONDQ("AWAIT SERVICE");
    SERVER :- NEW RES("SERVER", 1);
    NEXT   :- NEW NEGEXP("NEXT", 1.0);
    SERVE  :- NEW UNIFORM("SERVICE",2/3,1);
    P      :- NEW UNIFORM("IMPAT", 2.0, 5.0);
    NEW CUS("C").SCHEDULE(O.0);
    HOLD(240.0);
  END;
```

INDEX